SHORTLIST

Rome
2010

WHAT'S NEW | WHAT'S ON | WHAT'S BEST

www.timeout.com/rome

Contents

Published by Time Out Guides Ltd
Universal House
251 Tottenham Court Road
London W1T 7AB
Tel: + 44 (0)20 7813 3000
Fax: + 44 (0)20 7813 6001
Email: guides@timeout.com
www.timeout.com

Managing Director Peter Fiennes
Editorial Director Ruth Jarvis
Business Manager Daniel Allen
Editorial Manager Holly Pick
Assistant Management Accountant Ija Krasnikova

Time Out Guides is a wholly owned subsidiary of Time Out Group Ltd.

© **Time Out Group Ltd**
Chairman Tony Elliott
Chief Executive Officer David King
Group General Manager/Director Nichola Coulthard
Time Out Communications Ltd MD David Pepper
Time Out International Ltd MD Cathy Runciman
Time Out Magazine Ltd Publisher/Managing Director Mark Elliott
Production Director Mark Lamond
Group IT Director Simon Chappell
Marketing & Circulation Director Catherine Demajo

Time Out and the Time Out logo are trademarks of Time Out Group Ltd.

This edition first published in Great Britain in 2009 by Ebury Publishing
A Random House Group Company
Company information can be found on www.randomhouse.co.uk
Random House UK Limited Reg. No. 954009
10 9 8 7 6 5 4 3 2 1

Distributed in the US by Publishers Group West
Distributed in Canada by Publishers Group Canada

For further distribution details, see www.timeout.com

ISBN: 978-1-84670-137-5

A CIP catalogue record for this book is available from the British Library.

Printed and bound in Germany by Appl.

Rome Shortlist

The **Time Out Rome Shortlist 2010** is one of a series of annual guides that draws on Time Out's background as a magazine publisher to keep you current with everything that's going on in town. As well as Rome's key sights and the best of its eating, drinking and leisure options, it picks out the most exciting venues to have opened in the last year and gives a full calendar of annual events from September 2009 to December 2010. It also includes features on the important news, trends and openings, all compiled by locally based editors and writers. Whether you're visiting for the first time in your life or the first time this year, you'll find the *Time Out Rome Shortlist* contains all you need to know, in a portable and easy-to-use format.

The guide divides central Rome into six areas, each containing listings for Sights & Museums, Eating & Drinking, Shopping, Nightlife and Arts & Leisure, and maps pinpointing their locations. At the front of the book are chapters rounding up these scenes city-wide, and giving a shortlist of our overall picks. We also include itineraries for days out, plus essentials such as transport information and hotels.

Our listings give phone numbers as dialled from within Italy. Rome's prefix is 06; you must dial this prefix even if you're calling from within the city. The international code for Italy is 39. When calling from outside Italy do not drop the initial '0' of the Rome prefix. Listed numbers beginning with '3' are mobiles.

We have noted price categories by using one to four euro signs (€-€€€€), representing budget, moderate, expensive and luxury. Major credit cards are accepted unless otherwise stated. We also indicate when a venue is **NEW**, and give **Event highlights**.

All our listings are double-checked, but places do sometimes close or change their hours or prices, so it's a good idea to call a venue before visiting. While every effort has been made to ensure accuracy, the publishers cannot accept responsibility for any errors that this guide may contain.

Venues are marked on the maps using symbols numbered according to their order within the chapter and colour-coded as follows:

❶ Sights & Museums
❶ Eating & Drinking
❶ Shopping
❶ Nightlife
❶ Arts & Leisure

Map key	
Major sight or landmark	
Railway station	
Park	
Area name	TRIDENTE
Metro line	
Hospital	H
Church	

Time Out **Rome** Shortlist 2010

EDITORIAL
Editor Anne Hanley
Deputy Editor Anna Norman
Researcher Fulvia Angelini
Proofreader Patrick Mulkern
Indexer Rob Norman

DESIGN
Art Director Scott Moore
Art Editor Pinelope Kourmouzoglou
Senior Designer Henry Elphick
Graphic Designers Kei Ishimaru,
    Nicola Wilson
Advertising Designer Jodi Sher

Picture Editor Jael Marschner
Deputy Picture Editor Lynn Chambers
Picture Researcher Gemma Walters
Picture Desk Assistant Marzena Zoladz
Picture Librarian Christina Theisen

ADVERTISING
Commercial Director Mark Phillips
International Advertising Manager
    Kasimir Berger
International Sales Executive Charlie Sokol
Advertising Sales (Rome) Julie Simonsen,
    Magherita Tedone

MARKETING
Marketing Manager Yvonne Poon
**Sales & Marketing Director, North America
    & Latin America** Lisa Levinson
Senior Publishing Brand Manager
    Luthfa Begum
Art Director Anthony Huggins

PRODUCTION
Production Manager Brendan McKeown
Production Controller Damian Bennett
Production Co-ordinator Kelly Fenlon

CONTRIBUTORS
This guide was researched and written by Anne Hanley, with the exception of The Ideal
City, Rome in a Rush, Baroque trickery, Sampietrini, Viterbo medieval miracle (all Julia
Crosse); and Night Moves (Clara Marshall). The editor would like to thank all the writers
of the Time Out Rome Guide on which this guide is based.

PHOTOGRAPHY
Photography by Gianluca Moggi, except pages 7, 26, 29 Agnese Sanvito; pages 30, 40,
41 Getty Images PR; pages 25, 43, 44, 46, 48, 53, 54, 63, 111, 112, 124, 126, 137,
138, 152, 155, 156, 157, 158, 160, 163, 164 Alessandra Santorelli; page 147
AFP/Getty Images.

The following images were provided by the featured establishments/artists: pages 35,
36, 38, 88, 101, 166, 178.

Cover photograph: Piazza San Pietro and St Peter's Basilica, Vatican City. Credit: © Ian
Cumming/Axiom.

MAPS
LS International Cartography, via Decemviri 8, 20138 Milan, Italy (www.mapmovie.it).

About **Time Out**

Founded in 1968, Time Out has expanded from humble London beginnings into
the leading resource for those wanting to know what's happening in the world's
greatest cities. As well as our influential what's-on weeklies in London, New York
and Chicago, we publish nearly 30 other listings magazines in cities as varied as
Beijing and Mumbai. The magazines established Time Out's trademark style: sharp
writing, informed reviewing and bang up-to-date inside knowledge of every scene.

Time Out made the natural leap into travel guides in the 1980s with the City Guide
series, which now extends to over 50 destinations around the world. Written and
researched by expert local writers and generously illustrated with original photography,
the full-size guides cover a larger area than our Shortlist guides and include many
more venue reviews, along with additional background features and a full set of maps.

Throughout this rapid growth, the company has remained proudly independent,
still owned by Tony Elliott four decades after he started Time Out London as a single
fold-out sheet of A5 paper. This independence extends to the editorial content of all
our publications, this Shortlist included. No establishment has been featured because
it has advertised, and no payment has influenced any of our reviews. And, for our critics,
there's definitely no such thing as a free lunch: all restaurants and bars are visited
and reviewed anonymously, and Time Out always picks up the bill.
For more about the company, see www.timeout.com.

Don't Miss 2010

Roman Forum p59

Sights & Museums

If you come to Rome with a neat list of things to do, make sure it includes 'sitting at pavement cafés watching people go by' and 'strolling aimlessly through the alleys of the *centro storico*'. Of course, the city's museums, galleries and archaeological gems are second to none. But so is the spectacle that plays out on its streets 24/7.

It pays to approach the Eternal City knowing that you won't see everything: you can live here for decades and keep on being amazed by new finds. To appreciate Rome's treasures and its unique urban landscape, you'll need to walk, so bring comfy shoes. You'll also need to lounge – sitting at a pavement café may crank up the price of your cappuccino, but a front-row seat at the spectacle that is Rome is cheap at any price.

Rome today is looking good: many of its historic buildings have been restored and are gorgeously illuminated at night; streets and squares have been repaved with traditional *sampietrino* cobbles (see box p111). Parts of the *centro storico* have been pedestrianised; there are clean green electric buses and the metro is (very gradually) being extended.

Ancient sites

The area with the greatest density of remains lies between the Palatine, Capitoline, Esquiline and Quirinal hills. Located here are the Colosseum (p57), the Roman Forum (p59) and ancient

Rome's most desirable residential area, the Palatine (p59). But ancient Rome doesn't stop there: the Museo Nazionale Romano group (Palazzo Massimo alle Terme, p105; Palazzo Altemps, p78; Crypta Balbi, p65; and the Baths of Diocletian, p104; for all see www.archeorm.arti. beniculturali.it) houses a mind-boggling collection of ancient statuary, of which there's more in the Vatican and Capitoline museums (p146 and p56). And the Pantheon (p78) is a work of art in itself.

Churches

Down the centuries, popes, princes and aristocrats all commissioned architects and artists to build and adorn their preferred places of worship, with the result that central Rome is home to more than 400 churches, containing endless artistic treasures.

Churches are places of worship; though only the Vatican imposes its dress code rigidly (both in St Peter's and the Vatican Museums), very short skirts, bare midriffs, over-exposed shoulders and shorts are all frowned upon. Churches ask tourists to refrain from visiting during services. A supply of coins for the meters to light up the most interesting artworks is handy, as is a pair of binoculars.

Museums and galleries

Rome has long boasted some of the world's greatest galleries and museums, but the last few years have seen a rash of new permanent exhibits, and there are new showcases for old ones. The ancient, Renaissance and Baroque dominate, of course; but initiatives such as MACRO (p100)

S H O R T L I S T

Ancient monuments
- Ara Pacis Museum (p89)
- Colosseum (p57)
- Imperial Fora Museum (p58)
- Pantheon (p78)
- Roman Forum & Palatine (p59)

Ancient art
- Capitoline Museums (p56)
- Palazzo Altemps (p78)
- Palazzo Massimo alle Terme (p105)

Great Caravaggios
- *Flight into Egypt* at the Doria Pamphili Gallery (p78)
- *Judith and Holophernes* at the Palazzo Barberini (p98)
- *St Matthew* at San Luigi dei Francesi (p79)
- *St Paul* at Santa Maria del Popolo (p89)

Art meets industry
- Centrale Montemartini (p122)
- MACRO at the Birreria Peroni (p100)
- MACRO Future at the Mattatoio (p100)

Breathtaking views
- From the dome of St Peter's (p144)
- From the Gianicolo hill (p138)
- From the lift at the Vittoriano (p62)

Bustling *piazze*
- Campo de' Fiori (p65)
- Piazza Navona (p78)
- Piazza Vittorio (p101)

Leafy parks
- Villa Borghese (p93)
- Villa Sciarra (p138)
- Villa Torlonia (p100)

and MAXXI (p100) mean that the city is catering increasingly well for contemporary art.

Hours and information

In our listings we have given winter opening hours (*orario invernale*). In summer, opening hours may be extended significantly, with some major museums and sites keeping doors open as late as 11pm in high season. Most museums – though not churches – are closed on Mondays.

Note that ticket offices at many museums, galleries and ancient sites stop issuing tickets anything up to 75 minutes before gates shut.

Church opening times should be taken as rough guidelines. And whether doors are open or not often depends on anything from priestly whim to the availability of volunteer staff.

Regularly updated information – including timetable information – on all Rome's sights, shows and entertainments in general can be found on the excellent, exhaustive website www.060608.it. 06 0608 is also the phone number to call for information on just about anything that might interest visitors to Rome; all operators speak passable English. This phoneline will also arrange bookings.

Tickets

Entrance to publicly owned sites and museums is free (*gratuito*) or reduced (*ridotto*) for EU citizens (and citizens of other countries with bilateral agreements) aged under 18 or over 65; you must show photo-ID (for children too) at ticket offices to prove that you are eligible. Under-25s in full-time education may also be eligible for discounts, as may journalists, teachers,

Ara Pacis Museum p89

motoring association members and others. Carry a range of ID just in case.

Note that many sights now levy an extra charge, generally of €1.50-€3, when special exhibitions are taking place inside; visitors are given no option other than to pay the ticket-plus-exhibition price. In all cases, we have given the basic price in this guide.

Booking

Booking is mandatory for the Domus Aurea (p104) and Galleria Borghese (p94). It is also a good idea for big one-off shows if they have opened very recently.

Booking is possible – though really not necessary except for large groups – for many other sites and museums. Note that agencies charge a booking fee that further bumps up the price of tickets.

The official booking agencies for Rome's major sites are Pierreci (06 0608, www.060608.it or www.pierreci.it) and Ticketeria (06 32 810, www.ticketeria.it). Both accept MasterCard and Visa.

Discounts and passes

The Roma Pass is a multi-entrance card that costs €23 and is valid for three days. It gives free access to any two sights, reduced entry to all others, plus unlimited use of the city's public transport system. For further information, see www.romapass.it.

The Villa Borghese Card (€10) lasts for 12 months and allows free access to one of the many museums within this park (p93), as well as giving reduced entrance to the others and discounts at bookshops and bars. For further information, see www.villaborghese.it.

The following tickets can be bought (cash only) at any of the sites involved or online from www.ticketclic.it, which charges a €1.50 booking fee.

Appia Card (€6, €3 reductions, valid seven days) covers the Baths of Caracalla, Tomb of Cecilia Metella and Villa dei Quintili.

Archeologia Card (€23.50, €13.50 reductions, valid seven days) covers the Baths of Caracalla, Baths of Diocletian, Colosseum, Crypta Balbi, Palatine, Palazzo Altemps, Palazzo Massimo alle Terme, Tomb of Cecilia Metella and Villa dei Quintili.

Capitolini Card (€8.50, €6.50 reductions, valid seven days) covers the Capitoline Museums and Centrale Montemartini.

Museo Nazionale Romano Card (€7, €3.50 reductions, valid for three days) covers the Baths of Diocletian, the Crypta Balbi, the Palazzo Massimo alle Terme and the Palazzo Altemps.

Tours

Trambus's 110 Open bus (06 684 0901) leaves Termini station every 20mins (8.30am-8.30pm). It makes 11 stops on a two-hour circuit. Tours include commentary (in eight languages); an all-day stop-and-go ticket costs €20 (€15 reductions).

The Archeobus passes by the Baths of Caracalla (p118) and along via Appia Antica (Appian Way, p152), leaving Termini station about every 30mins from 8.30am to 4.30pm. Stop-and-go tickets cost €15 (€10 reductions); without stops, the trip takes about one-and-a-half hours.

Tickets for both can be bought at the booth in front of Termini, on board or online (www.trambus open.com). A variety of tickets combining these and other tours, and tours with a trip to or from Ciampino, are also available.

Freni e Frizioni p136

WHAT'S BEST
Eating & Drinking

Time was – not so long ago – when your average Roman family thought nothing of eating out a couple of times a week, mostly in the local pizzeria or the cheap-and-cheerful trattoria *sotto casa* (downstairs). But sharp price rises with the introduction of the euro left Italians feeling poorer, and they still hadn't recovered from that shock when the credit crunch hit in 2008. Few eateries feel cheap any more, and few Romans cheerful. But when they do go out, they are as determined as ever to get value (and that means quality) for money.

If restaurants are now no-go areas for some, the shabby neighbourhood bar with its excellent coffee and delicious *cornetti* (croissants) remains a favourite. And where the local trat has weathered the storm and kept prices in check, it will still attract local diners.

If, however, you're in the Eternal City to banish financial woes for a while, there's a host of addresses for sipping and dining in style. And if prices are now more or less on a par with many other European cities, the quality and authenticity of what's on offer here are hard to beat.

Eating

A swathe of designer restaurants opened in Rome around the turn of the millennium, but many have since closed, the survivors being those that offer real culinary excitement, rather than just a few twigs in a vase and the chance of spotting a once-famous TV starlet.

The growing demand for value for money, however, means that *trattorie* and *osterie* are weathering the storm much better. Some are unreconstructed family-run operations; others are recently

THE PERFECT BUN

Nachos.
Hamburger.
Spare Ribs.
Chicken Wings.
Chili con Carne.
Sunday Brunch.

Largo del teatro valle, 4 00186 - Roma   ph: +39 0645476337   info@theperfectbun.it   www.theperfectbun.it

opened places that take the trattoria formula and give it a twist by upping the creativity quotient in the kitchen.

What now sets Rome apart is the focus on the raw materials. Foodie enthusiasm has upped quality no end; the trickle-down effect of this means that even the most basic trat now generally offers decent extra-virgin olive oil with which to dress your salad and more-than-drinkable house wine.

Another recent novelty is the increasing variety. Once, the choice was between posh restaurant, humble trattoria or pizzeria. Today, there are wine bars, salad bars, gastropubs and deli-diners. Even the unchanging pizzeria has been shaken up by the arrival of gourmet pizza emporia. And Rome now has more decent Japanese and Indian restaurants than ever before... though moves in 2009 by some short-sighted councils in northern Italy to maintain culinary purity by banning the opening of 'foreign' food outlets showed a worrying national tendency towards foody protectionism.

It pays to be adventurous when eating in Rome – most of the best places don't have menus in six languages, and may not look like much on the outside. It's also worth getting away from the most heavily touristed parts of the *centro storico* to outlying areas like Testaccio, San Lorenzo or Il Pigneto, where you'll find some of the city's best-value creative *trattorie*.

Going the course

Traditionally, an Italian meal goes *antipasto* (starter), *primo* (usually pasta, sometimes soup), *secondo* (the meat or fish course) with optional *contorno* (vegetables or salad, served separately) and *dolce* (dessert). But locals these days rarely manage the whole routine,

SHORTLIST

Venues with views
- Bar in Capitoline Museums (p57)
- Caffè Bernini (p81)
- Il Ristoro (p149)

Alfresco dining
- Al Presidente (p99)
- Al Ristoro degli Angeli (p125)
- 'Gusto (p91)
- San Teodoro (p63)

Laid-back wine sipping
- Al Vino al Vino (p107)
- Antica Vineria (p71)
- Freni e Frizioni (p136)
- Il Goccetto (p75)
- Société Lutèce (p83)
- La Vineria (p75)

Ice-cream to remember
- Gelateria del Teatro (p82)
- Il Gelato (p119)
- Il Gelato di San Crispino (p82)

Lunch on the run
- Antico Forno Roscioli (p71)
- Burro e Alici (p90)
- Lo Zozzone (p83)
- Paninoteca da Guido (p149)
- Il Seme e la Foglia (p126)

Perfect pizza
- Baffetto 2 (p71)
- Bir & Fud (p135)
- Da Francesco (p82)
- Isola della Pizza (p151)
- Remo (p126)

Roman traditions
- Checchino dal 1887 (p125)
- Da Felice (p126)
- Enoteca Corsi (p82)
- Forno del Ghetto (p76)
- Sora Margherita (p75)

and you're under no obligation to order four courses either. It's perfectly normal to order a pasta dish followed by a simple *contorno*.

Top-flight restaurants will occasionally offer a special *menu degustazione* (taster menu), but any place with a *menu turistico*, especially if translated into many languages, should usually be avoided.

Drinks

One of the biggest changes over the last decade has been the way even humble eateries have started to have decent wine lists. More and more establishments are now offering a good selection of wine by the glass (*al bicchiere* or *alla mescita*). In pizzerias, the drink of choice is *birra* (beer) or soft drinks. Mineral water – *acqua minerale* – comes either *gassata* (sparkling) or *naturale* (still) and is usually served by the litre.

Prices, tipping and times

Places that add service to the bill are still in the minority; if in doubt, ask, '*il servizio è incluso?*' A good rule of thumb is to leave around five per cent in humbler places, or up to ten per cent in smarter eateries. If service has been slack or rude, you should have no qualms about leaving nothing – or checking the bill in detail, as there is still the occasional restaurateur who gets his sums wrong when dealing with foreigners. Most restaurants accept credit cards, but if there is no sticker on the door, ask, '*prendete le carte di credito?*'

Where we have specified '**Meals served**', this is the opening time of the kitchen: the establishment may remain open long after. In the evening, few serious restaurants open before 7.30pm. Pizzerias begin serving earlier, generally by 7pm.

In this guide, we have used the euro (€) symbol to indicate the average price range for a three-course meal without wine for one:

€ – €20 or less
€€ – €21 to €35
€€€ – €36 to €50
€€€€ – over €50

Children, women and (no) smoking

Taking children into restaurants – even the smartest – is never a problem in Rome. Waiters will usually produce a high chair (*un seggiolone*) and are generally happy to serve youngsters *una mezza porzione* – a half-portion.

Women dining alone will rarely encounter problems, though you have to get used to the local habit of staring. Single diners of either sex can have trouble getting a table at busy times: few proprietors want to waste a table that could hold four.

Smoking is now illegal in all restaurants except where there is a designated smoking area that meets stringent regulations.

Booking is recommended for Friday or Saturday evening or Sunday lunch, even in the more humble-looking places.

Pizza

Traditional Roman pizza is thin; Neapolitan pizza is puffier. Either way, make sure it comes from a wood-fired oven (*forno a legna*).

Pizza toppings are strictly orthodox: don't expect pineapple. Note that pizza is an evening thing – very few places serve it for lunch.

Wine bars

Neighbourhood *enoteche* (wine shops) and *vini e olii* (wine and oil) outlets have been around in Rome since time immemorial. Recently, a number of upmarket, international-style wine bars have also sprung up, offering snacks and even full meals to go with their wines.

GINA

eat & drink

restaurant

italian bistrò

wine & cocktail bar

tea room

sweets & ice cream

pic nic basket

music lounge

private party

Via San Sebastianello 7/A
(Next to Spanish Steps)
www.ginaroma.com
tel. 0039.06.678.02.51
Open 7/7 no stop 11 a.m 11 p.m
Gina's kitchen Via Plana 9/11
(piazza Euclide) Roma

GINA

eat & drink

Snacks

The city's snack culture lurks in unlikely places, such as the humble *alimentari* (grocer's) where they'll fill a crusty white roll (*rosetta*), or a slice of *pizza bianca* (focaccia) with ham, salami or cheese. *Pizza rustica* outlets serve pizza by the takeaway slab, while most bars have a range of sandwiches and filled rolls.

Vegetarians

Rome has few bona fide vegetarian restaurants; but even in traditional *trattorie*, there are plenty of meatless options to try – from *penne all'arrabbiata* (pasta in a tomato and chilli sauce) through to *tonnarelli cacio e pepe* (thick spaghetti with crumbly sheep's cheese and black pepper) to *carciofi alla giudia* (deep-fried artichokes). If you are at all unsure about the ingredients of any dish, ask if it has meat in it (*'c'è la carne?'*).

Pasticcerie and *gelaterie*

Most *pasticcerie* (cake shops) are bars where freshly baked goodies can be consumed in situ with a drink, or taken away.

Many bars have a freezer cabinet with a sign promising *produzione artigianale* (home-made ice-cream). This is often a con: it may mean industrial ice-cream mix whipped up on the premises. While this doesn't necessarily mean the ice-cream will be bad, you'll need to be selective when seeking a truly unique *gelato* experience. If the colours seem too bright to be real, then they aren't. Banana should be creamy-grey, not electric yellow.

As well as the two main choices of *frutta* and *crema* (fruit- or cream-based ice-cream), there's also *sorbetto* or *granita* (water ices). When you've exhausted these, sample a *grattachecca*, a rougher version of water ice.

Drinking

Cafés and bars

The average Roman starts his or her day with a coffee in a local café or bar (in Italy these amount to the same thing, since alcohol and coffee are served all day long in both). They will also have snacks, maybe cigarettes and bus tickets, and fabulous, cheap coffee.

In the touristy *centro storico*, things are different. Standing at the counter like the locals to knock back your tiny cupful is one thing; but occupy a table or, worse, a pavement table, and the bill will double or even treble. Of course, there are moments when nothing is more beguiling than sitting outside with a view of the Pantheon; just be aware that you'll pay for the luxury.

Besides the many variations of *caffè* (espresso) and cappuccino, most bars offer *cornetti* (croissants), *tramezzini* (sandwiches) and *panini* (filled rolls; one is a *panino*). A small bottle of still or sparkling mineral water (*acqua minerale naturale* or *gassata*) costs around €1.

By law, all bars must have a *bagno* (lavatory), which can be used by anyone, whether or not they purchase anything. Bars must also provide dehydrated passers-by with a glass of tap water, free and with no obligation to buy. Smoking is forbidden inside all bars and cafés.

Pubs and *enoteche*

Many of Rome's *enoteche* and *vini e olii* have recently become charming places to grab a drink and a slice of the *vita romana*. Some of these are chic venues with a *dopocena* (after-dinner) scene and a beautiful, see-and-be-seen crowd.

Rome's pubs are divided between a handful of long-standing British- and Irish-style institutions and a host of newer casual joints.

IL BACARO ROMA

sfizi ai fornelli

Via degli Spagnoli, 27
Roma
tel. 06.6872554
06.6864110
www.ilbacaro.com
**OPEN
TO LATE NIGHT**
(closed Sunday)
Reservations advisable

Via Condotti p89

WHAT'S BEST
Shopping

Shopping habits among Romans are changing rapidly, as locals head in droves for outlet malls in the city's hinterland peddling cut-price designer names. Regular malls with high-street fashion and household brands, plus a hypermarket or two, are also increasingly popular. And yet, Rome's *centro storico* shopping streets continue to teem with punters. In the Eternal City, there's something for all tastes.

As a visitor, you'll probably shop exclusively in the *centro*, where the first thing that will strike you is the dearth of malls and familiar chains (give or take a Benetton or two). Instead, there are corner grocery shops, dark and dusty bottle-lined wine shops, one-off boutiques catering to every imaginable taste… and, of course, the opulent outlets of Italy's fashion aristocracy.

Traditionalists can draw comfort from the fact that, for now, tiny boutiques and family-run stores are managing to retain their presence in Rome's retail sector. Just.

Because, in fact, the 'uniqueness' of Rome's shopping is skin-deep. Here, as elsewhere, the corner shop is being driven out by big-name mini-markets; there *are* clothing chains – it's just that they have different names here; and major international brands are colonising the Roman high street at a distressing pace.

Where to shop

Milan retains its crown as fashion centre, but the Eternal City is unquestionably a more picturesque place to shop. The major Italian names in *alta moda* are huddled around piazza di Spagna and via Condotti, in the Tridente. The main streets here are often packed, so wind your way through the pretty side streets and check out the smaller – though often costly – boutiques. Slicing through the Tridente from

Franchi p151

piazza del Popolo to piazza Venezia is via del Corso, home to mid-range outlets for everything from books and music to clothing and shoes.

Further south along via del Corso, the Galleria Alberto Sordi, a restored early 20th-century arcade, has fast become one of the city's prime shopping and meeting points. As well as the 20 retail outlets, there are a couple of *aperitivo* bars and frequent 'happenings' of a musical and artistic nature, all under one beautifully coloured glass roof.

There are more high street clothing retailers along traffic-clogged via Nazionale; while this street itself is no charmer, the nearby Monti neighbourhood packs unique boutiques and hip originals.

Across the river, beneath the Vatican walls in the Prati area, via Cola di Rienzo is a shorter and slightly less crowded version of via del Corso, with major retail chains, and some great food shopping.

For great independent designers and the city's best vintage gear, on the other hand, head west of piazza Navona to via del Governo Vecchio.

In order to sample those outlet malls, you'll need your own car. The largest ones are Castel Romano (www.mcarthurglen.it/castelromano), south of the city, Valmontone Fashion District (www.fashion district.it), off the A1 motorway heading south, and the new-for-2009 Soratte Outlet (www.soratteoutlet.it), off the A1 just north of Rome.

Opening times

Many Rome shop owners forgo the sacred siesta in favour of '*no-stop*' opening hours, from around 10am to 7.30pm, Monday to Saturday. The odd independent still clings to the 1-4pm shutdown. In the centre, lots of stores now open on Sundays.

Times given in this guide are winter opening hours; in summer

DON'T MISS: 2010

SHORTLIST

Take-home treats
- Bottega dei sapori della legalità (p63)
- Castroni (p151)
- Franchi (p151)
- Moriondo e Gariglio (p84)
- Said (p116)
- Valzani (p138)
- Volpetti (p127)

Clothes with class
- Arsenale (p84)
- Le Gallinelle (p109)
- Maga Morgana (p84)
- Momento (p76)
- Le Tartarughe (p84)

Reading matter
- Almost Corner Bookshop (p137)
- Feltrinelli International (p108)
- Libreria del Cinema (p136)
- Palazzo delle Esposizioni – basement bookshop (p105)

Shoe heaven
- Borini (p75)
- Loco (p76)

Divine scents
- Ai Monasteri (p83)
- L'Olfattorio – Bar à Parfums (p92)
- Roma – Store (p138)

Flea (etc) markets
- Micca Market, Sundays from 6pm at Micca Club (p114)
- Porta Portese (p137)
- La Soffitta sotto i Portici (p92)
- Testaccio market for shoes (p122)
- Via Sannio (p114)

Produce markets
- Campo de' Fiori (p65)
- Ex-Piazza Vittorio (p108)
- Testaccio (p127)

1000 ways to spend your weekends

From £12.99 / $19.95

Porta Portese p137

(June to September), shops that opt for long lunches tend to reopen later, at say 5.30pm, until around 8pm. Most food stores close on Thursday afternoons in winter, and Saturday afternoons in summer. The majority of non-food shops are closed Monday mornings. Many shops shut for at least two weeks in summer (usually in August) and almost all are shut for two or three days around the 15 August public holiday. If you want to avoid finding a particular shop *chiuso per ferie* (closed for holidays), be sure to ring ahead.

Service has improved a little but many shop assistants still seem hell-bent on either ignoring or intimidating customers. This is no time for Anglo-Saxon reticence; perfect the essential lines *'mi può aiutare, per favore?'* ('Can you help me, please?') and *'volevo solo dare un' occhiata'* ('I'm just looking') and you're ready for any eventuality.

Prices and paying

Italians bemoan the advent of the penury-inducing euro, but for Brits with much-devalued pounds, Italy may seem even more expensive than it does for euro-wielders.

Home-grown designer names are still a little easier on the wallet here than abroad, however. Bargaining belongs firmly at the flea market.

You should always be given a *scontrino* (receipt). If you aren't, then ask for it: by law, shops must provide one, and they and you are liable for a fine in the (wildly unlikely) event of your being caught without it. Major credit cards are accepted just about everywhere, but do check before getting to a till.

The rules on returning purchases are infuriatingly vague. Faulty goods, obviously, must be refunded or replaced. Many shops will also accept unwanted goods that are returned unused with a receipt within seven days of purchase, though this is not obligatory.

Tax rebates

Non-EU residents are entitled to a sales tax (IVA) rebate on purchases of personal goods worth over €155, if they are bought from a shop with the 'Europe Tax Free' sticker. The shop will give you a receipt and a 'Tax Free Shopping Cheque', which should be stamped by customs before leaving Italy.

Goa p128

Nightlife

After a bright start to the millennium, Rome's arts and entertainment scenes have entered a less jubilant phase as they watch to see which way the city's new right-wing administration will swing. It's unlikely, however, to encourage the emergence into the mainstream of formerly underground movements and projects, a development dear to the previous centre-left city council.

Those few years of frenetic activity have, however, left the city an important heritage. Dancing to the best international DJs and hearing the latest bands is still easier than it was, say, ten years ago. You will, however, need some inside information to avoid the Eurotrash dished out by the plethora of commercial venues.

Where to go, when to go

Compulsory closing times forcing most *centro storico* bars to shut at 2am have cancelled the unwritten 'open until the last punter stumbles out the door' rule that long gave Roman nights their uniquely relaxed feel.

Discos and live venues still stay open until the small hours, though, allowing Romans to maintain their habit of starting the evenings late and ending them even later.

Rome's nightlife venues tend to be concentrated mostly around a few easily accessible areas.

In Testaccio, nightlife action happens around Monte Testaccio (p120): – just walk around until you find the vibe you're after.

The area around via Libetta, off via Ostiense, teems with trendy clubs and is poised to become even more crowded: the whole area is slowly being developed as an arts hub.

Fashionistas head for the *centro storico*: spend an evening in the *triangolo della Pace* around via della Pace and you're part of trendy Roman life. The campo de' Fiori area, once another fashionista meeting spot, has become increasingly chaotic and, as the evening progresses, squalid.

Trastevere has lovely alleys packed with friendly, crowded bars, where English is the lingua franca. Note, though, that around piazza Trilussa, it can get pretty seedy in the wee hours.

Slightly further from the *centro*, artsy, studenty San Lorenzo is altogether less pretentious: drinks are cheaper, and there's always something interesting going on.

Not far from here, but further out still, is Il Pigneto (p117), fast becoming Rome's coolest night time hang-out of all. With only a couple of clubs – Circolo degli Artisti (p117) and Fanfulla 101 (via Fanfulla da Lodi 101, www.fanfulla.org) – the real attractions here are great restaurants, great late-night bars and a great atmosphere. Don't hang about too late though: it's a tough area and after 2am you may be made to feel unwelcome.

Clubbing

When picking a club for the night, bear in mind that many of Rome's mainstream venues serve up commercial house or 1980s retro on Fridays and Saturdays. Established places like Goa (p128), La Saponeria (p128) and Micca Club (p114) offer high-quality DJ sets; the focus in this last is on 1950s and '60s beats.

For something alternative, try dancing the night away at Screamadelica (Saturday at Circolo

SHORTLIST

Going live
- Circolo degli Artisti (p117)
- Dimmidisì (p116)
- Mads (p116)
- Palalottomatica (p45)

Alternative happenings
- Locanda Atlantide (p116)
- Rialtosantambrogio (p76)

Late late bars
- Caffè della Pace (p81)
- Friends Art Café (p136)
- Ombre Rosse (p137)
- Salotto 42 (p83)
- Il Tiaso (p117)

Dance till you drop
- Akab (p127)
- Alpheus (p128)
- Anima (p84)
- La Maison (p84)
- Micca Club (p114)
- La Saponeria (p128)

Best gay venues
- Coming Out (p114)
- Hangar (p109)
- Skyline (p114)

Best gay one-nighters
- Gorgeous I Am at Alpheus (Fri; p128)
- Muccassassina at Qube (Fri; p117)
- Omogenic at Circolo degli Artisti (Fri; p117)
- Venus Rising at Goa (last Sun of month; p128)

Jazz, Latin & Blues
- Alexanderplatz (p151)
- Big Mama (p138)
- Caruso-Café de Oriente (p128)
- Gregory's (p96)
- The Place (p151)

degli Artisti, p117), where global live acts are topped by DJs playing rock, pop and indie. On Tuesdays, DJ Andrea Esu and international guests spin their electro-house and tech sounds at L-Ektrica (Akab, p127). Vintage enthusiasts strike gold at Twiggy, Rome's best '60s night, where Italy's top live bands introduce DJs Luzy L and Corry X (at Mads, p116, in 2009, but check www.myspace.com/twiggy60sparty for updates). Micca Club (p114) hosts Dadumpa (Fri) and the Notte del Giaguaro (Sat), both with live gigs and DJ sets.

Going live

Gloriously eclectic programming at the Auditorium – Parco della Musica (p100) has helped seduce music-shy Romans into making live sounds a regular diary fixture.

But Rome's live music scene is also being boosted by a string of smallish clubs. In 2005, the city-sponsored Casa del Jazz (viale di Porta Ardeatina 55, 06 704 731, www.casajazz.it) opened in a villa confiscated from a local mobster. The cool Teatro Palladium (p128) hosts a daring programme too. And City Hall continues to fund the prestigious RomaEuropa Festival (p37). It remains to be seen whether the new administration will stump up for free mega-concerts in grand settings like its predecessor.

Concerts by huge international names are rare, but when they do happen, it's often in atmosphere-less mega-venues like the Stadio Olimpico (p100) or the PalaLottomatica (p45) in the suburb of EUR (p44).

Until not so long ago, much of Rome's alternative live action centred on very low-cost events hosted by *centri sociali* – disused buildings occupied by dissatisfied youth and transformed into spaces

for art, music and politics. With more opportunities elsewhere, their importance waned, but given the current climate, they may come back into their own... if, that is, Rome's mayor doesn't carry out his threat to shut them all down.

Summer in the city

Rome gives its best over the long summer: you'll be spoilt for choice between festivals, concerts, open-air cinema, theatre and discos, most of which come under the Estate Romana (p40) umbrella.

Gay Rome

Rome's gay community has been on an emotional roller-coaster over the past few years: it waited with bated breath in 2006-7 but parliamentary debate on civil unions eventually ground to a halt – thanks, many suspect, to Vatican intervention. Now, with a right-wing city administration, it's wondering whether the traditionally gay-friendly (or at least ostensibly tolerant) attitude of the city's rulers will be affected.

Gay life in the Italian capital continues to be mainstream, however, with new organisations, venues and facilities popping up. The historic Mario Mieli (www.mariomieli.org) group, flanked by the newer, hyperactive Di'Gay Project (www.digayproject. org), continues to add more social goodies to the shopping trolley.

Likewise, the gay going-out scene continues to diversify and cater for distinct clienteles, with restaurants, pubs, clubs and bars attracting punters of all ages. A proliferation of mixed one-nighters also mirrors the increasing number of places where men and women can have fun under the same roof. Or, for that matter, outdoors: one of the most notable successes in the Roman calendar is the summer Gay Village (p40). The www.gayvillage.it website is also a great source of year-round events info.

Many gay venues ask for an Arcigay card, which costs €15 for annual membership. The card can be bought at any participating venue.

Getting in

Getting into Rome's fashionable mainstream clubs can be stressful, no matter how well you're dressed. Intimidating bouncers will block your way, while PR luvvies smirk as they whisk supposed VIPs through the door past lines of frustrated would-be clients. But persistence and patience will get you in eventually.

Clubs and discobars generally charge an entrance fee at weekends but not on weekdays; be aware that on your first visit you will often have to buy a *tessera* (membership card) on top of, or sometimes instead of, the entrance fee. Tickets often include a 'free' drink, but you can expect the drinks you buy thereafter to be pricey. Another popular formula is to grant 'free' admission while forcing you to buy a (generally expensive) drink. To get out again you have to hand a stamped drink card to the bouncer, so hold on to whatever piece of paper staff give you or you'll be forced to pay twice.

Where we haven't specified a price for entrance, admission is free.

Finding out

For details of upcoming events, consult the listings magazines *Trovaroma* (Thursday with *La Repubblica*), *Roma C'è* (Wednesday) or *Zero6* (monthly, free in shops and pubs). Or visit www.romastyle.info, which is good for techno and drum 'n' bass, and www.2night.it or www.musicaroma.it for the latest gigs. Fans of indie and punk rock should take a look at www.myspace.com/romecityrockers and www.pogopop.it (in English, after a fashion).

Alexanderplatz p151

Rome International Film Festival p37

WHAT'S BEST

Arts & Leisure

A spell of arts optimism (and spending) after the turn of the millennium now appears to be slacking off after a new, less culture-friendly mayor was installed in City Hall in May 2008, and the credit crunch made money for 'frivolities' more scarce. Still, the after-effects of that golden age are still being felt, and Rome continues to offer much in the way of performing arts.

Fine arts – of the contemporary, commercial variety – also shifted swiftly up through several gears late in 2007 when top art dealer Larry Gagosian opened a stunning new gallery here.

Music

If Rome still enjoys its new-found place back on the music-lovers'

map of Europe, this is thanks mainly to activities at Auditorium – Parco della Musica (p100).

Inaugurated in 2002, this complex of exhibition and concert spaces, designed by Renzo Piano, has been hugely successful, enticing Romans of all tastes with a programme of such extraordinary breadth it is second only to New York's Lincoln Center for the variety of its offerings. This democratic eclecticism has cast its spell over citizens who had never set foot in a classical music venue in their lives: 2006 saw over a million presences. Even more miraculous, in a country where the arts are traditionally a financial black hole, the Auditorium is self-funding and firmly in the black.

But it is not the only venue in Rome for music. Many of the more traditional concert halls and locations also benefited from the surge of energy, and many of them offer high-quality programmes.

Opera, however, is one branch of the musical arts that continues to languish, with constipated programmes and generally mediocre productions. But like many other musical offerings in Rome, the settings for opera – the Teatro dell'Opera (p109) and the Baths of Caracalla (p118) – are so glorious that the quality doesn't always matter.

Not that it's always low – for instance, La Stravaganza (06 7707 2842, www.lastravaganzamusica.it) organises delightful chamber music concerts inside the Palazzo Doria Pamphili; during the interval the audience is invited to wander into the adjacent gallery (p78) to enjoy the superb art collection. On Sundays, there are noon recitals in the sumptuous Cappella Paolina of the president's residence, Palazzo del Quirinale (p98). There are also frequent (though badly publicised) concerts at the Museo Nazionale degli Strumenti Musicali (piazza Santa Croce in Gerusalemme 9A, 06 701 4796, www.museostrumentimusicali.it); during some, items from the museum's collection of antique instruments are played. And at the church of Sant'Anselmo (piazza Cavalieri di Malta 5) on the Aventine, Benedictine monks sing Gregorian chant evensong daily at 7.15pm.

Check the local press, and look out for wall posters for other such concerts. All musical events held in churches, and many held elsewhere, are free.

Theatre

If you're thinking of an evening at the theatre, don't expect daring

SHORTLIST

Gloriously eclectic music
- Auditorium - Parco della Musica (p100)

Unmissable festivals
- Estate Romana (p40)
- RomaEuropa Festival (p37)
- Rome International Film Festival (p37)
- Rome Literature Festival (p40)

Alfresco music
- Roma Incontra il Mondo world music festival in Villa Ada (p40)
- Teatro dell'Opera Summer season in the Baths of Caracalla (p41)
- Villa Celimontana Jazz Festival (p40)

Films in English
- Alcazar (p33)
- Metropolitan (p92)
- Nuovo Olimpia (p93)
- Nuovo Sacher (p33)

Virtual Rome
- Crypta Balbi (p65)
- Rewind Rome (p88 & p109)
- Terme di Diocleziano (p88)
- Time Elevator (p88 & p96)

Theatre & opera
- Teatro dell'Opera di Roma (p109)
- Teatro Palladium (p128)

Brand-new spas
- Acquamadre (p76)
- Kamispa (p99)

Sporting fixtures
- Athletics/swimming at the Foro Italico (p100)
- Football at the Stadio Olimpico (p100)
- Rugby at the Stadio Flaminio (p99)

CASINA VALADIER

Restaurant, lounge bar, live music

a charming place in the heart of rome,
romantic and trendy

OPEN ALL DAYS FROM 10.00 TO 2.00 PM

VILLA BORGHESE - PIAZZA BUCAREST - 00187 ROME
PH. + 39 06 69922090 Fax. + 39 06 6791280
INFO@CASINAVALADIER.IT

performances: the Italian school of drama, with its stiff style imposed by the stuffy dramatic arts academy, still holds sway.

One interesting project is the Casa dei Teatri (06 4544 0707, www. casadeiteatri.culturaroma.it), in a palazzo in Villa Pamphili. This centre integrates performances with workshops and research.

Dance

This Cinderella of Italian arts is allowed out of the kitchen more often nowadays, and features in seasonal programmes and festivals such as RomaEuropa (p37).

Galleries

Rome's commercial contemporary art world had been striving for some time to rival Turin and Naples. Now local dealers are wondering whether things have moved too fast.

The indefatigable Larry 'Gogo' Gagosian inaugurated his temple to art dealing (via Francesco Crispi 16, www.gagosian.com) in December 2007. While welcoming the international attention Gagosian attracts, locals are wondering whether there'll be any market share left for them.

Film

Italian dubbers are recognised as the world's best, but that's no consolation if you like to see films in the original language (*lingua originale* or *versione originale* – VO in listings). Little is left untampered with, but there are a handful of cinemas where some VO offerings appear more or less regularly on programmes. The Nuovo Olimpia (p93), just off via del Corso, and the Metropolitan (p92) usually show one or more

VO films, the former with slightly more recherché titles and the latter a little more mainstream. There are VO screenings at the Alcazar (via Merry del Val 14, Monday) and at the Nuovo Sacher (largo Ascianghi 1, Monday and/or Tuesday). The Warner Village Moderno (piazza Repubblica 43-45) hosts the occasional blockbuster in VO.

The Casa del Cinema (largo M Mastroianni 1, www.casadel cinema.it), inside Villa Borghese, screens an interesting selection of films for free.

Rome's annual film festival, Cinema – Festa Internazionale di Roma (aka Rome International Film Festival; p37), launched in 2006 and held in October, is one to look out for.

Sport

Many Romans have an aversion to physical activity, but they are passionate supporters.

Rome is home to two first-class football clubs: AS Roma (www.asroma.it) and SS Lazio (www.sslazio.it). The two teams share the Stadio Olimpico (p100) in the Foro Italico complex.

In 2007, a spate of stadium violence prompted tough new measures. Tickets can no longer be bought from the Stadio Olimpico box office: you must buy them from www.listicket.it or from specialist outlets. Tickets are personal (you'll need photo-ID to get into the stadium) and non-transferable.

Though most Romans reserve their enthusiasm for football, the city also has its rugby fans. Since 2000, the national side has been in the Six Nations' Championship, with home games played at the Stadio Flaminio (viale Tiziano, 06 3685 7309, www.federugby.it).

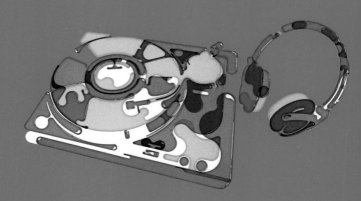

NYC

Ask New York City about New York City all night
nycgo.com

Calendar

Rome Marathon p39

Romans love their holidays, and are experts at making the best of whatever spare time comes their way. Any crisp, sunny winter weekend is good for a *scampagnata* (jaunt to the countryside); a mid-week public holiday can be made into a lengthy break by what is known as *fare il ponte* (doing a bridge), or taking off the days between the holiday and the nearest weekend. If the current ten annual public holidays look paltry next to the ancient Romans' 150, citizens of the Eternal City will make them feel like far, far more.

Religious holidays (and the Easter week in particular) turn the city centre into a heaving mass of visiting humanity; only *Ferragosto* (the Assumption) on 15 August shuts the city down. Different districts of Rome hold smaller-scale celebrations of their own

patron saints in their own way, from calorific blowouts and costume parades to extravagant firework displays.

Throughout the year, Rome offers small-scale independent festivals and big-budget citywide events that make ample use of the city's endless supply of photogenic venues.

Keep an eye on local press and wall posters for the occasional huge free concert, and also major exhibitions, which tend to be announced at short notice. The websites of the cultural heritage ministry (www.beniculturali.it), the Rome city council (www.comune.roma.it), the city's information site www.060608.it and the Rome tourist board (www.turismoroma.it) are useful sources of information.

Dates highlighted in **bold** are public holidays.

Palazzo delle Esposizioni

September 2009

Until 13 Sept **Bulgari: 150 years of Italian jewellery**
Palazzo delle Esposizioni (p105)

Until 10 Jan 2010 **The Divine Vespasian. Bi-millennium of the Flavian Dynasty**
Venues around the
Roman Forum (p59)

Sept-Jan 2010 **Caravaggio/Bacon**
Galleria Borghese (p94)
www.galleriaborghese.it
Works by the two 'tortured' artists placed side by side for the first time.

24 Sept-17 Jan **Roman Painting: Colours of the Empire**
Scuderie del Quirinale (p98)
www.scuderiequirinale.it
Artworks from the first to the fourth centuries.

Late Sept-early Dec
RomaEuropa Festival
Various locations
www.romaeuropa.net
Rome's most prestigious performing arts festival.

October 2009

Ongoing The Divine Vespasian;
Roman Painting: Colours
of the Empire; RomaEuropa
Festival (for all, see Sept)

Oct-Feb 2010 **Alexander Calder**
Palazzo delle Esposizioni (p105)
www.palazzoesposizioni.it
Over 100 works by the American artist.

15-23 **Rome International Film Festival**
Auditorium – Parco della Musica (p100) and other venues
www.romacinemafest.org
The fourth edition of Rome's international film festival.

Late Oct **Mostra dell'Antiquariato**
Via de' Coronari
This antiques fair is packed with dealers.

November 2009

Ongoing The Divine Vespasian;
Roman Painting: Colours
of the Empire; RomaEuropa
Festival (for all, see Sept);
Alexander Calder (see Oct).

1-2 **All Saints/All Souls**
Cimitero del Verano,
piazzale del Verano
Romans visit family graves.

December 2009

Ongoing The Divine Vespasian;
Roman Painting: Colours
of the Empire; RomaEuropa
Festival (for all, see Sept);
Alexander Calder (see Oct).

8 **Immacolata Concezione**
Piazza di Spagna (p90)
Immaculate Conception.

25-26 **Natale & Santo Stefano**
Nativity scenes are set up inside churches and on St Peter's square (p141), and a Christmas fair is held in piazza Navona.

31 **San Silvestro**
Free concert in piazza del Popolo (p85); much street partying.

January 2010

Ongoing The Divine Vespasian;
Roman Painting: Colours
of the Empire; RomaEuropa
Festival (for all, see Sept);
Alexander Calder (see Oct).

1 **Capodanno**
New Year's Day.

6 **Epifania – La Befana**
Piazza Navona (p79)
A fair dedicated to *La Befana* – the old witch – who brings Epiphany treats for all the children.

17 **Sant'Eusebio**
Sant'Eusebio, via Napoleone III
Animal lovers have pets blessed.

MAXXI

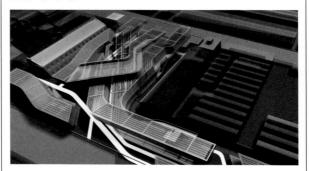

In 1999, a design by Anglo-Iraqi architect Zaha Hadid was selected to house Rome's answer to the Tate Modern: **MAXXI** (Museo nazionale delle arti del Secolo XXI – 21st Century Arts Museum, p100). Since then, mooted inauguration dates have come and gone, as the powers that be failed repeatedly to put up funding to match their enthusiasm. But – scaled down, pared back and with a permanent collection somewhat lacking in pzazz – MAXXI was nearing completion as this guide went to press, and was slated to open in early 2010. By which time, its dynamic directors hope, it will have gathered enough momentum to launch Rome firmly on to the contemporary arts circuit.

Occupying the site of a former army barracks in the northern Flaminio suburb, the new complex is a snaking design that will house museums of art and architecture, a library, resource centre, café, bookshop... all the trappings of the 21st-century arts facility. From an original budget of around €57 million, the cost of building the first, main structure has shot up to around €150 million.

But this is par for the course, and there seems to be general relief that the high walls of an incongruous military zone in the heart of this residential area will finally be torn down. With its pedestrian through-routes, this will be, the MAXXI Foundation's director general Pio Baldi has said, 'a living urban space'.

The importance of relating to the surrounding city was underscored in *Dialoghi con la città* (Conversations with the City), a series of site-specific installations prepared for accessible areas of MAXXI in the run-up to the grand opening.

And MAXXI's directors describe the complex as a 'campus'. There are plans to work closely with schools and attract locals with seminars and workshops.

All of which may turn Hadid's design into a hive of art-centred activity. It may also conceal the fact that MAXXI will never be the Tate Modern, and that Rome, with its antique glories, is unlikely to draw international crowds with its contemporary ones.
■ www.maxxi.darc.beniculturali.it

February 2010

Ongoing Alexander Calder (see Oct).

6-16 **Carnevale**
Around the city centre
Kids dress up and throw confetti in the run-up to Lent.

10 Feb-30 June **Renaissance Forms: Sculpture in Rome in the 15th Century**
Palazzo Venezia (p59)
Works by Donatello, Bregna and Michelangelo.

March 2010

Ongoing Renaissance Forms (see Feb).

9 **Feast of Santa Francesca Romana**
Monastero Oblate di Santa Francesca Romana, via Teatro di Marcello 32 & 40
Rare opportunity to visit this medieval nunnery; Romans have cars blessed at Santa Francesca Romana church in the Roman Forum.

16 **Palazzo Massimo alle Colonne**
Corso Vittorio Emanuele 141
Once-a-year opening of the patrician palace, 8am-1pm.

19 **Feast of San Giuseppe**
Around via Trionfale
Partying and batter-ball eating to mark St Joseph's day.

21 **Maratona della Città di Roma**
Around the city centre
www.maratonadiroma.it
The marathon begins and ends in via dei Fori Imperial. There's a 5km fun-run for those not up to the whole 42km.

Dates tbc **Giornate FAI**
Various locations
www.fondoambiente.it
For one weekend each spring, private and institutional owners of interesting, historic properties reveal their spectacular interiors that are usually off-limits to the public.

29 Mar-5 Apr **Holy Week & Easter**
Vatican (p140), Colosseum (p57)
Palm Sunday mass at St Peter's and Pope's Via Crucis at Colosseum on Good Friday.

April 2010

Ongoing Renaissance Forms (see Feb); Holy Week & Easter (see Mar).

April-May **FotoGrafia**
Various locations
www.zoneattive.it
Rome's international festival of photography was threatened by the withdrawal of city funding in 2009, but seemed determined to continue in 2010.

21 **Natale di Roma**
Campidoglio (p56)
Rome celebrates its 2,763rd birthday with an immense display of fireworks.

25 **Liberation Day**

Late Apr **Mostra delle Azalee**
Piazza di Spagna (p90)
Spring arrives early in Rome, bringing masses of blooms. Some 3,000 vases of azaleas sit on the Spanish Steps.

Date tbc **Settimana della Cultura**
www.beniculturali.it
For one week in April, all state-owned museums are free and many otherwise closed sites are open. Dates vary from year to year.

May 2010

Ongoing Renaissance Forms (see Feb).

1 **Primo Maggio**
Piazza San Giovanni
www.primomaggio.com
Trade unions organise this huge, free rock concert for May Day. Performers are mainly Italian.

Rome International Film Festival p37

Mid May-late June
Rome Literature Festival
Basilica di Massenzio, Roman
Forum (p60)
www.festivaldelleletterature.it
Book launches and readings.

Mid May-late June
Roseto Comunale
Via Valle Murcia/clivo dei Pubblici
Annual opening of Rome's municipal
rose garden.

Late May **Piazza di Siena**
Piazza di Siena,
Villa Borghese (p93)
www.piazzadisiena.com
The city's ultra-smart four-day show-
jumping event.

June 2010

Ongoing Renaissance Forms (see
Feb); Roseto Comunale (see May).

Early June-end Sept
Estate Romana
Various locations
www.estateromana.comune.roma.it

Piazze, palazzi and parks come alive
with music, and films are shown on
outdoor screens. Many events are free.

Early June-Aug
Villa Celimontana Jazz Festival
Villa Celimontana (p109)
www.villacelimontanajazz.com
Jazz concerts take place beneath the
trees of this lovely park.

Mid June-early Aug
Roma Incontra il Mondo
Villa Ada, via di Ponte Salario
www.villaada.org
World music is performed by the lake
in this park in the northern suburbs.

Mid June-mid Aug **Fiesta!**
Via Appia Nuova 1245
www.fiesta.it
Latin American music fest at the
Capanelle racecourse near Ciampino.

Late June-early Sept **Gay Village**
Venue varies
www.gayvillage.it
A ten-week open-air bonanza with
bars, restaurants, live acts, discos,

cinema, for boys and girls. Venue moves from year to year: check the website.

Late June-mid Aug **Teatro dell'Opera Summer Season**
Baths of Caracalla (p118)
www.operaroma.it
Rome's opera company stages grand performances in these Roman ruins.

Late June-early Sept
Cosmophonies
www.cosmophonies.com
Roman Theatre, Ostia Antica (p159)
World music, light entertainment and opera amid the ruins.

29 Santi Pietro e Paolo
Basilica di San Paolo
fuori le Mura (p123)
Street fair outside St Paul's basilica and mass at St Peter's for the feast day of Rome's patron saints.

July 2010

Ongoing Estate Romana, Villa Celimontana Jazz Festival, Roma Incontra il Mondo, Gay Village, Fiesta!, Teatro dell'Opera Summer Season, Cosmophonies (for all, see June)

Mid July **Festa di Noantri**
Piazza Santa Maria in Trastevere, piazza Mastai
Two weeks of arts events, street performances and fairground attractions.

August 2010

Ongoing Estate Romana, Villa Celimontana Jazz Festival, Roma Incontra il Mondo, Gay Village, Fiesta!, Teatro dell'Opera Summer Season, Cosmophonies (for all, see June)

1 **Festa delle Catene**
San Pietro in Vincoli (p105)
The chains that bound St Peter are displayed in a special mass.

5 **Festa della Madonna della Neve**
Santa Maria Maggiore (p105)
A blizzard of rose petals flutters down on festive mass-goers.

10 Notte di San Lorenzo
San Lorenzo in Panisperna,
via Panisperna 90
Nuns distribute bread and candles
on this, the night of shooting stars.

15 Ferragosto
Rome closes down for the feast of the
Assumption. Many locals head to the
coast for the long weekend.

September 2010

Ongoing Estate Romana,
Gay Village, Cosmophonies
(for all, see June)

Sept-Nov **RomaEuropa Festival**
Various locations
www.romaeuropa.net
Rome's most prestigious performing
arts festival, with an eclectic mix of
music, dance and theatre performances.

October 2010

Ongoing RomaEuropa Festival
(see Sept)

Late Oct **Mostra dell'Antiquariato**
Via de' Coronari
Antiques fair in this collector's mecca.

Oct 29-Nov 6 **Rome
International Film Festival**
Auditorium – Parco della Musica
(p100) and other venues
www.romacinemafest.org
The fifth edition of Rome's international film festival.

November 2010

Ongoing RomaEuropa Festival
(see Sept); Rome International
Film Festival (see Oct)

1-2 All Saints/All Souls
Cimitero del Verano
Romans visit family graves.

December 2010

8 Immacolata Concezione
Piazza di Spagna (p90)
Immaculate Conception.

25-26 Natale & Santo Stefano
Nativity scenes in churches; Christmas
fair in piazza Navona.

31 **San Silvestro**
Free concert in piazza del Popolo; much
street partying.

Natale

Itineraries

Centro dei Congressi p46

The Ideal City

There's ancient Rome, and there's Baroque Rome. And then there's *La Terza Roma* (the Third Rome) – the immense modern metropolis stretching from the Aurelian walls to the sea that Benito Mussolini dreamed of, then went some way towards creating, setting to work on it soon after he swept to power in 1922.

Even in today's increasingly right-wing Italy, the legacy of the Fascist dictator is still a bit of an embarrassment. But if the ancient and the Baroque begin to pall, half a day spent studying the regime's impressive exercises in futuristic town planning and architecture will show that, behind the bombast, repression and artifice, some interesting urban experiments were taking place.

Il Duce's aims were simple: he would rid Italy of backwardness and poverty, and found a new Fascist Italian Empire – complete with rich foreign colonies – based

on an updated vision of the Roman Empire. The best of modern architecture, he decided, would express the regime's grandeur and dynamism.

Rome itself was difficult to modernize: *il Duce* tried hard with various set pieces, sweeping away picturesque medieval housing here and experimenting with vast boulevards there. But when the historic fabric proved too difficult to mould to his own plans, Mussolini simply started again, down the road towards the sea. Our main, half-day itinerary takes us to that 'ideal city': the suburb of **EUR** (p155). But a couple of pre-emptive visits to regime-linked venues in the city centre will give you an idea of the dictator's ambitions.

Mussolini himself wielded a pick – to commence demolition of the warren of Renaissance housing in the Borgo (p140), to make way for via della Conciliazione, the boulevard that sweeps majestically up to St Peter's. The artist Raphael's house was one of the first to go.

The dictator also bulldozed an absurd six-lane thoroughfare – now called via dei Fori Imperiali – through archaeological marvels and medieval dwellings in the Imperial fora (p58). This was to create a half-mile road link between the Colosseum (p57) and his office in Palazzo Venezia (p59), from the balcony of which he harangued his people and exchanged stiff-armed salutes with his troops.

Adolf Hitler's 1938 visit to Rome was the excuse for a torch-lit Fascist extravaganza in Mussolini's purpose-built new Foro Italico (p100) athletics complex. The gigantic male nude sculptures surrounding the stadium, and the 1932 obelisk – which still bears the legend *Mussolini Dux* – are well worth inspecting. So is piazza Augusto Imperatore, which was given a makeover when *il Duce* decided he too should one day lie at rest in the great emperor's mausoleum (p89).

But for a real taste of the Fascist Ideal City – hub of an Ideal Empire – you must go to EUR. This unlovely acronym stands for *Esposizione universale romano*, the intended site of events planned for 1942 to mark the 20th anniversary of the Fascist March on Rome (in fact, the district was originally known as E42). Getting there is easy: take the metro (linea B) to EUR Fermi; or bus number 30 and get off at the large ornamental lake. This is a business district, so a Sunday visit will reveal a relatively car-free EUR in all its eerie glory. Come in the morning to visit the district's museums (they close at 2pm, and all day Monday), which afford a glimpse inside the lofty halls of grandiloquent Fascist planning.

In spirit, EUR today lies somewhere between Brasilia and Milton Keynes. Well-heeled foreign residents settle in the expensive villas and apartment blocks in EUR's leafy residential fringes. Business people trek out to clinch deals or haggle in the ministries, state bodies and nationalised companies based here. And officials of the current right-wing city administration nurture nostalgic plans to complete EUR's master plan, recently mooting, for instance, the erection of Adalberto Libera's immense (and hugely kitsch) entrance arch designed for E42.

Italy's best architects were called to work on the E42 project, the design committee for which was headed by architect Marcello Piacentini. Endless squabbles held works up drastically. And World War II put an end to E42 (and to Mussolini). When Allied troops liberated Rome, they briefly occupied EUR's grandiose exhibition halls, the only part of the site then completed. It wasn't until Rome won its bid to host the 1960s Olympics that anyone thought of finishing EUR: it was the perfect site for the games.

The lake by the EUR Fermi metro station was built for the rowing events. The perfectly circular PalaLottomatica sports stadium behind the lake was designed by Pierluigi Nervi; it now doubles as a venue for major rock concerts.

From the northern shore of the lake, peer up the main via Cristoforo Colombo for Arturo Dazzi's obelisk-monument to radar and telephone pioneer Guglielmo Marconi, and head towards it. The first few blocks take you through the newer end of EUR. Even today, construction is still under way. On your right you'll pass the spot where architect Massimiliano Fuksas' *Nuvola* (cloud) is taking shape: this futuristic congress centre and hotel is scheduled to open in 2010.

Continue north along via Colombo for the area designed for E42. Buildings to your right on arcaded, classically inspired piazzale G Marconi house museums such as the **Museo dell'Alto Medievo** (p156), where exquisite artefacts prove that the Dark Ages were really quite bright, and the **Museo Nazionale Preistorico Etnografico L Pigorini** (p157), home to a 30ft canoe, carved from a single oak and paddled on Lake Bracciano some 10,000 years ago.

One block further along via Colombo is the intersection with via della Civiltà del Lavoro. Turn left for the **Palazzo della Civiltà del Lavoro**, inaugurated in 1940 and known to locals – for obvious reasons – as the square Colosseum. Around the top of the building a piece of doggerel, specially composed for this spot, defines Italians as a nation of poets, artists, heroes, navigators and

Palazzo della Civiltà del Lavoro

'transmigrators', a reference to the transatlantic seaplane flights of 1933 by aviator and Fascist hero Italo Balbo.

A short detour to piazzale K Adenauer will bring you to chic bar **Palombini** (06 591 1700, www.palombini.com), which offers cappuccino, dozens of flavours of ice-cream or light lunches beneath its beautiful bougainvillea pergola.

Doubling back along via Ciro il Grande, you'll spot the EUR builders' mission statement – 'the Third Rome will expand over other hills along the banks of the sacred river to the shores of the Tyrrhenian' – inscribed around what were the E42 offices in piazzale dell'Agricoltura. Many mosaics and sculptures were commissioned to decorate the exhibition site, including the somewhat comical bronze *Spirit of Fascism* here, and the splendid bas relief illustrating the history of Rome from Romulus and Remus through Emperor Augustus to *il Duce*.

Back across the main drag, and returning to via della Civiltà Romana, make for architect Adalberto Libera's fine Centro dei Congressi on piazza JF Kennedy. It was intended as a perfect cube, but Piacentini insisted on tacking on the wider bit at the bottom.

It's just one block south-east from here to piazza G Agnelli, home to the **Museo della Civiltà Romana** (p157) with its imposing colonnade. This is perhaps the most impressive of EUR's museums, if only for its huge scale model of fourth-century Rome. Archeologist Italo Gismondi began work on the plaster model in 1935 and tinkered with it until just before his death in 1974. Also here are plaster casts of the reliefs on the column in Trajan's Forum (p58).

From via Colombo, the 30 bus will whisk you back to largo Argentina in the *centro storico*.

Campo de' Fiori p49

Night Moves

A Roman 'night out' will probably be very different from one where you come from.

Romans go out for company and endless chat. If this can be done somewhere where you happen to bump into a variety of friends and acquaintances, so much the better. It might all strike the uninitiated as aimless wandering. Romans, though, have made it into a fine art. To increase the possibility of chance encounters, different groups tend to drift to their own particular areas: late twenty- and thirtysomethings to the clubs dug into Monte Testaccio (p122), university students with a yen for dancing to via Ostiense (p122) and perambulating students and hipsters to the streets and locali of San Lorenzo (p114).

Whatever your final night-out goal, your evening is likely to begin in the *centro storico* (p54) or in Trastevere (p129), and is quite likely to involve going off on the occasional tangent to a Roman monument or beauty spot: the inhabitants of the Eternal City never tire of admiring their home town. Our itinerary starts with *aperitivi* in Trastevere, and can be drawn out to fill a long long evening, or even spread over two.

Freni e Frizioni (p136) is a great bar to fuel up for the night ahead – which, for the locals, means eating, not drinking: drinking is, on the whole, secondary to conversation. Many Italians think of alcohol as something to be sipped with meals; most simply can't see the point of drinking yourself senseless. So the alternative crowd you'll find any clear evening on the riverside pavement outside Freni are attracted not so much by the mainly very ordinary wine by the glass (at very fair prices) as by the high-piled snacks that weigh down a long table from

Piazza dell'Immacolata

about 7pm and are free to anyone with a drink in their hand.

If you're feeling energetic, this might be followed by a hike up the Gianicolo hill to watch the sun set from the **Fontana Paola** (p138). Or you might just follow the crowds across the river on the pedestrian Ponte Sisto bridge, right opposite Freni, and wiggle through the medieval streets of the *centro storico* to check out the action in **campo de' Fiori** (p65).

Once upon a time, the campo was *the* Roman nightlife spot. Nowadays, it's just about bearable before dinner, perhaps for a quick drink at **La Vineria** (p75) where pavement tables provide a ringside seat for the spectacle of locals shutting up for the day, planning their evenings or just rushing home. After dinner, however, the square is invaded by visiting Anglo students on pub crawls, a generally raucous crowd which turns the area decidedly squalid. Unless a degenerating frat-party ambience appeals, stay just long enough to plan your next move. Which will probably mean dinner.

After your *aperitivo* snacks, a quick pizza may well suffice. The *centro* is packed with *pizzerie*, though many are sub-standard and overpriced: this is, after all, a heavily touristed area and, at the cheaper end of the market, that generally means minimum effort. (**Da Francesco**, p82, and **Baffetto 2**, p71, are possible options here.) If the clubs of Monte Testaccio or via Ostiense are your final destination, hop on bus number 30 in largo Argentina and get off in via Marmorata for **Da Remo** (p126), a cavernous Testaccio classic churning out inconceivable quantities of thin-crust pizzas.

If you're a San Lorenzo type, on the other hand, take bus 492 from corso Vittorio to via Tiburtina. Lining this road are numerous pizza joints, any of them better by far than the tourist-trap eateries of the *centro*. Take a right off via Tiburtina into via degli Equi and make for **Formula Uno** (via degli Equi 13, 06 445 3866, closed Sun). It's huge, terribly scruffy and you'll probably have to wait 15 minutes or so for a table, but the heaving masses of students tucking into the excellent pizzas in this humming food factory always seem perfectly satisfied.

At this point, the ambling begins. The bars along via dei Volsci are cheap and eternally popular, with crowds of loungers drifting from one to the other in search of old and new friends. When the weather permits, the San Lorenzo district's main square, **piazza dell'Immacolata**, is the epicentre of activity. There are no bars to mention on this irregularly shaped piazza, and by Rome standards, there's nothing very beautiful about it either. But the multitudes lazing and mingling here, perhaps with drink in hand bought in some bar nearby, are too caught up in their networking to mind this.

Occasionally, parties will hive off – for laid-back live music at clubs such as **Mads** (p116) or the eclectic offerings at **Locanda Atlantide** (p116). The more ambitious will hike out to larger music venues such as the **Circolo degli Artisti** (p117; backtrack to Termini station, and take bus 105) or **Qube** (p117; take bus 409 from piazza del Verano).

Whether your evening winds up at 1am or 6am, chances are that the finishing touch will be hot *cornetti* (croissants) munched en route to bed. At via dei Volsci 44/45, **Pasticci di Fefè** feeds hungry night owls into the wee hours.

ITINERARIES

Colosseum

Rome in a Rush

Taken at a leisurely pace and delved into thoroughly, Rome's sights and cultural offerings could keep you busy for weeks or even months. But if all you have is a few hours in transit, or a free morning during a hectic business trip, don't despair. The *centro storico* is compact and it is here that most of the city's treasures lie. This three-hour whistlestop tour will give you a real feel for the place and a primer for your next visit.

Understanding what you're looking at is very simple – as long as you remember that Rome experienced three great outbursts of art and architecture, all of which feature on this lightning tour. First came the Classical period (100 BC-AD 300) from which an amazing amount survives, albeit in ruins; next up is the Renaissance (c1420-1527) when a colourful succession of bellicose, megalomaniac, billionaire popes threw their ill-gotten gains into an orgy of

exquisite church and palace building; and as a grand finale came the outrageously overblown Baroque period (c1620-1680), which put fruity festoons on every last theatrical façade.

Get your taxi driver to drop you at the top of the **Spanish Steps** (p90). (Or take Metro A to Spagna.) You've seen it in the movies, but the view of the city from the top of the Spanish Steps is still spectacular: straight ahead is super-smart via Condotti, lined with the flagship stores of Italy's top designers. Flocks of loungers follow the sun as it moves across the staircase. The Spanish Embassy to the Holy See still stands in **piazza di Spagna**. Romantic poet John Keats breathed his last in the pink house on the left at the foot of the Steps, now a museum (p89).

Resist basking in the sun on the Steps, or bunking off with your credit card. Instead, after glancing at the pretty boat-shaped fountain at the bottom of the Steps, turn right into via del Babuino, one of the three prongs of the Tridente district.

At the far end of this upmarket street, lined with antiques shops and galleries, is **piazza del Popolo**, hub of Pope Sixtus V's striking 17th-century urban planning scheme. Before you get there, duck right into picturesque via Margutta, home to a string of galleries.

From a pavement table at **Rosati** (p92), cappuccino in hand, you'll notice that piazza del Popolo holds fine examples of all Rome's artistic periods. In the centre of this great neo-classical square stands an Egyptian obelisk purloined by Emperor Augustus from the Temple of the Sun at Heliopolis. Twin pepperpot Baroque churches mark the start of the Tridente, while the church of **Santa Maria del Popolo** (p89) (you absolutely must dash into it, if only to gawp at the matching pair of paintings by Baroque master Caravaggio) is a Renaissance gem. The mighty gate in the ancient Roman city walls was hastily built to welcome prestigious convert to Catholicism, Queen Christina of Sweden in 1655.

Busy via del Corso, the central prong of the Tridente, was where Carnevale horse races were held in papal Rome. Today, Roman youth deck themselves out in the low-cost fashion emporia lining this thoroughfare. Rush past them all, stopping only to glimpse at some of Rome's most splendid *palazzi*.

The ultra-aristocratic Ruspoli and Borghese families still live in their grand city palaces. You can often get into **Palazzo Ruspoli** (p89x) for exhibitions, but you will have to content yourself with a glimpse of the courtyard of vast 17th-century **Palazzo Borghese** (via Fontanella Borghese). Napoleon Bonaparte's sister, the beautiful

Paolina, lived here with her husband Prince Camillo Borghese.

Further down via del Corso is the even more spectacular **Doria Pamphili Gallery** (p78). You may like to spend an hour exploring its jaw-dropping art collection.

Alternatively, check which way the political wind is blowing in nearby piazza Colonna (named after Marcus Aurelius' immense column, at the centre of the square). The prime minister's office is in 16th-century **Palazzo Chigi** here; nearby in 17th-century **Palazzo Montecitorio** is the Italian lower house of parliament. The obelisk in the centre of the piazza was the needle of the outsized sundial set up here by Emperor Augustus.

It's only a two-minute walk from here to piazza Augusto Imperatore. The emperor built a huge circular mausoleum, now sadly stripped of its marble, for himself and his family. By the river is the Richard Meier building housing Augustus' **Ara Pacis** (p89, Altar of Peace); the Imperial family is depicted in stunning, delicate reliefs, and a long Latin inscription lists the scholar-emperor's achievements.

You'll probably be flagging by now, so reward yourself with the remarkably reasonable buffet lunch at **'Gusto** (p91; insist on an outside table). After which – if you still have sufficient time and energy – hop on the 81 bus right outside the restaurant. In about 20 minutes, it will whisk you past those Roman landmarks you haven't yet seen: through **piazza Venezia**, past the **Capitoline** (p56), down to the **Bocca della Verità** (p62), along the side of the **Circus Maximus** (p57) and back past the **Palatine** (p61) to the **Colosseum** (p57). You can hop off here and head back to your hotel (or the train station, or the airport) feeling that you really have seen (just about) everything.

ITINERARIES

The Legendary Harry's Bar

Legendary Harry's Bar is the unique place that evokes the "Dolce Vita" as if it were a clip from the film, creating a vivid flashback to the golden era of the Via Veneto, when Frank Sinatra sang at the piano and all the stars made their appearance in this bar/restaurant full of glamour and style. As in the roaring sixties, you can still sip an aperitif, enjoy the live piano bar every evening and dive into the magic of the Via Veneto from the exclusive and fascinating Harry's Bar. The refined cuisine recalls the freshness of Mediterranean flavours based on prime ingredients. Tradition and fantasy inspire the elegant dishes, accompanied by the most prestigious labels and a high class service.

Reservations Recommended

Via V. Veneto 150 - 00187 Roma – www.harrysbar.it - info@harrysbar.it
Tel. +39 06 48 46 43/ +39 06 47 42 103 – Fax. +39 06 48 83 117
Open from: 11:00 – to 2:00am – Piano Bar 22:00 – 2:00am (Mon - Sat)

Rome by Area

Il Centro

Il centro archeologico

Rome took a few centuries to transform itself from a huddle of huts on a hill overlooking the River Tiber into the ancient world's most powerful city.

But by the fifth century BC, magnificent palaces had replaced that eighth- or ninth-century settlement on the **Palatine** hill. The frescoes with their gem-like colours in the recently opened **House of Augustus** give an idea of the beauty with which wealthy ancients surrounded themselves.

The Palatine overlooked the bustling **Roman Forum** below. It was from here that the Republic – and later the Empire – was run and justice administered, in grandiose buildings around richly decorated public squares. The facing hill – the **Capitoline** – was Rome's most sacred, with imposing temples. Flanking the Roman Forum,

successive emperors strove to assert their own particular importance and munificence in the **Imperial Fora**. Also in this history-packed area, emperors kept public discontent at bay with gory diversions and heart-stopping sports at the **Colosseum** and the **Circus Maximus**.

The Capitoline (Campidoglio) was the site of two major temples; to Jupiter Capitolinus – chunks of which are visible inside the **Capitoline Museums** – and Juno Moneta, 'giver of advice', where the church of **Santa Maria in Aracoeli** now stands.

The splendid piazza that now tops the Capitoline was designed in the 1530s by Michelangelo; the best approach is via the steps called the *cordonata*, also by Michelangelo, with two giant Roman statues of the mythical twins Castor and Pollux at the top. The building directly opposite is Rome's city hall; on either side are the *palazzi*

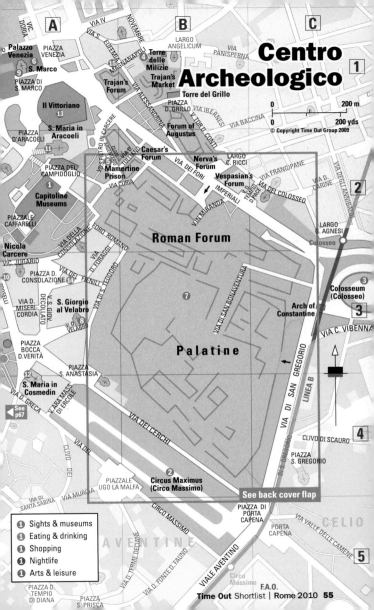

Centro Archeologico

A **B** **C**

1

VIC. DORIA
VIA IV NOVEMBRE
VIA S. EUFEMIA
VIA S. MAGNANAPOLI
VIA IV NOVEMBRE
LARGO ANGELICUM
VIA PANISPERNA

Palazzo Venezia
PIAZZA VENEZIA
S. Marco
PIAZZA DI S. MARCO
Trajan's Forum
Torre delle Milizie
Trajan's Market
Torre del Grillo
PIAZZA D. GRILLO
VIA N. TOR D. CONTI
VIA IBERNESI
VIA BACCINA

Il Vittoriano
S. Maria in Aracoeli
PIAZZA D'ARACOELI
Forum of Augustus
Caesar's Forum
Nerva's Forum
Vespasian's Forum

0   200 m
0   200 yds
© Copyright Time Out Group 2009

2

PIAZZA DEL CAMPIDOGLIO
Capitoline Museums
PIAZZALE CAFFARELLI
Mamertine Prison
VIA CURIA
VIA DEI FORI
VIA IN MIRANDA
IMPERIALI
VIA DEL COLOSSEO
VIA FRANGIPANE
VIA D. CARINE
VIA DELL'ANNIBALDI
LARGO C. RICCI

Nicola Carcere
VIC. IUGARIO
Roman Forum
VIA DELLA CONSOLAZIONE
VIA D. FORO ROMANO
VIA D. FORAGGI
PIAZZA D. CONSOLAZIONE
VIA DEI FIENILI
LARGO G. AGNESI
Colosseo

3

S. Giorgio al Velabro
V.S. GIOV. DECOLLATO
V.D. VELABRO
VIA D. MISERICORDIA
Colosseum (Colosseo)
VIA C. VIBENNA

Palatine
Arch of Constantine
VIA DI SAN BONAVENTURA
VIA DI S. TEODORO

4

PIAZZA BOCCA D.VERITA
S. Maria in Cosmedin
VIA D. GRECA
V. ARA MASS. DI ERCOLE
PIAZZA S. ANASTASIA
VIA DI SAN GREGORIO
LINEA B
CLIVO DI SCAURO
PIAZZA S. GREGORIO
See p67

CLIVO DEI
VIA DEL
VIA DEL CERCHI
PIAZZALE UGO LA MALFA
Circus Maximus (Circo Massimo)

5

VIA DI SANTA SABINA
VIA MURCIA
CIRCO MASSIMO
PIAZZA DI PORTA CAPENA
PORTA CAPENA
VIA VALLE DELLE CAMENE
CELIO
AVENTINE
VIA D. TERME DECIANE
VIA D. FONTE D. FAUNO
VIALE AVENTINO
Circo Massimo
F.A.O.
PIAZZA D. TEMPIO DI DIANA
PIAZZA S. PRISCA

Sights & museums
Eating & drinking
Shopping
Nightlife
Arts & leisure

Temple of Jupiter

housing the Capitoline museums. The equestrian statue of Marcus Aurelius in the centre is a computer-generated copy; the second-century gilded bronze original is inside the museum.

At the bottom of the *cordonata* is piazza Venezia. Dominating this dizzying roundabout is the **Vittoriano**, a piece of nationalistic kitsch that outdoes anything dreamed up by the ancients. Just around the corner at via IV Novembre 119A, the provincial government occasionally opens the archaeological digs in its cellars in Palazzo Valentini: any chance to see this site with its excellent high-tech multilingual explanations should be seized immediately.

South of the Capitoline, on low ground by the river, was the *velabrum*, the marshy area where Remus and Romulus were, according to Rome's foundation

myth, found floating in a basket and then suckled by a she-wolf. Two delightful Republican-age temples still stand here, and the area is dotted with remains of the *forum boarium* and *forum holitorium* (cattle and vegetable markets) that occupied this space.

Sights & museums

Capitoline Museums

Piazza del Campidoglio 1 (06 6710 2475/06 0608/www.museicapitolini.org). **Open** 9am-8pm Tue-Sun. **Admission** €6.50; €4.50 reductions; extra charge during exhibitions. See also p12. **Map** p55 A2 ❶

Housed in two *palazzi* opposite each other on Michelangelo's piazza del Campidoglio, the Capitoline Museums (*Musei capitolini*) are the oldest museums in the world, opened to the public in 1734, though the collection was begun in 1471 by Pope Sixtus IV. His successors continued to add ancient sculptures and, later, paintings.

Entry is through the Palazzo dei Conservatori (to the right at the top of the steps). The courtyard contains parts of a colossal statue of Constantine that originally stood in the Basilica of Maxentius in the Roman Forum. Inside, ancient works are mixed with statues by the Baroque greats Gian Lorenzo Bernini. In Rm7 (Sala della Lupa) is a fourth-century BC Etruscan she-wolf and suckling twins (added during the Renaissance).

In a smart modern section on the first floor, the second-century statue of Marcus Aurelius has been given a suitably grand space. Also here are chunks of the Temple of Jupiter.

The second-floor gallery contains paintings by greats such as Titian, Tintoretto and Caravaggio. Across the piazza (or through the underground *Tabularium*, the ancient Capitoline archive building), the Palazzo Nuovo houses one of Europe's greatest collections of ancient sculpture, including the coy *Capitoline Venus*, the *Dying Gaul* and countless portrait busts of emperors and their families.

A top-floor café and restaurant (accessible without paying the museum entrance fee) are rather overpriced but offer a magnificent view over the city.

Circus Maximus

Via del Circo Massimo. **Map** p55 B4 ❷

Little of the actual structure remains at the Circus Maximus, ancient Rome's major chariot-racing venue, but it's still possible to visualise the flat base of this long grassy basin as the racetrack, and the sloping sides as the stands. At the southern end are some brick remains of the original seating (the tower is medieval). The oldest and largest of Rome's ancient arenas, the Circus Maximus hosted chariot races from at least the fourth century BC. It was rebuilt by Julius Caesar to hold as many as 300,000 people. Races involved up to 12 rigs of four horses each; the circus was also flooded for mock sea battles.

Colosseum

Piazza del Colosseo (06 700 5469). **Open** 8.30am-sunset daily.

Admission (includes Roman Forum & Palatine) €9; €4.50 reductions; extra charge during exhibitions. No credit cards. **Map** p55 C3 ❸

Note: if the queue at the Colosseum is daunting, get your ticket from the Palatine entrance at via di San Gregorio 30, bypass the line and go straight in.

Built in AD 72 by Emperor Vespasian, *il Colosseo* hosted gory battles between combinations of gladiators, slaves, prisoners and wild animals of all descriptions. Properly called the *Amphitheatrum flavium*, the building was later known as the Colosseum not because it was big, but because of a gold-plated colossal statue, now lost, that stood alongside. The arena was about 500m (a third of a mile) in circumference and could seat over 50,000 people. Nowhere in the world was there a larger setting for mass slaughter. In the 100 days of carnage held to inaugurate the amphitheatre in AD 80, 5,000 beasts perished. Sometimes, animals got to kill people: a common sentence in the Roman criminal justice system was *damnatio ad bestias*, where miscreants were turned loose, unarmed, into the arena.

Marcus Aurelius

ROME BY AREA

After the fall of the Roman Empire, authorities banned games here and the Colosseum became a quarry for stone and marble to build Roman *palazzi*. The pockmarks on the Colosseum's masonry date from the ninth century, when the lead clamps holding the stones together were pillaged. This irreverence didn't stop until the mid 18th century, when the Colosseum was consecrated as a church.

Standing beside the Colosseum, Constantine's triumphal arch was erected in AD 315, shortly before the emperor abandoned the city for Byzantium.

Imperial Fora Museum

Via IV Novembre 94 (06 6992 3521/ www.mercatiditraiano.it). **Open** 9am-7pm Tue-Sun. **Admission** €6.50: €4.50 reductions; extra charge during exhibitions. **Map** p55 B1 ❹

When the Roman Forum (p59) became too small to cope with the growing city, emperors combined philanthropy with propaganda and created new fora of their own in what is now known collectively as the *Fori imperiali* (Imperial Fora). Along the via dei Fori Imperiali (sliced cavalierly through the ruins in the early 20th century) are five separate fora – each one was built by a different emperor.

Excavations in the 1990s unearthed great swathes of this archaeological space. It's not easy to interpret the ruins, most of which are visible from street level. A pre-emptive visit to the scale model of the *fori* at the visitors' centre (via dei Fori Imperiali, open 9.30am-6.30pm daily) will help.

The best-preserved and unquestionably most impressive part of the complex is Trajan's forum and the towering remains of Trajan's markets behind. Two years of restoration work came to an end in October 2007, giving Trajan's markets a gloriously cleaned-up interior, a beautifully lit collection of marble artefacts and a new name: *il Museo dei fori imperiali*. Moreover, it opened up atmospheric stretches of the ancient streets and medieval buildings surrounding the market itself.

If you enter Trajan's markets from via IV Novembre, the first room is the Great Hall, a large space possibly used for the corn dole in antiquity. To the south of the Great Hall are the open-air terraces at the top of the spectacular Great Hemicycle, built in AD 107. To the east of the Great Hall, stairs lead down to the so-called via Biberatica, an ancient street flanked by well-preserved shops; these were probably *tabernae* (bars); hence the name (*bibere* is Latin for 'to drink'). More stairs lead down through the various layers of the Great Hemicycle, where most of the 150 shops or offices are still in perfect condition, many with doorjambs still showing the grooves where shutters would have slid into place when the working day was over.

Below the markets, at the piazza Venezia end of via dei Fori Imperiali, is **Trajan's forum**, laid out in the early second century AD. It's dominated by Trajan's column (AD 113), with detailed spiralling reliefs showing victories over Dacia (modern-day Romania). The rectangular foundation to the south of Trajan's column, where several imposing granite columns still stand, was the basilica Ulpia, an administrative building.

Across the road from Trajan's forum, **Caesar's forum** was the earliest of the *Fori imperiali*, built in 51 BC by Julius Caesar. Three columns of the *Venus generatrix* temple have been rebuilt. Back on the same side as Trajan's forum, **Augustus' forum** was inaugurated in 2 BC. Three columns from the Temple of Mars Ultor still stand, as does the towering wall separating the forum from the sprawling Suburra slum behind. **Nerva's forum** (AD 97) lies mainly beneath via dei Fori Imperiali. On the south side of the road, **Vespasian's** forum (AD 75) was home to the Temple of Pax (Peace), part of which is now incorporated into the church of Santi Cosma e Damiano. Maps placed on a wall here by Mussolini show how Rome ruled the world.

Mamertine Prison

Via del Tulliano (06 679 2902). **Open** 9am-5pm daily. **Admission** donation expected. **Map** p55 A2 ⑤

Anyone thought to pose a threat to the security of the ancient Roman state was thrown into the *Carcere mamertino* (Mamertine Prison), a dank, underground dungeon, between the Roman Forum and present-day via dei Fori Imperiali. The prison's most famous inmates, legend has it, were Saints Peter and Paul. Peter head-butted the wall in the ground-level room leaving his features impressed on the rock, and is said to have caused a miraculous well to bubble up.

Palazzo Venezia

Via del Plebiscito 118 (06 699 941). **Open** 8.30am-7.30pm Tue-Sun. **Admission** €4; €2 reductions; extra charge during exhibitions. No credit cards. **Map** p55 A1 ⑥

This collection contains a hotchpotch of anything from terracotta models by Baroque sculptor Gian Lorenzo Bernini (for the angels that now grace Ponte Sant'Angelo), to medieval decorative art. Major exhibitions are staged regularly; they often give access to the huge Sala del Mappamondo, used by Mussolini as his office.

On the upper level of the cloister of Pope Paul II's 'secret garden', a lapidarium houses ancient, medieval and Renaissance sarcophagi, coats of arms, funerary monuments and assorted fragments.

Roman Forum & Palatine

Via di San Gregorio 30/largo della Salaria Vecchia 5/6 (06 3996 7700/ 06 699 841). **Open** 8.30am-1hr before sunset daily. **Admission** (includes

Capitoline wolf p56

Colosseum) €9; €4.50 reductions; extra charge during exhibitions. No credit cards. **Map** p55 B3 ⑦

Note: Letters ⓐ in the text refer to the Roman Forum and Palatine map on the back cover flap.

From March 2008, the Forum and Palatine once again became a single site, visited on the same ticket, which also allows entrance to the Colosseum. We recommend entering from the quieter via di San Gregorio entrance, visiting the Palatine first, then making your way down to the Forum.

However, guided tours (€4, in Italian) of parts of the Forum that are generally off-limits to visitors depart from the largo della Salaria Vecchia ticket office (formerly largo Remo e Romolo, off via dei Fori Imperiali); if you wish to join these, you should book your tour and enter from there. If you want to arrange a visit (free) to Augustus' house on the Palatine, you will need to organise a time at this entrance too.

Vitti

There delights,
one beautiful
square

**Restaurant
– Gelateria
– Pastry Shop**
Since 1878

**Piazza San
Lorenzo in Lucina
33 - 00186 Roma**

Palatine

Legend relates that a basket holding twin babes Romulus and Remus was found in the swampy area near the Tiber to the west of here, and that the twins had been suckled by a she-wolf in a cave. In 753 BC, having murdered his brother, Romulus scaled the Palatine hill and founded Rome. In fact, archaeological evidence shows that proto-Romans had settled on *il Palatino* a century or more before that. Later, the Palatine became the Beverly Hills of the ancient city, where movers and shakers built their palaces. On the southern side of the Palatine, overlooking the Circus Maximus, are the remains of vast Imperial dwellings, including Emperor Domitian's *Domus augustana* , with what may have been a private stadium in the garden. Next door, the Museo Palatino  charts the history of the Palatine from the eighth century BC.

Immediately west of here is the House of Augustus (*Domus augusti*, , four spectacularly frescoed rooms of which were opened to the public in March 2008.

With Rome's decline the Palatine became a rural backwater; in the 1540s, much of the hill was bought by Cardinal Alessandro Farnese, who created a pleasure villa. His gardens – the *Horti farnesiani*  – are still a lovely, leafy – if unkempt – place to wander on a hot day. Beneath the gardens is the *cryptoporticus* , a semi-subterranean tunnel built by Nero.

Roman Forum

During the early years of the Republic, this was an open space with shops and a few temples, and it sufficed; but by the second century BC ever-conquering Rome needed to convey authority and wealth. Out went the food stalls; in came law courts, offices and immense public buildings with grandiose decorations. The *Foro romano* was the symbolic heart of the Empire.

Descending from the Palatine, the Forum is framed by the Arch of Titus (AD 81; ), built to celebrate the sack of Jerusalem. To the right are the towering ruins of the Basilica of Maxentius , completed in AD 312. Below on the left is the house of the Vestal Virgins . Along the via Sacra , the Forum's high street, are (right) the great columns of the Temple of Antoninus and Faustina ; the giant Basilica Emilia (right; ) – once a bustling place for administration, courts and business; the Curia , the home of the Senate, begun in 45 BC by Julius Caesar; and the Arch of Septimius Severus , built in AD 203. Beside the arch are the remains of an Imperial rostra , from where Mark Antony supposedly asked Romans to lend him their ears.

Roman Forum

San Giorgio in Velabro

Via del Velabro 19 (06 6920 4534/ www.oscgeneral.org). **Open** 8am-6.30pm daily. **Map** p55 A3 ❽

This austere little church of the seventh century has 16 Roman columns pilfered from the Palatine and the Aventine hills in its nave, and pieces of an eighth- or ninth-century choir incorporated into the walls. In the apse is a much-restored 13th-century fresco of St George. Outside to the left is the Arco degli Argentari, built in AD 204; it was a gate on the road between the main Forum and the *forum boarium* (cattle market), along which moneychangers (*argenteri*) plied their trade.

San Marco

Piazza San Marco 48 (06 679 5205/ www.sanmarcoevangelista.it). **Open** 4-7pm Mon; 8.30am-noon, 4-7pm Tue-Sun. **Map** p55 A1 ❾

Founded, tradition says, in 336 on the site of the house where St Mark the Evangelist stayed, this church was rebuilt by Pope Paul II in the 15th century when the neighbouring Palazzo Venezia was constructed, and was given its Baroque look in the mid 18th century. Remaining from its earlier manifestations are the 12th-century bell tower, and the ninth-century mosaic of Christ in the apse. In the portico is the gravestone of Vanozza Catanei, mother of the notorious Cesare and Lucrezia Borgia.

San Nicola in Carcere

Via del Teatro di Marcello 46 (06 686 9972). **Open** 7am-7pm Mon-Sat; 9am-7pm Sun. **Map** off p55 A3 ❿

The 12th-century San Nicola was built over three Roman temples, dating from the second and third centuries BC; a guide (donation appreciated) takes you down to these. On the outside of the church, six columns from the Temple of Janus can be seen on the left; the ones on the right are from the Temple of Spes (Hope).

Santa Maria in Aracoeli

Piazza del Campidoglio 4 (06 679 8155). **Open** 9.30am-12.30pm, 2.30-5.30pm daily. **Map** p55 A2 ⓫

Up a daunting flight of steps, the Romanesque Aracoeli ('altar of heaven') stands on the site of an ancient temple to Juno Moneta. The current basilica-form church was designed in the late 13th century. The first chapel on the right has scenes by Pinturicchio from the life of St Francis of Assisi's helpmate St Bernardino (1486). To the left of the altar, a round chapel contains relics of St Helena, mother of the Emperor Constantine. At the back of the transept, the Chapel of the Holy Child contains a much-venerated disease-healing *bambinello*, which is often whisked to the bedside of moribund Romans.

Santa Maria in Cosmedin & the Mouth of Truth

Piazza della Bocca della Verità 18 (06 678 1419). **Open** 9.30am-5pm daily. **Map** p55 A3 ⓬

Built in the sixth century and enlarged in the eighth, Santa Maria was embellished with a glorious Cosmati-work floor, throne and choir in the 11th-13th centuries. In the sacristy is a fragment of an eighth-century mosaic of the Holy Family, brought here from the original St Peter's. The church is better known as the *bocca della verità* (the mouth of truth), after the great stone mask of a man with a gaping mouth on the portico wall – probably an ancient drain cover. Anyone who lies while their hand is in the mouth will have that hand bitten off, according to legend. On the little green opposite stand the first-century BC Temples of Hercules (round) and Portunus (square).

Vittoriano

Piazza Venezia (06 699 1718). **Open** *Monument* 10am-4pm daily. *Museo Centrale del Risorgimento* 9.30am-6pm daily. *Complesso del Vittoriano* (06 678 0664) 9.30am-6.30pm daily. **Admission** varies. **Map** p55 A1 ⓭

Bottega dei sapori della legalità

Variously known as 'the wedding cake' and 'the typewriter', this eyesore is a monument to united Italy, constructed between 1885 and 1911. You can climb the steps (free) for a good view over the city, or check out the exhibitions – mainly of 19th- and 20th-century art – held regularly in the gallery along the left side of the monument as you look at it. Along the right side, a door leads to a space that hosts exhibits on Italian history, and a collection of memorabilia from the Unification struggle.

Also through this entrance – and best of all – is a new lift (€7, €3.50 reductions) that whizzes you up to the very top of the monument for an unmissable, breathtaking 360-degree panorama across the whole of Rome and far beyond... from the only spot where the spectacle isn't marred by the Vittoriano itself. There's a (comparatively pricey) café on one of the lower terraces.

Eating & drinking

San Teodoro
Via dei Fienili 49-51 (06 678 0933/ www.st-teodoro.it). **Meals served** 12.45-3.15pm, 8-11.30pm Mon-Sat.

Closed 3wks Dec-Jan; 1wk Aug. €€€€.
Creative Italian. Map p55 A3 ⓮

Of a summer's evening, there are few more pleasant places in Rome for an alfresco meal than this seafood-oriented restaurant around the back of the Forum, in a pretty residential piazza. Come prepared to splash out, though. Some dishes are pure *cucina romana*; others, like the *tonnarelli San Teodoro* (with shrimps, courgettes and cherry tomatoes) are lighter and more creative. It opens on Sundays during the summer. San Teodoro's light lunches (€€) are also available in its caffè-tavola calda next door at number 53.

Shopping

Bottega dei sapori della legalità
Via dei Prefetti 23 (06 6992 5262)/ www.libera.it). **Open** 10am-1pm, 3-6.30pm Mon-Fri. Closed 2wks Aug. **Map** p55 A1 ⓯

Discreetly tucked away beneath Trajan's forum, this shop may look like any other upmarket food emporium, with delicious olive oil, wine and organic foodstuffs. What sets it apart is that everything is produced by

ROME BY AREA

ristorante settembrini

settembrini is our street

settembrini is a character from "the enchanted mountain"

settembrini is our home, your home

it is our wager and our hope to have made a place that offers prime ingredients in quality dishes at reasonable prices.

one is tempted to say superb dishes but we'll let you be the judge of that.

via Settembrini 27, 00197 Rome
phone: +39 06 3232617
www.ristorantesettembrini.it
closed saturday lunch, sunday all day

SETTEMBRINI
vino e cucina

co-operatives of young people on land confiscated from organised crime outfits.

The Ghetto & Campo de' Fiori

From the earliest of ancient times, the area in the great loop of the River Tiber was the *campus martius* (field of war), where Roman males did physical jerks to stay fighting fit. As time went on, the area became packed with theatres providing lowbrow fun for ancient Romans. After barbarian hordes rampaged through Rome in the fifth and sixth centuries, the area fell into ruin. By the late Middle Ages, it was densely populated and insalubrious.

That part of the *campus martius* that today stretches south from busy corso Vittorio Emanuele (aka corso Vittorio) to the Tiber saw its fortunes improve when the pope made the Vatican – just across the river – his main residence in the mid 15th century. Nowadays, its tightly wedged buildings, narrow cobbled alleys and mixture of graceful Renaissance columns and chunky blocks of ancient travertine form the perfect backdrop to everyday Roman streetlife.

The area is one of contrasts: **campo de' Fiori** – with its lively morning market and livelier partying crowds at night – stands next to solemn, dignified **piazza Farnese**, with its grand Palazzo Farnese, partly designed by Michelangelo. Top-end antique dealers in via Giulia rub along with craftsmen plying their trades in streets with names (via dei Leutari – lutemakers; via dei Cappellari – hatmakers) that recall the jobs of their medieval ancestors.

In the south-east, **largo Argentina** is a polluted transport

Santa Maria in Cosmedin p62

hub with a chunk of ancient Rome at its heart: visible when you peer over the railings are columns, altars and foundations from four temples, dating from the mid third century BC to c100 BC.

On the southern side of the square lies the **Ghetto**: its picture-postcard winding alleys mask a sorrowful history. Rome's Jews occupy a unique place in the history of the diaspora, having maintained a presence in the city uninterrupted for over 2,000 years. The Ghetto was walled off from the rest of the city in 1556, and remained that way until the 1870s. In piazza Mattei stands the beautiful, delicate Turtle Fountain, erected overnight in the 1580s, though the turtles may have been an afterthought.

Sights & museums

Crypta Balbi
Via delle Botteghe Oscure 31 (06 678 0167). Open 9am-7.45pm Tue-Sun.

ROME BY AREA

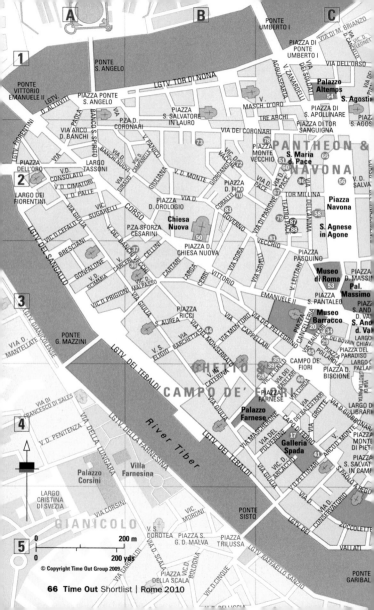

© Copyright Time Out Group 2009

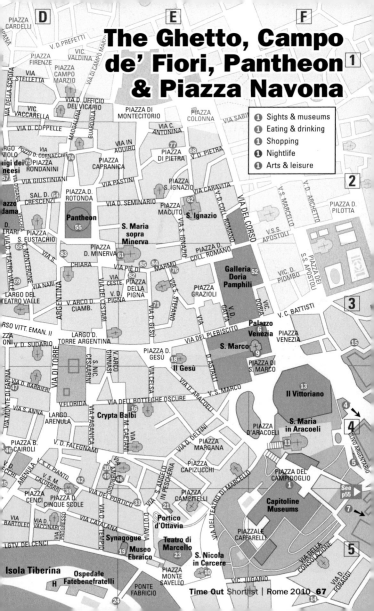

The Ghetto, Campo de' Fiori, Pantheon & Piazza Navona

- **1** Sights & museums
- **1** Eating & drinking
- **1** Shopping
- **1** Nightlife
- **1** Arts & leisure

Pantheon 55

S. Maria sopra Minerva

S. Ignazio

Galleria Doria Pamphilj 52

Palazzo Venezia

S. Marco 9

Il Gesù 18

Crypta Balbi

Il Vittoriano 13

S. Maria in Aracoeli

Capitoline Museums

PIAZZA DEL CAMPIDOGLIO

Portico d'Ottavia

Synagogue

Museo Ebraico 19

Teatro di Marcello 23

S. Nicola in Carcere

Isola Tiberina

Ospedale Fatebenefratelli

Admission €7; €3.50 reductions; extra charge during exhibitions; see p9 Museo Nazionale Romano. No credit cards. **Map** p67 E4 ⑯

The Crypta Balbi – the foyer of the ancient Theatre of Balbus – is packed with displays, maps and models that explain (in English) Rome's evolution from a bellicose pre-Imperial era, to early Christian times and on through the dim Middle Ages. Frequent tours take visitors down to the digs beneath the museum; a special guided tour at 3pm on Sundays allows a glimpse of newly excavated sections beyond the museum. Tours (in Italian) are free.

Galleria Spada

Piazza Capo di Ferro 13 (06 683 2409/ www.galleriaborghese.it). **Open** 8.30am-7.30pm Tue-Sun. **Admission** €5; €2.50 reductions. No credit cards. **Map** p66 C4 ⑰

This gem of a palace – alas, showing signs of neglect – was acquired by art collector Cardinal Bernardino Spada in 1632; the walls are crammed with paintings. There are some impressive names here: Domenichino, Guercino, Guido Reni plus the father-daughter Gentileschi duo, Orazio and Artemisia. The main attraction of the museum, however, is the Borromini Perspective, where perspective trickery makes a 9m-long (30ft) colonnade look much longer.

Il Gesù

Piazza del Gesù (06 697 001/www. chiesadelgesu.org). **Open** *Church* 7am-12.30pm, 4-7.30pm daily. *Loyola's rooms (06 6920 5800)* 4-6pm Mon-Sat; 10am-noon Sun. **Map** p67 E3 ⑬

The Gesù, built in 1568-84, is the flagship church of the Jesuits, and was designed to involve the congregation as closely as possible in services, with a nave unobstructed by aisles. One of Rome's great Baroque masterpieces – *Triumph in the Name of Jesus* by Il Baciccia (1676-79) – decorates the ceiling of the nave. On the left is the ornate chapel of Sant'Ignazio (1696; see box p69). Outside the church, at piazza del Gesù 45, you can visit St Ignatius' rooms.

Jewish Museum of Rome

Lungotevere Cenci (06 6840 0661/ www.museoebraico.roma.it). **Open**

Via Giulia p65

Baroque trickery

Flashing lights and piped heavenly choirs herald an eye-popping performance of religious theatricality at the **Gesù** (p68), Rome's most exuberant Baroque church. A bizarre daily *son et lumière* on the life, but mostly the death, of the Jesuits' founder, Spaniard Ignatius Loyola, offers 15 minutes' respite from the dizzying frescoes on the vast church's ceiling and the sheer opulence of the gold, silver and precious marbles of the Gesù's fixtures and fittings. Be there at 5.30pm prompt: proceedings start with mechanical precision.

The Jesuits were the richest Catholic order, and the most energetic, sending teams of fired-up missionaries to the four corners of the (then) known world. This church is their showcase, and Loyola's final resting place.

After the recent discovery of the original 30ft altarpiece painted by Jesuit brother Andrea Pozzo, depicting the saint's apotheosis, a full-scale restoration began of the complex Baroque mechanics once used to raise and lower the giant altarpiece. These were designed as a saintly spectacle to inspire awe and reverence in amazed on-lookers. In the 16th century, manpower turned the levers; now the priest likens the motor harnessed to the antique wooden framework to the sort of thing 'which opens a garage door'.

After a bit of Baroque sacred music and lights dancing over Pozzo's massive canvas while excerpts are read (in Italian) from St Ignatius' *Spiritual Exercises*, the altarpiece begins to disappear, winched down soundlessly into the bowels of the church. Revealed in its place on the lapis lazuli and gold altar is a huge silver-plated statue of the Spanish mystic.

Baroque art is all about magic, trickery, delight and astonishment. Pozzo here (and at nearby Sant'Ignazio, p80) showed himself to be a master. For more examples of Baroque playfulness, take a day trip to the Villa d'Este (p160) at Tivoli to see Baroque pranks at the service of nature: ingenious hidden jets that spray unwary visitors, and a fantastic musical fountain.

Campo de' Fiori p65

Portico D'Ottavia

Via Portico D'Ottavia. Map p67 E5 ㉑
Great ancient columns and a marble
frontispiece, held together with rusting
iron braces, now form part of the
church of Sant'Angelo in Pescheria, but
they were originally the entrance of a
massive colonnaded square (portico)
containing temples and libraries, built
in the first century AD by Emperor
Augustus and dedicated to his sister
Octavia. A walkway (open 9am-6pm
daily) has been opened through the
forum piscarium – the ancient fish
market; it continues past a graveyard
of broken columns and capitals to the
Teatro di Marcello, passing by three
towering columns that were part of the
Temple of Apollo (433 BC).

Sant'Andrea della Valle

Piazza Vidoni 6 (06 686 1339).
Open 7.30am-12.30pm, 4.30-7.30pm
daily. Map p66 C3 ㉒
Perhaps from an original design by
Giacomo della Porta, this church was
taken in hand in the mid 17th century
by Carlo Maderno, who stretched the
plan upward, creating a dome that is
the highest in Rome after St Peter's.
Puccini set the opening act of *Tosca* in
the chapel on the left.

Theatre of Marcellus

Via Teatro di Marcello. Map p67 E5 ㉓
The *Teatro di Marcello* is one of Rome's
strangest and most impressive sights –
a Renaissance palace grafted on to an
ancient theatre. Julius Caesar began
building the theatre, but it was finished
in 11 BC by Augustus, who named it
after his favourite nephew. It originally
had three tiers and seated up to 20,000
people. Abandoned in the fourth
century AD, it was turned into a fortress
in the 12th century and then into a palazzo in the 16th by the Savelli family.

Tiber Island & Ponte Rotto

Map p67 D5 ㉔
When the last Etruscan king was driven from Rome, the Romans uprooted

10am-5pm Mon-Thur, Sun; 9am-2pm
Fri. **Admission** €7.50; €4 reductions.
Map p67 E5 ⑲
As well as luxurious crowns, Torah
mantles and silverware, the Museo
ebraico presents vivid reminders of the
persecution suffered by Rome's Jews
at various times through history, with
copies of the 16th-century papal edicts
that banned Jews from many activities, and heart-rending relics from
the World War II concentration
camps. Refurbished and extended in
2005, the museum now displays
exquisite carvings from long-gone
Roman synagogues.

Museo Barracco

Corso Vittorio 166A (06 6821 4105/
www.museobarracco.it). **Open** 9am-
7pm Tue-Sun. **Admission** €3; €1.50
reductions; extra charge during exhibitions.
No credit cards. Map p66 C3 ⑳
This small collection of mainly pre-
Roman art was amassed in the first
half of the 20th century. Don't miss the
copy of the *Wounded Bitch* by the
fourth-century BC sculptor Lysippus,
on the second floor.

the wheat from his fields and threw it in baskets into the river. Silt accumulated and formed an island where Aesculapius, the Roman god of medicine, founded a sanctuary in the third century BC. That's what the legend says, and the island has always had a vocation for public health. Today, a hospital occupies the north end. The church of San Bartolomeo is built over the original sanctuary; the columns in the nave are from that earlier building. Remains of the ancient building can also be seen from the riverside footpath, from where there's also a fine view over the *ponte rotto* (broken bridge). This stands on the site of the *Pons aemilius*, Rome's first stone bridge, built in 142 BC. It was rebuilt many times before 1598, when they gave up trying. To the east of the bridge is a tunnel in the embankment: the gaping mouth of the city's great *cloaca maxima* sewer, built in the sixth century BC.

Eating & drinking

See also p81 *Casa Bleve*.

Alberto Pica

Via della Seggiola 12 (06 686 8405).
Open 8.30am-2am Mon-Sat. Closed 2wks Aug. No credit cards. **Bar/ice-cream**. Map p67 D4 ㉕
Horrendous neon lighting, surly staff and some very good ice-cream are the hallmarks of this long-running bar: *riso alla cannella* (cinnamon rice) is particularly delicious. Open Sunday evenings in summer and December.

Antica Vineria

Via Monte della Farina 37 (06 6880 6989). **Open** 10.30am-3pm, 6.30-11.30pm Mon-Sat. No credit cards. **Wine bar**. Map p67 D4 ㉖
Aka Vineria di Marco e Giancarlo, this is a laid-back boho-chic stop with standing-only customers spilling out into the picturesque street to sip wine by the glass at very reasonable prices.

Antico Forno Roscioli

Via dei Chiavari 34 (06 686 4045/ www.anticofornoroscioli.it). **Open** 6am-8pm Mon-Sat. **Bakery**. Map p66 C4 ㉗
The pizza bianca (oiled and salted pizza base) at this bakery makes a great snack in itself but the crowded lunch counter provides a greater choice (see box p73). The Roscioli dynasty's smarter restaurant (€€) nearby at via dei Giubbonari 21 is good but not cheap, and staff could definitely be cheerier.

Ar Galletto

Piazza Farnese 102 (06 686 1714).
Meals served 12.15-3pm, 7.15-11pm Mon-Sat. Closed 2wks Dec-Jan. €€€.
Roman. Map p66 C4 ㉓
With a ringside view of stately piazza Farnese, Ar Galletto serves unpretentious Roman dishes without the horribly inflated prices charged by other restaurants around here. Dishes like *penne all'arrabbiata* or *spaghetti alle vongole* are appetising. There are tables on the square in summer.

Baffetto 2

Piazza del Teatro di Pompeo 18 (06 6821 0807/www.pizzeriabaffetto. it). **Meals served** 12.30-3.30pm, 6.30pm-1am daily. €. **Pizzeria**.
Map p66 C3 ㉙
Both branches of the legendary Baffetto serve good pizzas and decent pasta. The newest branch has tables outside on a bustling square near campo de' Fiori, and longer opening hours than the original at via del Governo Vecchio 114 (which is only open in the evening).

Bartaruga

Piazza Mattei 9 (06 689 2299). **Open** 6pm-midnight Mon-Thur, Sun; 6pm-2am Fri, Sat. No credit cards. **Bar**.
Map p67 D4 ㉚
This baroque locale, in peach and midnight blue with divans and candelabra, is the haunt of the beautiful, the eccentric and those too entranced by

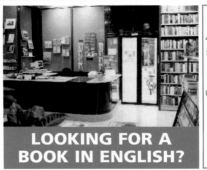

the lovely square outside to move on elsewhere. Staff can be surly.

Bernasconi

Piazza Cairoli 16 (06 6880 6264).
Open 7am-8.30pm Tue-Sun. Closed Aug. No credit cards. **Café/bar**.
Map p67 D4 ③

It's worth fighting your way inside this cramped, inconspicuous bar for unbeatable chewy, yeasty *cornetti* (croissants).

Crudo

Via degli Specchi 6 (06 683 8989/ www.crudoroma.it). **Open** *Bar & lounge* 7.30pm-2am Mon-Sun; *meals served* 12.30-3.30pm Mon; 12.30-3.30pm, 8-11.30pm Tue-Fri; 8-11.30pm Sat. Closed Aug. **Bar/Creative Italian**. Map p67 D4 ②

With a dazzling designer interior with art installations, plasma screens and DJs, Crudo offers some of the best *aperitivi* in town, plus dining that is sometimes more glam than good (€€€).

Da Giggetto

Via Portico d'Ottavia 21A-22 (06 686 1105/www.giggettoalportico.it). **Meals served** 12.30-3pm, 7.30-11pm Tue-Sun. Closed 2wks July. €€€. **Roman Jewish**. Map p67 E5 ③

This old standby in the Ghetto serves up decent versions of Roman-Jewish classics like *carciofi alla giudia* (fried artichokes) and fried *baccalà* (salt cod), mostly to tables of jolly tourists. The atmosphere is warm and bustling, the helpings plentiful.

Ditirambo

Piazza della Cancelleria 75 (06 687 1626/www.ristoranteditirambo.it). **Meals served** 7.30-11.30pm Mon; 1-3pm, 7.30-11.30pm Tue-Sun. Closed 2wks Aug. €€. **Creative Italian**. Map p66 C3 ③

This funky trattoria serves up good-value pan-Italian dishes based on fresh, mainly organic ingredients. The chef specialises in traditional fare with a creative kick, as in the excellent baby

Stand-up fare

It's a while since Romans reluctantly abandoned the daily three-course lunch ritual and reconciled themselves to a swift *panino* between appointments. All *alimentari* (grocers') will put some salami and/or cheese inside the bread roll of your choice. And most bars have savoury goodies, of varying freshness and tastiness.

But Romans being the foodies they are, even lunch-on-the-wing was bound to move upmarket. Now, a range of specialist delis et al offer something rather superior to the limp roll. Perch and peck, and your brief lunch stopover can be a gourmet treat.

Antico Forno Roscioli (p71) is a heaving mass of humanity at lunchtime as clued-in locals fight to have this bakery's excellent pizza bianca (pizza base) filled, or to order a plate of one of the delicious pastas of the day.

In the Tridente, the hole-in-the-wall **Bisciù** (p90) offers a few varieties of cured meat, plus some vegetables preserved in jars. But the real point of this place is *mozzarella di bufala*, and it's as good as you'll get this side of Naples. Have it between two chunks of country bread, or beside a minimalist salad in a plastic dish.

Burro e Alici (p90), on the other hand, has a fine selection of hams and salamis, cheeses and preserved vegetables from all over Italy, plus an enticing choice of sandwiches, including their trademark open sandwich of salted anchovies (*alici*) with lashings of butter (*burro*) – a traditional Roman treat.

The Flavians

A new exhibition honours the Roman dynasty.

Roman Forum

If the Roman Empire enjoyed a relatively peaceful second century, it was due in large part to the short-lived Flavian dynasty: a father-and-two-sons act that shook up the troubled super-state after the death of Nero, taxing, rebuilding and securing borders in order that the daily skulduggery of caput mundi could carry on without shaking the foundations of Empire.

In 2009-10, a series of major exhibitions on the Flavians is being organised under the banner *Divus Vespasianus*.

Generally portrayed as a gruff soldier with a healthy sense of humour, Vespasian (AD 9-79, ruled from 69) was down-to-earth about the need to replenish the public purse. The proverb *pecunia non olet* ('money doesn't smell')

was, it is said, coined by him when his son Titus objected to a decree taxing the contents of public urinals – the contents of which were vital for the tanning industry.

With sons Titus (ruled 79-81) and Domitian (ruled 81-96), Vespasian also changed the face of Rome, giving the city many of its best-known monuments.

The great fire of 64 – the one during which Nero supposedly fiddled – left large swathes of the city empty. Land which Nero had made into an artificial lake was drained by Vespasian for the construction of the Colosseum (p57), inaugurated under Titus; Vespasian's Temple of Peace in the Imperial Fora (p58) was inaugurated in 75; Titus' victory over/destruction of Jerusalem was celebrated in the Arch of Titus (p61); and with his favourite architect Rabirio, Domitian built the magnificent Domus Flavia palace on the Palatine. He also gave the city a spectacular athletics stadium (now piazza Navona, p77).

Tending towards the (generally) benign-despotic, the three Flavians did all they could to undermine the powers of the previously powerful Senate, underscored the centrality of the emperor and firmly established the principle that anyone wanting to rule Rome had to be firmly in control of the army.

For information on the exhibitions, which includes a are opening of the Curia in the Roman Forum (p61), go to www.pierreci.it, and search for 'Divus Vespasianus'.

squid with a purée of *cicerchie* beans or the veal silverside braised in coffee.

Forno Campo de' Fiori

Campo de' Fiori 22/vicolo del Gallo 14 (06 6880 6662/www.fornocampode fiori.com). **Open** 7.30am-2.30pm, 5-8pm Mon-Sat. Closed 2wks Aug. No credit cards. **€**. **Takeway pizza**. **Map** p66 C3 ⊕

Spread over two premises, this bakery does excellent takeaway sliced pizza. Its plain pizza bianca base is delicious in itself, but check out the one with *fiori di zucca* (courgette flowers) too.

Il Goccetto

Via dei Banchi Vecchi 14 (06 686 4268). **Open** 6.30pm-midnight Mon; 11.30am-2pm, 6.30pm-midnight Tue-Sat. Closed 1wk Jan, 3wks Aug. **Wine bar**. **Map** p66 B3 ⊕

One of the more serious *centro storico* wine bars, with dark wood-clad walls and a cosy, private-club feel. Wine is the main point here, with a satisfying range of Italian and French labels by the glass from €4.

Il Pagliaccio

Via dei Banchi Vecchi 129A (06 6880 9595/www.ristoranteilpagliaccio.it). **Meals served** 8-10.30pm Mon, Tue; 1-2.30pm, 8-10.30pm Wed-Sat. Closed 1wk Jan, 2wks Aug. **€€€€**. **Creative Italian**. **Map** p66 B3 ⊕

Though its second Michelin star in 2009 is bound to push prices up, chef Anthony Genovese's restaurant still offers one of the best-value gourmet dinners in Rome. A seasonally changing menu encompasses Far Eastern influences and fresh approaches to Mediterranean classics. Leave plenty of space for the excellent desserts.

Sora Margherita

Piazza delle Cinque Scole 30 (06 687 4216). **Meals served** 12.30-3pm Tue-Thur, Sun; 12.30-3pm, 8-9.30pm Fri, Sat. Closed Aug. **€€**. No credit cards. **Roman Jewish**. **Map** p67 D5 ⊕

This hole-in-the-wall trattoria is not for health freaks, but no one argues with serious Roman Jewish cooking at these prices. The classic pasta and meat dishes on offer include a superlative *pasta e fagioli* (pasta with beans), *tonnarelli cacio e pepe* (pasta with cheese and pepper) and *ossobuco* washed down with rough-and-ready house wine. On Friday and Saturday evenings, you have to book for one of two sittings.

Le Piramidi

Vicolo del Gallo 11 (06 687 9061/ www.cucinaraba.com). **Open** 10am-midnight Tue-Sun. Closed Aug. **€**. **Middle Eastern takeaway**. No credit cards. **Map** p66 C4 ⊕

Le Piramidi makes for a welcome change from takeaway pizza if you're just in the mood for a quick snack. The range of Middle Eastern takeaway fare is fresh, cheap and tasty.

La Vineria

Campo de' Fiori 15 (06 6880 3268). **Open** 8.30am-1am Mon-Sat. Closed 2wks Aug. **Wine bar**. **Map** p66 C4 ⊕

Known variously as Vineria Reggio or just plain La Vineria, this is the longest-running wine bar on the campo, and where locals flock to plan the evening ahead over a glass of wine. (Very small) glasses start from just €1.50.

Shopping

See also above **Forno Campo de' Fiori**.

Borini

Via dei Pettinari 86 (06 687 5670). **Open** 3.30-7.30pm Mon; 9.30am-1pm, 3.30-7.30pm Tue-Sat. Closed 3wks Aug. **Map** p66 C4 ⊕

Franco Borini's busily chaotic shop is piled high with durable footwear ranging from classical to outrageous, in rainbow colours. Shoes come at prices that won't make you gasp.

Forno del Ghetto

Via Portico d'Ottavia 1 (06 687 8637).
Open 7am-2pm, 3.30-7.30pm Mon-
Thur; 8am-2pm Fri; 7.30am-5pm Sun.
Closed 3wks Aug & Jewish holidays.
No credit cards. **Map** p67 D4 ㉒
This tiny bakery staffed by a gaggle
of tight-lipped women has no sign but
is immediately recognisable by the
line of slavering regulars outside.
Among lots of other goodies, they
come here for the unforgettable dam-
son and ricotta tart.

Ibiz

Via dei Chiavari 39 (06 6830 7297).
Open 9.30am-7.30pm Mon-Sat. Closed
2wks Aug. **Map** p66 C4 ㊸
Elisa Nepi's leather bags are fast becoming classics: you can decide which suits
you as you watch them being made in
the on-site workshop. There are brief-
cases, belts and even chairs too.

Ilaria Miani

*Via Monserrato 35 (06 683 3160/
www.ilariamiani.it).* **Open** 4.30-8pm
Mon; 10.30am-1.30pm, 4.30-8pm Tue-
Sat. Closed Aug. **Map** p66 B3 ㊹
Interior designer Ilaria Miani's country-
chic furniture and *objets* grace many of
Italy's most stylish homes. Pick some
up for yourself in her richly coloured
retail space.

Loco

Via dei Baullari 22 (06 6880 8216).
Open 3.30-8.30pm Mon; 10.30am-8pm
Tue-Sat. Closed 2wks Aug. **Map** p66
C3 ㊺
If you like your shoes avant-garde, this
small copper and wood decorated store
is the place for you. From classy to wild
and eccentric, its pieces are always one
step ahead of the flock.

Momento

Piazza Cairoli 9 (06 6880 8157). **Open**
10.30am-1.30pm, 3.30-7.30pm Mon-Sat;
noon-7.30pm Sun. **Map** p67 D4 ㊻
The poshest of princesses and her boho
cousin will be equally awed by the

collection of clothes and accessories at
this treasure trove. There's something
here for the fearless and the flamoyant,
and all at very approachable prices.

Spazio Sette

Via dei Barbieri 7 (06 686 9747).
Open 3.30-7.30pm Mon; 9.30am-1pm,
3.30-7.30pm Tue-Sat. Closed 3wks Aug.
Map p67 D4 ㊼
A stalwart of the Roman design circuit since it opened in the 1970s,
Spazio Sette is a coolly chic treasure
trove of kitchenware, table decorations, rugs, furniture and lights occupying three floors of a delightful
17th-century palazzo.

Nightlife

Rialtosantambrogio

*Via Sant'Ambrogio 4 (06 6813 3640/
www.rialto.roma.it).* **Open** times
& days vary. Closed July-mid Sept.
Admission free-€7. No credit cards.
Map p67 E4 ㊽
This *centro sociale* (squat) in the Ghetto
hosts performances, art exhibitions, live
music and disco nights along with cutting-edge electronica DJs and VJs, especially at the weekend. It's a meeting
point for a radical crowd.

Arts & leisure

Acquamadre

NEW *Via di Sant'Ambrogio 17
(06 686 4272/www.acquamadre.it).*
Open 2-9pm Tue; 11am-9pm Wed-
Sun. Closed Aug. **Map** p67 D4 ㊾
What better way to remove the grime of
Roman traffic than to sweat it out in this
modern take on an ancient bath house:
calm, steamy and offering a selection of
massages and beauty treatments.

The Pantheon & Piazza Navona

Like its counterpart to the south
(The Ghetto & Campo de' Fiori;

p65-76), this area of picturesque alleys in the loop of the river north of corso Vittorio Emanuele was part of the ancient *campus martius*.

After the Empire fell, the *campus* was prime construction territory and every medieval wall tells a tale of primitive recycling: grand *palazzi* were built from stolen marble; humbler souls constructed their little houses among the ruins. It's still a democratic area, where mink-coated contessas mingle with pensioners, craftsmen and tradesmen. After dark, smart restaurants, hip bars and, increasingly, tourist-trap rip-offs, fill to bursting, especially around Santa Maria della Pace.

Two squares – both living links to ancient Rome – dominate the district: **piazza della Rotonda** – home to the **Pantheon** – and magnificent **piazza Navona**.

West of piazza Navona, piazza Pasquino is home to a truncated classical statue; for centuries, Romans have pinned satirical verse (pasquinades) to this sculpture. Further north, elegant, antiques-shop-lined via dei Coronari was once the haunt of pilgrim-fleecing rosary-makers (*coronari*).

When corso Vittorio was hacked through the medieval fabric in the 1870s, only the most grandiose of homes were spared: Palazzo Massimo at no.141, with its curved façade following the stands in Domitian's *odeon* (small theatre), is one.

To the east of the Pantheon, **Galleria Doria Pamphili** contains one of Rome's finest art collections, while the charmingly rococo **piazza Sant'Ignazio** looks like a stage set. In neighbouring piazza di Pietra, the columns of the Temple of Hadrian can be seen embedded in the walls of Rome's ex-stock exchange.

Bernini's elephant p80

Sights & museums

Chiesa Nuova/Santa Maria in Vallicella

Piazza della Chiesa Nuova (06 687 5289/www.vallicella.org). **Open** 8am-noon, 4.30-7.15pm daily. **Map** p66 B2 ⑳

Filippo Neri (1515-95) was a wealthy Florentine who abandoned commerce to live among the poor in Rome. He founded the Oratorian order in 1544. In 1575, work began on the order's headquarters, the Chiesa Nuova. Neri wanted a large, simple building; the walls were covered with the exuberant frescoes and multicoloured marbles only after his death. Pietro da Cortona painted the *Assumption of the Virgin* (1650) in the apse, Rubens the *Virgin and Child* (1608) over the altar.

Chiostro del Bramante

Via della Pace 5 (06 6880 9036/ www.chiostrodelbramante.it). **Open** 10am-8pm Tue-Fri; 10am-9pm Sat,

Sun. **Admission** €10; €7 reductions. No credit cards. **Map** p66 C2 ⑤

Attached to the church of Santa Maria della Pace (p79) is this beautifully harmonious cloister designed by Donato Bramante, his first work after arriving in Rome in the early 16th century. The space hosts one-off exhibitions that are usually of high quality. The café-restaurant upstairs (no need to buy a ticket to get in; credit cards accepted) is a delightful place to rest and refuel.

Doria Pamphilj Gallery

Via del Corso 305 (06 679 7323/www. doriapamphilj.it). **Open** 10am-5pm daily. **Admission** €9; €6 reductions. No credit cards. **Map** p67 F3 ㉒

If the most impressive exhibition spaces of this treasure-filled, privately owned gallery are situated around the central courtyard, it is in rooms off the long Galleria degli Specchi that the highlights of the collection are to be found; the tiny Gabinetto di Velázquez contains that artist's dramatic portrait of the Pamphili Pope Innocent X; there's also a splendid bust by Bernini of the same pontiff next to it; off the other end of the *galleria* are four smaller rooms ordered by century. In the 17th-century room, Caravaggio is represented by the *Rest on the Flight into Egypt* and the *Penitent Magdalene*; the 16th-century room includes Titian's shameless *Salome* and a *Portrait of Two Men* by Raphael. There's also a sequence of plush state apartments.

Museo di Roma

Palazzo Braschi, via di San Pantaleo 10 (06 8207 7304/06 0608/www.museo diroma.it). **Open** 9am-7pm Tue-Sun. **Admission** €6.50; €4.50 reductions; extra charge during exhibitions. No credit cards. **Map** p66 C3 ㉓

A moderately interesting rotating collection recounts the evolution of the city from the Middle Ages to the early 20th century. Sculpture, clothing, furniture and photographs help to put the city's monuments in a human context. One-off exhibitions on Roman themes can be enlightening.

Palazzo Altemps

Piazza Sant'Apollinare 46 (06 687 2719). **Open** 9am-7.45pm Tue-Sun. **Admission** €7; €3.50 reductions; extra charge during exhibitions; see p9 Museo Nazionale Romano. No credit cards. **Map** p66 C1 ㉔

The 15th-century Palazzo Altemps houses part of the state-owned stock of Roman treasures: gems of classical statuary purchased from the Boncompagni-Ludovisi, Altemps and Mattei families. The Ludovisis liked 'fixing' statues: an *Athena with Serpent* was revamped in the 17th century by Alessandro Algardi, who also 'improved' the *Hermes Loghios*. The museum's greatest treasure is the Ludovisi Throne, a fifth-century BC work from Magna Grecia... though some believe it to be a fake.

Pantheon

Piazza della Rotonda (06 6830 0230). **Open** 8.30am-7.30pm Mon-Sat; 9am-6pm Sun; 9am-1pm public holidays. **Map** p67 D2 ㉕

The Pantheon was built by Hadrian in AD 119-125 as a temple to the most important deities; the inscription on the pediment records a Pantheon built 100 years before by General Marcus Agrippa (which confused historians for centuries). Its fine state of preservation is due to the building's conversion to a church in AD 608, though its bronze cladding was stolen over the centuries: part is now in Bernini's *baldacchino* in St Peter's. The bronze doors are the original Roman ones. Inside, the Pantheon's glory lies in its dimensions. The diameter of the hemispherical dome is exactly equal to the height of the building. At the centre of the dome is the oculus, a circular hole 9m (30ft) in diameter, a symbolic link between the temple and the heavens. Until the 18th century, the portico was used as a marketplace: supports for the stalls

Fountain of the Four Rivers

Map p66 C2 56

4-7pm Mon-Wed, Fri-Sun; 10am-12.30pm Thur. **Map** p67 D2 57
Completed in 1589, San Luigi/St Louis is the church of Rome's French community. In the fifth chapel on the left are Caravaggio's spectacular scenes from the life of St Matthew (1600-02). But make sure you don't overlook the lovely frescoes of St Cecilia by Domenichino (1615-17), in the second chapel on the right.

Sant'Agnese in Agone

Piazza Navona (06 6819 2134/ www.santagneseinagone.org). **Open** 9.30am-12.30pm, 4-7pm Tue-Sat; 10am-1pm, 4-7pm Sun. **Map** p66 C2 58
Legend says that teenage St Agnes was cast naked into the stadium of Domitian around AD 304 when she refused to renounce Christ and marry a powerful local. Her pagan persecutors chopped her head off (the implausibly small skull is still here), supposedly on the exact spot where the church now stands. Begun in 1652, the church was given its splendidly fluid concave façade by Borromini. Concerts are held in the sacristy at 6pm most Friday evenings during winter.

Sant'Agostino

Piazza Sant'Agostino 80 (06 6880 1962). **Open** 8am-noon, 4-7.30pm daily. **Map** p66 C1 59
This 15th-century church has one of the earliest Renaissance façades in Rome, made of travertine filched from the Colosseum. Inside, the third column on the left bears a fresco of Isaiah by Raphael (1512). In the first chapel on the left is Caravaggio's depiction of the grubbiest pilgrims ever to present themselves at the feet of the startlingly beautiful *Madonna of the Pilgrims* (1604).

Santa Maria della Pace

Arco della Pace 5 (06 686 1156). **Open** 9am-noon Mon, Wed, Sat. **Map** p66 C2 60
Built in 1482, Santa Maria della Pace was given its theatrical Baroque façade

were inserted into the notches that today are still visible in the columns.

Piazza Navona

Map p66 C2 56
This tremendous theatrical space owes its shape to an ancient athletics stadium, built in AD 86 by Emperor Domitian. Just north of the piazza, in piazza di Tor Sanguigna, remains of the original arena are visible from the street. Piazza Navona acquired its current form in the mid 17th century. The central fountain of the Four Rivers, finished in 1651, is one of the most extravagant masterpieces designed by Bernini; in 2008, it re-emerged after a lengthy restoration. Its main figures represent the longest rivers of the four continents known at the time; Ganges of Asia, Nile of Africa, Danube of Europe and Plata of the Americas, all with appropriate flora. The figure of the Nile is veiled, because its source was unknown.

San Luigi dei Francesi

Piazza San Luigi dei Francesi 5 (06 688 271). **Open** 10am-12.30pm,

by Pietro da Cortona in 1656. Just inside the door is Raphael's *Sybils* (1514). See also p77 Chiostro del Bramante.

Santa Maria sopra Minerva

Piazza della Minerva 42 (06 679 3926/ www.basilicaminerva.it). **Open** 7am-7pm daily. **Map** p67 E3 ⑥

Rome's only Gothic church was built on the site of an ancient temple of Minerva in 1280. Its best works of art are Renaissance: on the right of the transept is the Carafa chapel, with frescoes by Filippino Lippi (1457-1504). Also here is the tomb of the Carafa Pope Paul IV (1555-59), famous for enclosing the Jewish Ghetto and having loincloths painted on the nudes of Michelangelo's *Last Judgement* in the Sistine Chapel. A bronze loincloth was also ordered to cover Christ's genitals on a work here by Michelangelo, a Christ holding up

a cross. The *Madonna and Child*, an earlier work believed by some to be by Fra Angelico though probably by Benozzo Gozzoli, is in the chapel to the left of the altar, close to the artistic monk's own tomb. The father of modern astronomy, Galileo Galilei, who dared suggest that the earth revolved around the sun, was tried for heresy in the adjoining monastery in 1633. In the square in front of the church is a charming marble elephant bearing an obelisk on its back, by Bernini.

Sant'Ignazio di Loyola

Piazza Sant'Ignazio (06 679 4406/ www.chiesasantignazio.org). **Open** 8am-12.15pm, 3-7.15pm daily. **Map** p67 E2 ⑥

Sant'Ignazio was begun in 1626 to commemorate the canonisation of St Ignatius, founder of the Jesuits. Trompe l'oeil columns soar above the nave, and architraves by Andrea Pozzo open to a cloudy heaven. When the monks next door claimed that a dome would rob them of light, Pozzo simply painted a dome on the ceiling. The illusion is fairly convincing if you stand on the disc set in the floor of the nave. Walk away, however, and it collapses.

Sant'Ivo alla Sapienza

Corso Rinascimento 40 (06 361 2562). **Open** 9am-noon Sun. **Map** p67 D3 ⑥

In this crowning glory of Borromini's tortured imagination, completed in 1660, the concave façade is countered by the convex bulk of the dome, which terminates in a bizarre corkscrew spire. Inside, the convex and concave surfaces on the walls and up into the dome leave you feeling like someone spiked your cappuccino. Opens, erratically, at other times too.

Eating & drinking

See also **Baffetto 2** (p71), **Chiostro del Bramante** (p77) and **Friends Art Café** (p136).

Bar Sant'Eustachio

Armando al Pantheon

Salita de' Crescenzi 31 (06 6880 3034/ www.armandoalpantheon.it). **Meals served** 12.30-3pm, 7-11pm Mon-Fri; 12.30-3pm Sat. Closed Aug. **€€**. **Roman**. Map p67 D2 ㉞

Armando's charming sons continue to serve up the kind of simple no-frills Roman fare at honest prices that has been on offer here since 1961: a miracle, in this neighbourhood of po-mo makeovers and tourist rip-offs. The only concessions to changing times are some vegetarian and gluten-free dishes.

Bar Sant'Eustachio

Piazza Sant'Eustachio 82 (06 6880 2048/www.santeustachioilcaffe.it). **Open** 8.30am-1am Mon-Thur, Sun; 8.30am-1.20am Fri, Sat. No credit cards. **Café**. Map p67 D3 ㉟

This is one of the city's most famous coffee bars and its walls are plastered with celebrity testimonials. The coffee is quite extraordinary, if expensive. Try the *gran caffè*: the *schiuma* (froth) can be slurped out afterwards with spoon or fingers.

Caffè Bernini

Piazza Navona 44 (06 6819 2998/ www.caffebernini.com). **Open** 8.30am-12.30am daily. Closed 2wks Jan. **Café/Creative Italian**. Map p66 C2 ㊱

Hordes of hawkers and a plethora of tourist rip-off eateries can make a visit to glorious piazza Navona a trial. So full marks to the recently relaunched Caffè Bernini where the pan-Med food is good and fairly priced (for the area; **€€€**), and sitting outside for a coffee or *aperitivo* is an affordable pleasure.

Caffè della Pace

Via della Pace 3/7 (06 686 1216/ www.caffedellapace.it). **Open** 4pm-3am Mon; 8.30am-3am Tue-Sun. **Café/bar**. Map p66 C2 ㊲

Eternally à la mode with the bronzed and well-heeled, Caffè della Pace has warm, antiques- and flower-filled

Casa Bleve

rooms for the colder months, and (comparatively pricey) pavement tables, beneath the trademark ivy-clad façade, for sunny weather.

La Caffettiera

Piazza di Pietra 65 (06 679 8147). **Open** 7am-9pm Mon-Sat; 8am-9pm Sun. **Café**. Map p67 E2 ㊳

Politicians from the nearby parliament buildings lounge in the sumptuous tea room of this temple to Neapolitan goodies, while lesser mortals bolt coffees at the bar. The rum babà reigns supreme, but ricotta-lovers rave over the crunchy *sfogliatella*.

Casa Bleve

Via del Teatro Valle 48-49 (06 686 5970/www.casableve.it). **Meals served** 12.30-3pm, 7.30-10pm Tue-Sat. Closed 3wks Aug. **€€€**. **Wine bar/Italian**. Map p67 D3 ㊴

The main room of this elegant wine bar is a huge colonnaded roofed-in courtyard in a palazzo near to the

ROME BY AREA

Green T

The menu changes daily at this 1940s wine shop – you'll find it written up on the board at the entrance. Dishes follow the traditional Roman culinary calendar – potato *gnocchi* on Thursdays and stewed *baccalà* (salt cod) on Fridays.

Etabli

Vicolo delle Vacche 9 (06 9761 6694/ www.etabli.it). **Open** 10am-4pm, 6pm-2am Tue-Sun. Closed 3wks Aug. **Bar**. Map p66 B2 **72**

This new-ish locale in the super-chic *triangolo della pace* area is already drawing Rome's bright young things with its pared-back decor, twiddly chandeliers and deep armchairs around the fireplace. The welcome is suave-warm, the feeling intimate. In one room light meals are served at appropriate times; there's a restaurant (€€€) upstairs.

Gelateria del Teatro

Via di San Simone 70 (06 4547 4880). **Open** noon-10.30pm Mon-Thur, Sun; noon-11.30pm Fri, Sat Tue-Sat; noon-4pm, 6pm-2am Sun. Closed 3wks Aug. **Ice-cream**. Map p66 B2 **73**

See box p126.

Il Gelato di San Crispino

NEW *Piazza della Maddalena 3 (06 9760 1190/www.ilgelatodisan crispino.com).* **Open** 11am-8.30pm Mon, Wed, Thur, Sun; 11am-12.30am Fri, Sat. **Ice-cream**. Map p67 D2 **74**

Like its forerunner – still going strong at via della Panetteria 42, near the Trevi fountain – this new branch of Il Gelato di San Crispino serves some of the best ice-cream to be found in Rome. Flavours change according to what's in season. The place is open daily from mid March to mid September. See also box p126.

Grano

NEW *Piazza Rondanini 53 (06 6860 4099/www.ristorantegrano.it).*

Pantheon. The buffet option offers a vast choice of cheese, cured meat, smoked fish and salads, and there's also an impressive selection of wines. The first Bleve off-licence/eaterie in the Ghetto (La Vecchia Bottega del Vino, via Santa Maria del Pianto 9-11, www.lavecchiabottegadelvino.com) has a more intimate vibe.

Da Francesco

Piazza del Fico 29 (06 686 4009). **Meals served** *Nov-Mar* 11.50am-3pm, 7pm-12.30am Mon, Wed-Sun. €€. No credit cards. **Pizzeria**. Map p66 B2 **70**

Da Francesco is the genuine *centro storico* pizzeria article. It serves tasty pizzas and a range of competent, classic dishes in a warm, traditional ambience. Open Tuesday evenings in summer. Service is brisk but friendly. Bookings often go astray.

Enoteca Corsi

Via del Gesù 87-88 (06 679 0821). **Meals served** noon-3.30pm Mon-Sat. Closed Aug. €. **Roman**. Map p67 E3 **71**

Open 12.30-3pm, 7.30pm-midnight daily. €€€. **Creative Southern Italian**. Map p67 D2 🥈

The name (which means wheat in Italian) suggests a concept restaurant, but pasta and delicious homemade bread make their presence felt in this country-chic restaurant with southern Italian influences.

Green T

Via Pie' di Marmo 28 (06 679 8628/ www.green-tea.it). **Meals served** 12.30-3pm, 7.30pm-midnight Mon-Sat. Closed 2wks Aug. €€€. **Chinese**. Map p67 E3 🥈

Stylishly pared back in its decor, this Chinese restaurant has a coolly hushed air that comes as a welcome break after a hot morning's sightseeing and when you just can't take another plate of pasta. At €7 and €17, the set-lunch menus are a good deal. The place reopens at 6pm for a wide and excellent choice of teas.

Salotto 42

Piazza di Pietra 42 (06 678 5804/ www.salotto42.it). **Open** 10am-2am Tue-Sat; 10am-midnight Sun. Closed Aug. **Bar**. Map p67 E2 🥈

Incredibly comfortable chairs and sofas give a cosy feel to Salotto 42 during the day, when a smörgåsbord of nibbles is available. By night, the sleek room becomes a gorgeous cocktail bar with a great soundtrack and excellent cocktails. There's also a selection of books and magazines on fashion, art and design.

Société Lutèce

Piazza di Montevecchio 17 (06 6830 1472/www.societe-lutece.it). **Open** 6pm-2am Tue-Sun. Closed 2wks Aug. **Bar**. Map p66 C2 🥈

Société Lutèce is popular with eclectic Roman hipsters, the bar's cramped quarters often cause a spill-over into the small piazza. The *aperitivo* buffet (from 7pm) is plentiful and the vibe is decidedly laid-back.

Lo Zozzone

Via del Teatro Pace 32 (06 6880 8575). **Open** 9am-9pm Mon-Fri; 9am-11pm Sat. Closed Aug. €. No credit cards. **Takeaway pizza**. Map p66 C2 🥈

The 'dirty old man' (that's what the name means) serves Rome's best *pizza bianca ripiena* – which, as a sign explains, is 'White Pizza With Any Thing You Like Inside'. Fillings range from classics like prosciutto and mozzarella to exotic combinations. Pay at the till for a standard slab (€3.50); then join the receipt-waving hordes to get served. In summer, it also opens on Sundays.

Shopping

Ai Monasteri

Corso Rinascimento 72 (06 6880 2783/www.aimonasteri.it). **Open** 10am-1pm, 3.30-7.30pm Mon-Wed, Fri, Sat; 10am-1pm Thur. Closed Aug. Map p66 C2 🥈

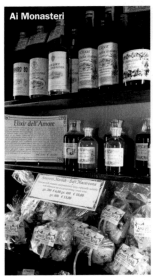

Ai Monasteri

ROME BY AREA

This richly perfumed old shop, founded in 1894, sells jams, chocolates, cosmetics and cure-all potions produced by religious orders around Italy.

Arsenale
Via del Governo Vecchio 64 (06 686 1380/www.patriziapieroni.it). **Open** 3.30-7.30pm Mon; 10am-7.30pm Tue-Sat. Closed 2wks Aug. **Map** p66 C2 ③①

Patrizia Pieroni's wonderful garments make for great window displays – not to mention successful party conversation pieces – and have been going down well with the Roman boho-chic luvvy crowd for years.

Ditta G Poggi
Via del Gesù 74-75 (06 679 3674/ www.poggi1825.it). **Open** 9am-1pm, 4-7.30pm Mon-Sat. Closed 2wks Aug. **Map** p67 E3 ③②

This wonderfully old-fashioned shop has been selling paints, brushes, canvases and artists' supplies of every description since 1825.

Maga Morgana
Via del Governo Vecchio 27 (06 687 9995). **Open** 10am-7.30pm Mon-Sat. **Map** p67 D3 ③③

Designer Luciana Iannace's quirky one-of-a-kind women's clothes include hand-knitted sweaters, skirts and dresses. More knitted and woollen items are sold at the sister shop down the road at no.98.

Moriondo & Gariglio
Via del Piè di Marmo 21 (06 699 0856). **Open** 9am-7.30pm Mon-Sat. Closed Aug. **Map** p67 E3 ③④

This fairytale chocolate shop with beautiful gift boxes is especially lovely close to Christmas, when you will have to fight to get your hands on the excellent marrons glacés.

Le Tartarughe
Via Pie' di Marmo 17 (06 679 2240/ www.susannalisoperletartarughe.it).

Open 3.30-7.30pm Mon; 10am-7.30pm Tue-Sat. Closed 3wks Aug. **Map** p67 E3 ③⑤

Designer Susanna Liso's sumptuous classic-with-a-twist creations range from cocktail dresses to elegant workwear, all in eye-catching colours. For gorgeous accessories, head across the road to no.33. There's a new branch at via Mastrogiorgio 70, in Testaccio.

Nightlife

See also **Friends Art Café** (p136), **Salotto 42** (p83) and **Société Lutèce** (p83).

Anima
Via Santa Maria dell'Anima 57 (347 850 9256). **Open** 6pm-4am daily. **Map** p66 C2 ③⑥

With improbably baroque gilded mouldings, this small venue has a buzzing atmosphere and serves very good drinks. It caters for a mixed crowd of all ages and nationalities. Expect to hear hip hop, R&B, funk, soul and reggae.

Bloom
Via del Teatro Pace 30 (06 6880 2029). **Open** 11.30pm-3am Mon, Tue, Thur-Sun. Closed Aug. **Map** p66 C2 ③⑦

A bar and disco (generally on Friday and Saturday), Bloom is cooler than ice: eat sushi, sip a cocktail, dance or simply relax and join your fashionable fellow guests checking out each others' outfits.

La Maison
Vicolo dei Granari 3 (06 683 3312/ www.lamaisonroma.it). **Open** 11pm-4am Wed-Sat. Closed June-Sept. **Map** p66 C2 ③⑧

One of the clubs of choice of Rome's fashion victims, La Maison is dressed to impress. Huge chandeliers, dark red walls and curvy sofas give it an opulent, courtly feeling. Surprisingly, the music on offer is not banal and the atmosphere is buzzing. The doormen are picky, however.

Ara Pacis Museum p89

Tridente, Trevi & Borghese

Il Tridente

With its English banks and English bookshops, the wedge-shaped Tridente was a home-from-home for the Grand Tourists of the 18th and 19th centuries. English '*milords*' took lodgings in and around piazza di Spagna. When venturing beyond the familiar streets, they resorted to guides to help them avoid pitfalls.

Even today there are visitors who never make it further than the Tridente's plethora of glorious fashion retailers: from Armani to Zegna, there's hardly a big name in *moda* that hasn't staked a claim in the narrow streets of the Tridente.

The whole area was built as a showpiece. At the head of the wedge is **piazza del Popolo**. It was given its oval form by architect Giuseppe Valadier in the early 19th century.

Leading out centrally from the square is the Tridente's principal thoroughfare, via del Corso, which passes high-street clothing retailers en route to the towering column of Marcus Aurelius (piazza Colonna) – which was built between AD 180 and 196 to commemorate the victories on the battlefield of that most intellectual of Roman emperors – and piazza Venezia.

Via Ripetta veers off down the riverside, leading to Augustus' **mausoleum** and the **Ara Pacis**.

The third street, chic via del Babuino, runs past a series of tempting antique and designer stores to the **Spanish Steps**.

Parallel to via del Babuino, tucked right below the Pincio hill, is via Margutta, fondly remembered as the focus of the 1960s art scene and 'home' to Gregory Peck in the 1953 classic *Roman Holiday*. Fellini also lived on this artsy alley.

Criss-crossing the three main arteries are streets such as via

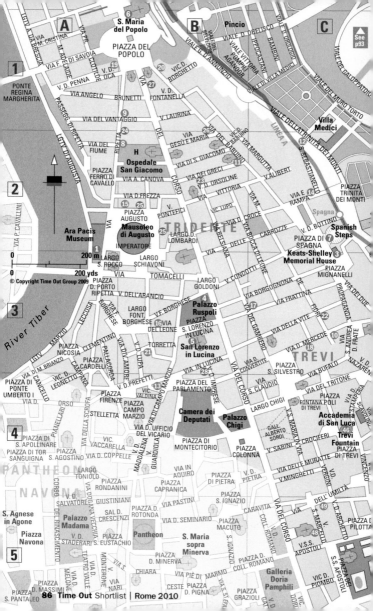

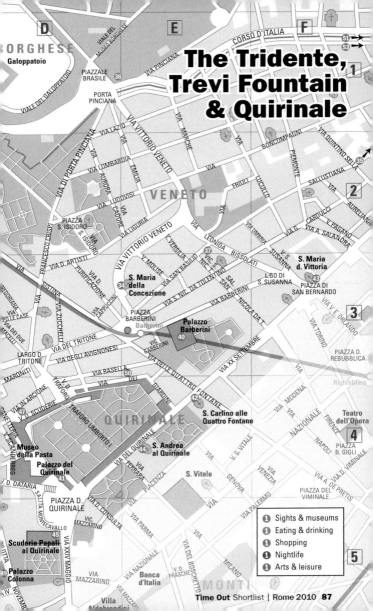

The Tridente, Trevi Fountain & Quirinale

D **E** **F**

CORSO D'ITALIA

1

BORGHESE

Galoppatoio

PIAZZALE BRASILE

PORTA PINCIANA

VENETO

PIAZZA S. ISIDORO

S. Maria della Concezione

PIAZZA BARBERINI

Barberini

S. Maria d. Vittoria

PIAZZA DI SAN BERNARDO

L.GO DI S. SUSANNA

S. Maria d. Vittoria

2

3

PIAZZA D. REBUBBLICA

Repubblica

Palazzo Barberini

S. Carlino alle Quattro Fontane

QUIRINALE

Teatro dell'Opera

PIAZZA B. GIGLI

4

Museo della Pasta

Palazzo del Quirinale

S. Andrea al Quirinale

S. Vitale

PIAZZA DEL VIMINALE

PIAZZA D. QUIRINALE

Scuderie Papali al Quirinale

Palazzo Colonna

Banca d'Italia

MONTI

5

Villa Aldobrandini

1 Sights & museums
1 Eating & drinking
1 Shopping
1 Nightlife
1 Arts & leisure

Virtual Rome

Rewind Rome

For tourism in Rome, 2008 was not a good year. After a decade of soaring figures, a fall-off in visitors of six to seven per cent was predicted. City Hall, therefore, is keen to get tourists back into the Eternal City. But are they going about it in the right way?

Selling Rome, one would think, would not be a difficult task: with so much history and culture oozing from the very masonry, all you need to do is provide adequate infrastructure and a guiding hand.

But City Hall is not looking to improve, but renew, with plans for a vast ancient Rome-themed amusement park somewhere just outside the city.

For those who prefer their culture to come digitally packaged, Rome already has an attraction or two: the flight-simulator **Time Elevator** (p96) offers a bumpy 20-minute ride through two millennia of history, while the new **Rewind Rome** (p109) takes the latest in 3D imaging wizardry and mixes video game technology and rather cheesy virtual guides for a romp through *Caput mundi*.

On a more erudite note, computers in the **Crypta Balbi** (p65) offer an interactive guide to how rubbish raised Rome's street levels, while the **Terme di Diocleziano** (p104) has an animated explanation (in Italian only) of how the ancient via Flaminia would have looked.

The new park – to cover 300 hectares, with five hotels and recreations of all ancient Rome's key sites – would be built on (still unspecified) council-owned land, privately financed and would attract, the council says, eight million visitors annually, to add to the 20-odd million who already come to the Eternal City each year.

In the meantime, skeptics point out that the Appian Way is unkempt and label-less, museums complain of serious underfunding, a handful of gardeners struggle to keep parks presentable and little has been done to render the Roman Forum more 'legible'. Many hotels continue to charge high prices for bad service, and the spread of tourist-trap restaurants goes on practically unchecked. Orlando has little else to offer besides its Disney extravaganza: Rome, well managed, is one of the world's greatest attractions in itself.

Condotti that have given Rome its reputation as a major fashion centre.

Sights & museums

Ara Pacis Museum

Via Ripetta/lungotevere in Augusta (06 0608/www.arapacis.it). **Open** 9am-7pm Tue-Sun. **Admission** €6.50; €4.50 reductions; extra charge during exhibitions. **Map** p86 A2 ❶

The *Ara pacis augustae* ('Augustan Altar of Peace') was inaugurated in 9 BC to celebrate the security that the Emperor Augustus' victories had brought. The altar was rebuilt in the early 20th century from fragments amassed through a long dig and a trawl through the world's museums. The altar itself sits inside an enclosure carved with exquisitely realistic reliefs. The upper band shows the ceremonies surrounding the dedication of the altar. The carved faces of Augustus and his family have all been identified. The monument resides in a container designed by US architect Richard Meier, with an exhibition space below.

The forlorn brick cylinder next door in piazza Augusto Imperatore was originally a mausoleum covered with marble pillars and statues, begun in 28 BC. Augustus was laid to rest in the central chamber on his death in AD 14. The square is currently being refurbished.

Explora – Museo dei Bambini di Roma

Via Flaminia 82 (06 361 3776/ www.mdbr.it). **Open** sessions at 10am, noon, 3pm, 5pm Tue-Sun. **Admission** €6; €7 3-12s. **Map** p97 A2 ❷

This children's museum provides educational fun for under-12s. The 3pm and 5pm sessions on Thursday afternoons cost €5 for all. Booking is essential.

Keats-Shelley Memorial House

Piazza di Spagna 26 (06 678 4235/ www.keats-shelley-house.org). **Open** 10am-1pm, 2-6pm Mon-Fri; 11am-2pm,

3-6pm Sat. Closed 1wk Dec. **Admission** €4; €3 reductions. **Map** p86 C3 ❸

The house at the bottom of the Spanish Steps where the 25-year-old John Keats died of tuberculosis in 1821 is crammed with mementos: a lock of Keats's hair and his death mask, an urn holding tiny pieces of Shelley's charred skeleton, and copies of documents and letters.

Palazzo Ruspoli-Fondazione Memmo

Via del Corso 418 (06 687 4704/ www.fondazionememmo.com). **Open** times vary. **Admission** varies. No credit cards. **Map** p86 B3 ❹

The palace of one of Rome's old noble families is used for touring exhibitions of art, archaeology and history. The basement rooms often host photo exhibitions; admission is sometimes free.

San Lorenzo in Lucina

Piazza San Lorenzo in Lucina 16A (06 687 1494). **Open** 8am-8pm daily. **Map** p86 B3 ❺

This 12th-century church – built on the site of an early Christian place of worship – incorporates Roman columns into its exterior. The 17th-century interior has Bernini portrait busts, a kitsch 17th-century *Crucifixion* by Guido Reni and a monument to French artist Nicolas Poussin, who died in Rome in 1665. In the first chapel on the right is a grill, reputed to be the one on which St Lawrence was roasted to death.

Santa Maria del Popolo

Piazza del Popolo 12 (06 361 0836). **Open** 7.30am-noon, 4-7pm Mon-Sat; 7.30am-1.30pm, 4.30-7.30pm Sun. **Map** p86 B1 ❻

According to legend, Santa Maria del Popolo occupies the site where the hated Emperor Nero was buried. In 1099, Pope Paschal II built a chapel here to dispel demons still believed to haunt the spot. In 1472, Pope Sixtus IV rebuilt the chapel as a church. In the apse are Rome's first stained-glass windows (1509). The apse was designed by

Bramante, while the choir ceiling and first and third chapels in the right aisle were frescoed by Pinturicchio. The Chigi Chapel was designed by Raphael for wealthy banker Agostino Chigi, and features Chigi's horoscope. The church's most-gawped-at possessions, however, are the two masterpieces by Caravaggio to the left of the main altar, showing the stories of Saints Peter and Paul.

Spanish Steps & Piazza di Spagna

Map p86 C2 **7**

Piazza di Spagna has been considered a compulsory stop for visitors to Rome since the 18th century. The square takes its name from the Spanish Embassy, but is most famous for the Spanish Steps (Scalinata di Trinità dei Monti), an elegant cascade down from the church of Trinità dei Monti. The steps (completed in 1725) were, in fact, funded by a French diplomat. At the foot of the stairs is a boat-shaped fountain, the *barcaccia*, designed in 1627 by either Gian Lorenzo Bernini or his less-famous father Pietro.

Eating & drinking

Bisciù

NEW *Via Ripetta 40 (06 3265 2670/ www.bisciu.it).* **Open** 10am-6pm Mon-Wed, Fri, Sat; 10am-2pm Thur. Closed Aug. €. **Snack bar**. Map p86 B2 **8**
See box p73.

Buccone

Via Ripetta 19-20 (06 361 2154/ www.enotecabuccone.com). **Open** *Shop* 9am-8.30pm Mon-Thur; 9am-11.30pm Fri, Sat. **Meals served** 12.30-3pm Mon-Thur; 12.30-3pm, 7.30-10.30pm Fri, Sat. Closed 3wks Aug. €€. **Enoteca**. Map p86 B1 **9**
Originally – and still – a bottle shop, Buccone has tables squeezed between its high wooden shelves. The fare – a few pasta dishes, meaty seconds and creative salads – is simple but good, the prices very reasonable.

Burro e Alici

NEW *Via della Mercede 34 (06 699 0778/www.burroealici.com).* **Open** 10.30am-7.30pm Mon-Sat. Closed 2wks Aug. €. **Snack bar**. Map p86 C3 **10**
See box p73.

Caffè Canova-Tadolini

Via del Babuino 150A (06 3211 0702/ www.museoateliercanovatadolini.it). **Open** 8am-8.30pm daily. Closed 3wks Aug. **Café**. Map p86 B2 **11**
Once the studio of 19th-century sculptor Antonio Canova, this café has tables among its sculpture models and a refined and elegant old-world feel.

Ciampini – Café du Jardin

Piazza Trinità dei Monti (06 678 5678/ www.caffeciampini.com). **Open** 8am-1am Mon, Tue, Thur-Sun. (Daily in spring and autumn.) Closed mid Oct-Mar. **Café**. Map p86 C2 **12**
This open-air café and restaurant (€€€) near the top of the Spanish Steps is surrounded by creeper-curtained trellises, with a pond in the centre. There's a spectacular view, especially at sunset.

Da Gino

Vicolo Rosini 4 (06 687 3434). **Meals served** 1-2.45pm, 8-10.45pm Mon-Sat. Closed Aug. €€. **Roman**. No credit cards. Map p86 B4 **13**
In a hard-to-find lane just off piazza del Parlamento, this old-style *osteria* champions the lighter side of the local tradition in dishes like *tonnarelli alla ciociara* (pasta with mushrooms and tomatoes), and pasta and chickpeas in ray sauce; desserts include an excellent tiramisù.

GiNa

Via San Sebastianello 7A (06 678 0251/www.ginaroma.com). **Open** 11am-8pm daily. Closed 2wks Aug. €€. **Italian/bar**. Map p86 C2 **14**
This bright and artsy light-lunch and dinner bar is a rather good option for snacking by the Spanish Steps. The menu is homely: a couple of soups, four or five daily pasta dishes, a range of

Spanish Steps & Piazza di Spagna

creative and gourmet salads, wine by the glass or bottle. You can also order a gourmet picnic hamper.

'Gusto

Piazza Augusto Imperatore 9 (06 322 6273/www.gusto.it). **Open** *Wine bar* noon-2am daily. **Meals served** *Pizzeria* 12.30-3pm, 7.30pm-1am daily. *Restaurant* 12.45-3pm, 7.45pm-midnight daily. **€€-€€€. Pizzeria/ Italian/Wine bar.** Map p86 B2 ⑮
'Gusto is a multi-purpose, split-level pizzeria, restaurant and wine bar, with a kitchen shop and bookshop next door. The ground-floor pizza and salad bar is always packed; the buffet lunch is good value. Upstairs, the more expensive restaurant applies oriental techniques to Italian models, not always convincingly. The wine bar out back is buzzing and stylish, with a good choice of wines by the glass and nibbles. Around the corner at via della Frezza 16, the mod L'Osteria is part of the same outfit. 'Gusto's newest outpost – 'Gusto al 28 – is a minimal-chic fish restaurant and wine bar at piazza Augusto Imperatore 28.

Matricianella

Via del Leone 4 (06 683 2100/www. matricianella.it). **Meals served** 12.30-3pm, 7.30-11pm Mon-Sat. Closed 3wks Aug. **€€€. Roman.** Map p86 B3 ⑯
A friendly, bustling place with good prices. The Roman imprint is most evident in classics such as the *bucatini all'amatriciana* (pasta with spicy sausage sauce) or *abbacchio a scottadito* (thin strips of lamb), but there are lots of creative options. The well-chosen wine list is a model of honest pricing. Book ahead.

Palatium

Via Frattina 94 (06 6920 2132/ www.enotecapalatium.it). **Open** 11am-11pm Mon-Sat. Closed 2wks Aug. **€€. Wine bar/Italian.** Map p86 C3 ⑰
Though it's backed by the Lazio regional government, this wine bar and eaterie is more than a PR exercise, offering the chance to go beyond the Castelli romani clichés to explore lesser-known local vintages such as Cesanese or Aleatico. After *aperitivi* from 6-8pm, Palatium switches into restaurant mode, offering light creative dishes.

Pizza Ciro

Via della Mercede 43 (06 678 6015/ www.pizzaciro.it). **Meals served** 11am-2am daily. **€**. **Pizzeria**. **Map** p86 C3 ⑱
From outside this may look like a modest, touristy pizza parlour, but Ciro is, in fact, one enormous eating factory. The pizzas are not at all bad, and *primi* such as *tubetti alla Ciro* (pasta with rocket and mussels) provide a decent alternative.

Rosati

Piazza del Popolo 4/5A (06 322 5859). **Open** 7am-11pm daily. **Café/bar**. **Map** p86 A1 ⑲
Frequented by Calvino and Pasolini, this bar's elegant interior has remained unchanged since 1922. Try the *Sogni romani* cocktail: orange juice with liqueurs in red and yellow – the colours of the city.

Stravinskij Bar

Via del Babuino 9 (06 328 881/06 689 1694/www.hotelderussie.it). **Open** 9am-1am daily. **Café/bar**. **Map** p86 B1 ⑳
Within the swanky De Russie hotel, this chic bar has an inside area with comfy armchairs and a fabulous patio where tables are surrounded by orange trees.

Vic's

Vicolo della Torretta 60 (06 687 1445). **Meals served** 12.30-3pm Mon; 12.30-3pm, 7.30-10.30pm Tue-Sat. Closed 2wks Aug. **€**. No credit cards. **Italian**. **Map** p86 B3 ㉑
This wine and salad bar offers a range of creative salads such as radicchio, pine nuts, sultanas and parmesan. Pared-back Roman *osteria* decor, charming service and a fairly priced wine list complete the picture.

Shopping

The Tridente is Rome's chic shopping area *per eccellenza*. In this wedge you'll find the big names of Italian fashion: Prada, Fendi, Gucci, Dolce & Gabbana et al.

Anglo-American Book Co

Via della Vite 102 (06 679 5222/ www.aab.it). **Open** 3.30-7.30pm Mon; 10am-7.30pm Tue-Sat. Closed 3wks Aug. **Map** p86 C3 ㉒
A good selection of books in English.

Lion Bookshop

Via dei Greci 36 (06 3265 4007/ www.thelionbookshop.com). **Open** 3.30-7.30pm Mon; 10am-7.30pm Tue-Sun. **Map** p86 B2 ㉓
This friendly shop is a great place for modern fiction and children's books.

L'Olfattorio – Bar à Parfums

Via Ripetta 34 (06 361 2325/ www.olfattorio.it). **Open** 3.30-7.30pm Tue-Sat. Closed Oct. **Map** p86 B1 ㉔
A scent-mixing expert will awaken your olfactory organs and guide you towards your perfect perfume.

La Soffitta Sotto i Portici

Piazza Augusto Imperatore (06 3600 5345). **Open** 9am-sunset 1st & 3rd Sun of mth. Closed Aug. **Map** p86 B2 ㉕
A street market with collectibles of all kinds, ranging from magazines to jewellery, at non-bargain prices. There's a multilingual information desk.

TAD

Via del Babuino 155A (06 3269 5131/ www.taditaly.com). **Open** noon-7.30pm Mon; 10.30am-7.30pm Tue-Fri; 10.30am-8pm Sat; noon-8pm Sun. **Map** p86 B1 ㉖
The idea behind this 'concept store' is that you can shop for clothes, shoes, flowers, household good, CDs, mags and perfumes, get your hair done, eat fusion Thai-Italian and drink – all in one place.

Arts & leisure

Metropolitan

Via del Corso 7 (06 320 0933). **Tickets** €4-€7. **Map** p86 B1 ㉗
This cinema shows the latest big-budget movies in the original language.

Galleria Borghese p94

Nuovo Olimpia

Via in Lucina 16G (06 686 1068).
Tickets €5-€7. **Map** p86 B3 ㉓
High-ish profile arthouse movies are
likely to turn up on this cinema's screens
in the original language.

Villa Borghese & Via Veneto

Until the 1870s, when Rome became
the capital of newly united Italy and
speculators set to work to house the
soaring population, the the city was
dotted with splendid private estates.
An act of unusual foresight by the
state in 1901 saved Villa Borghese
from the carve-up, and left us with
this delightful green space.

The area has always been green.
Ancient aristocrats built sprawling
villas here, and noble families and
monastic orders continued the
tradition right up until the 1800s.
Now the city's most central public
park, it offers a great art repository
– the superb **Galleria Borghese**,
plus one of Rome's greatest views

– from the Pincio, over piazza del
Popolo to the dome of St Peter's.

Descending south from the park,
via Vittorio Veneto (known simply
as via Veneto) was the haunt of the
famous and glamorous in the *dolce
vita* years of the 1950s and '60s.
These days, it's home to insurance
companies, luxury hotels and
visitors wondering where the
stars and paparazzi went.

At the southern end of via Veneto
is piazza Barberini. In ancient times,
erotic dances were performed here
to mark the coming of spring. The
square's magnificent centrepiece,
Bernini's Triton fountain, was once
in open countryside. Now he sits –
his two fish-tail legs tucked beneath
him on a shell supported by four
dolphins – amid thundering traffic.
The bees around him are the
Barberini family emblem.

Sights & museums

Bioparco-Zoo

*Piazzale del Giardino Zoologico 20
(06 360 8211/www.bioparco.it).*

ROME BY AREA

Piazza del Popolo p85

Open 9.30am-5pm daily. **Admission** €10; €8 reductions. **Map** p97 D1/D2 ㉙ Slightly more sprightly since its makeover from 'zoo' to 'biopark', this place will keep your kids happy for an afternoon. Next door – and accessible through the zoo – is the Museo Civico di Zoologia di Roma, with sections on biodiversity and extreme habitats.

Galleria Borghese
Piazzale del Museo Borghese 5 (06 32 810/www.galleriaborghese.it). **Open** 9am-7.30pm Tue-Sun. **Admission** €8.50; €5.25 reductions; extra charge during exhibitions. **Map** p97 E2 ㉚ **Note**: booking (€2) is obligatory.

Begun in 1608, the Casino Borghese was designed to house the art collection of Cardinal Scipione Borghese, Bernini's greatest patron. The interior decoration (1775-90) was restored in the 1990s. A curved double staircase leads to the imposing entrance salon, with fourth-century AD floor mosaics showing gladiators fighting wild animals. In room 1

is Antonio Canova's 1808 waxed marble figure of Pauline, sister of Napoleon and wife of Prince Camillo Borghese, as a topless *Venus*; Prince Camillo thought the work so provocative that he forbade even the artist from seeing it after completion. Rooms 2-4 contain some wonderful sculptures by Gian Lorenzo Bernini: the *David* (1624) in room 2 is a self-portrait of the artist; room 3 houses his *Apollo and Daphne* (1625); room 4 his *Rape of Proserpine* (1622). Room 5 contains important pieces of classical sculpture, including a Roman copy of a Greek dancing faun and a sleeping hermaphrodite. Bernini's *Aeneas and Anchises* (1620) dominates room 6, while room 7 has an Egyptian theme: included among the classical statues is a second-century Isis. The six Caravaggios in room 8 include the *Boy with a Basket of Fruit* (c1594) and the *Sick Bacchus* (c1593), believed to be a self-portrait.

Upstairs, the picture gallery holds a surfeit of masterpieces. Look out for: Raphael's *Deposition* and Pinturicchio's *Crucifixion with Saints Jerome and Christopher* (room 9); Lucas Cranach's *Venus and Cupid with Honeycomb* (room 10); and Rubens's spectacular *Pietà* and *Susanna and the Elders* (room 18). Titian's *Venus Blindfolding Cupid* and *Sacred and Profane Love*, recently restored but still difficult to interpret, are the stars of room 20, which also contains a stunning *Portrait of a Man* by Antonello da Messina.

Event highlights Caravaggio/Bacon: from the Galleria Borghese's ongoing 'ten great artists in ten years' programme, 2009 is dedicated to these two masters (late 2009-early 2010).

Galleria Nazionale d'Arte Moderna e Contemporanea
Viale delle Belle Arti 131 (06 3229 8221/www.gnam.beniculturali.it). **Open** 8.30am-7.30pm Tue-Sun. **Admission** €9; €7. No credit cards. **Map** p97 C2 ㉛ This collection begins with the 19th century: an enormous statue of *Hercules* by Canova dominates the central hall of the

left wing; elsewhere are charming views of the 19th-century Italian landscape. The 20th-century component includes works by de Chirico, Modigliani, Morandi and Marini. International stars include *The Three Ages* by Klimt and *The Gardener* and *Madame Ginoux* by Van Gogh. Cézanne, Braque, Rodin and Henry Moore are also represented.

Museo Carlo Bilotti

Viale Fiorello La Guardia (06 0608/ www.museocarlobilotti.it). **Open** 9am-7pm Tue-Sun. **Admission** €4.50; €2.50 reductions; extra charge for exhibitions. No credit cards. **Map** p97 C3 ㉜

This museum houses the collection of billionaire art tycoon Carlo Bilotti: Giorgio de Chirico, Larry Rivers, Jean Dubuffet and Andy Warhol all feature.

Museo Nazionale di Villa Giulia

Piazzale di Villa Giulia 9 (06 300 0562/ www.villaborghese.it). **Open** 8.30am-7.30pm Tue-Sun. **Admission** €4; €2 reductions. No credit cards. **Map** p97 B1 ㉝

This collection, in a villa designed by Michelangelo and Vignola for Pope Julius III in the mid 1500s, records the pre-Roman peoples of central Italy, and the sophisticated, mysterious Etruscans in particular. The Etruscans went well prepared to their graves, and most of the collection comes from excavations of tombs: the museum has hundreds of vases, pieces of furniture and models of buildings made to accompany the dead. In the courtyard, stairs descend to the nymphaeum; in an adjacent room is the sixth-century BC terracotta *Apollo of Veio*. In the garden there is a reconstruction of an Etruscan temple and a café.

Santa Maria della Concezione

Via V Veneto 27 (06 487 1185/ www.cappucciniviaveneto.it). **Open** *Church* 7am-noon, 3-7pm daily. *Crypt* 9am-noon, 3-6pm daily. **Admission** *Crypt* donation expected. **Map** p87 E3 ㉞

Commonly known as *i cappuccini* (the Capuchins) after the long-bearded, brown-clad Franciscan sub-order to which it belongs, this Baroque church's attraction lies in the crypt: the skeletons of over 4,000 monks have been dismantled and arranged in swirls and curlicues through four chapels. Ribs hang from the ceiling in the form of chandeliers, and inverted pelvic bones make the shape of hour-glasses – a reminder (as a notice states) that 'you will be what we now are'.

Eating & drinking

Cantina Cantarini

Piazza Sallustio 12 (06 485 528). **Meals served** 12.30-2.45pm, 7.30-10.45pm Mon-Sat. Closed 3wks Aug, 2wks Dec-Jan. €€€. **Roman**. **Map** off p87 F2 ㉟

This good-value high-quality trattoria is meat-based for the first part of the week, then turns fishy thereafter. The atmosphere is as *allegro* as seating is tight – though outside tables take off some of the pressure in summer.

Cinecaffè – Casina delle Rose

Largo M Mastroianni 1 (06 4201 6224/www.cinecaffe.it). **Open** *Café* 9am-8pm daily; *restaurant* 12.30-3.30pm daily. **Café/Italian**. **Map** p87 D1 ㊱

This ultra-civilised café at the via Veneto end of Villa Borghese serves excellent coffee, drinks and wallet-friendly light lunches to office workers, tourists and cinema aficionados. The restaurant (€€€), serving mod-Med fare, is pricier.

Moma

Via San Basilio 42-43 (06 4201 1798/ www.momaristorante.com). **Open** 7.30am-12.30am Mon-Sat. **Meals served** 12.30-3.30pm, 8-11pm. **Café/ Italian/ Wine bar**. **Map** p87 E2 ㊲

As the name suggests, this busy, tiny café/wine bar/restaurant (€€€) aims for a New York ambience. Tiny overall, there's a bar area downstairs and seating upstairs. The lunchtime snack-sized gourmet salads and hot dishes – some on edible 'plates' of crunchy pastry – make a pleasant change from the usual bar sandwich.

Nightlife

Gregory's
Via Gregoriana 54A (06 679 6386/ www.gregorysjazz.com). **Open** 7pm-2am Tue-Sun. Closed Aug. **Map** p86 C3 ③⑧
This cosy little venue oozes jazz culture from every pore; it has top live acts and a jam session on Wednesdays. Book ahead for the restaurant.

Trevi Fountain & Quirinale

Water is the dominant theme in the area nestling beneath the immense **Quirinal palace**, once home to popes and kings and now the official residence of Italy's president. The water that cascades into the **Trevi Fountain** is *acqua vergine,* said to be Rome's best, and used by Grand Tourists to make their tea. (Don't try drinking straight from the fountain: it's full of coins and chlorine.)

The surrounding medieval streets conceal many other testimonies to the importance of water: from the 'miraculous' well in the church of Santa Maria in Via (via Mortaro 24), from where cupfuls of healing liquid are still dispensed, to the Città d'Acqua (vicolo del Puttarello 25), where the *acqua vergine* can be heard rushing below a recently excavated ancient Roman street.

The Trevi district was a service area for the palace: here were the printing presses, bureaucratic departments and service industries that oiled the machinery of state. Aristocratic families, such as the Barberinis and Colonnas, built their palaces close by; their art collections are now on view.

Another fine collection lurks inside the Accademia di San Luca (piazza dell'Accademia 77, www.accademiasanluca.it). A slow-moving *restauro* has been going on for years, and is due for completion in 2011. In the meantime, you'll have to settle for a peek at Borromini's glorious spiral staircase in the courtyard and the third-floor display of plaster casts – 'sketches' for sculptures by Antonio Canova et al.

For an altogether more 21st-century take on the Eternal City, catch the 45-minute flight-simulator projection on Rome's history at Time Elevator (via dei SS Apostoli 20, www.time-elevator.it, from €17, €15 reductions; see box p88).

Sharing the Quirinal hill with the president's palace are two of Rome's finest small Baroque churches, **San Carlino** and **Sant'Andrea**, and a crossroads with four fountains (1593) representing river gods.

Sights & museums

Galleria Colonna
Piazza SS Apostoli 66 (06 678 4350/ www.galleriacolonna.it). **Open** 9am-1pm Sat. Closed Aug. **Admission** €10; €8 reductions. No credit cards. **Map** p87 D5 ③⑨
This splendid six-room gallery was completed in 1703 for the Colonna family, whose descendants still live in the palace. The immense frescoed ceiling of the mirrored Great Hall pays tribute to family hero Marcantonio Colonna, who led the papal fleet to victory against the Turks in the Battle of Lepanto in 1571. The gallery's most famous picture is Annibale Caracci's earthy peasant *Bean Eater*, but don't miss Bronzino's wonderfully sensuous *Venus and Cupid*. Private visits can be arranged on other days.

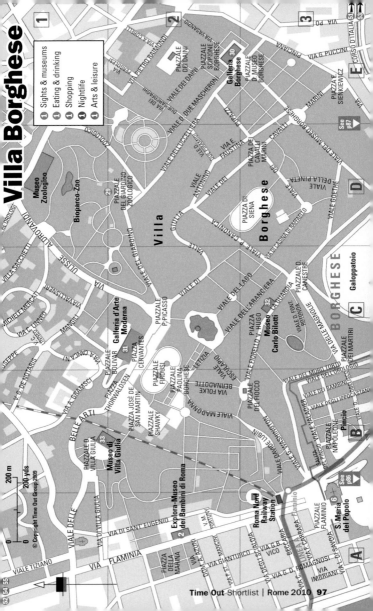

Villa Borghese

Legend:
- Sights & museums
- Eating & drinking
- Shopping
- Nightlife
- Arts & leisure

Labels on map:

Museo Zoologico
Bioparco-Zoo
Galleria d'Arte Moderna 31
Galleria Borghese 30
Museo Carlo Bilotti 32
Museo di Villa Giulia 33
Explora-Museo dei Bambini di Roma 2
Roma Nord Railway Station
S. Maria del Popolo 6
Pincio
Villa Borghese
Galoppatoio

PIAZZALE DEI DAINI
PIAZZALE SCIPIONE BORGHESE
PIAZZA DI SIENA
PIAZZALE P.PICASSO
PIAZZALE CERVANTES
PIAZZA CAVALLI MARINI
PIAZZALE CANESTRE
PIAZZA FIORELLO T.HUGO
PIAZZA DI GIARDIA
PIAZZALE DEI MARTIRI
PIAZZA BOLIVAR
PIAZZALE THORWALDSEN
PIAZZALE JOSE DE SAN MARTIN
PIAZZA SHAWKY
PIAZZA FIRDUSI
PIAZZALE PAOLINA BORGHESE
PIAZZALE DELFIOCCO
PIAZZALE D. VILLA GIULIA
PIAZZALE FLAMINIO
PIAZZA DELLA MARINA

VIA PO
VIA G. PUCCINI
CORSO D'ITALIA
VIALE TIZIANO
VIA FLAMINIA

See p87
See p86

200 m
200 yds

© Copyright Time Out Group 2009

52 53 54 55

Palazzo Barberini – Galleria Nazionale d'Arte Antica

Via delle Quattro Fontane 13 (06 481 4591/bookings 06 32 810/www.galleria borghese.it). **Open** 9am-7.30pm Tue-Sun. **Admission** €5; €3 reductions. No credit cards. **Map** p87 E3 ④

This vast Baroque palace, built by the Barberini Pope Urban VIII, houses one of Rome's most important art collections. Top architects like Maderno, Borromini and Bernini worked on this pile, which was completed in just five years (1627-33). Entrance is now up Borromini's graceful oval staircase and through the grand reception room where the ceiling is adorned with Pietro di Cortona's magnificent *Allegory of Divine Providence* (1639). Highlights of the collection include Filippo Lippi's *Madonna* (with possibly the ugliest Christ-child ever painted); an enigmatic portrait by Raphael of a courtesan believed to be his mistress; a *Nativity* and *Baptism of Christ* by El Greco; Tintoretto's *Christ and the Woman taken in Adultery*; Titian's *Venus and Adonis*; Caravaggio's *Judith beheading Holofernes* and the beautiful *Narcissus*; a Holbein portrait, *Henry VIII Dressed for his Wedding to Anne of Cleves*; and a bust by Bernini of Pope Urban VIII.

Palazzo del Quirinale

Piazza del Quirinale (06 46 991/ www.quirinale.it). **Open** 8.30am-noon Sun. Closed late June-early Sept. **Admission** €5. No credit cards. **Map** p87 D4 ④

The popes still hadn't finished the new St Peter's when (in 1574) they started building a summer palace on the Quirinal hill. In case an elderly pope died on his hols and had to be replaced, the Cappella Paolina was built as a replica of the Vatican's Sistine Chapel minus the Michelangelos. On Sunday mornings, when parts of the presidential palace open to the public, you may be fortunate enough to catch one of the noon concerts held in this chapel.

San Carlino alle Quattro Fontane

Via del Quirinale 23 (06 488 3261/ www.sancarlino-borromini.it). **Open** 10am-1pm, 3-6pm Mon-Fri; 10am-1pm Sat; noon-1pm Sun. July, Aug 10am-1pm Mon-Sat, noon-1pm Sun. **Map** p87 E4 ④

This was Borromini's first solo piece (built in 1638-42), and the one he was proudest of. The oval dome is remarkable: its geometrical coffers decrease in size towards the lantern to give the illusion of added height; hidden windows make the dome appear to float in mid air.

Santa Maria della Vittoria

Via XX Settembre 17 (06 4274 0571). **Open** 8.30am-noon, 3.30-6pm daily. **Map** p87 F3 ④

This early Baroque church, designed by Carlo Maderno, holds one of Bernini's most famous works. *The Ecstasy of St Teresa*, in the Cornaro chapel (fourth on the left), shows the Spanish mystic floating on a cloud in a supposedly spiritual trance after an androgynous angel has pierced her with a burning arrow. The result is more than a little ambiguous.

Sant'Andrea al Quirinale

Via del Quirinale 29 (06 474 0807). **Open** 8.30am-noon, 4-7pm Mon-Sat; 9am-noon, 4-7pm Sun. **Map** p87 E4 ④

Pope Alexander VII (1655-67) was so pleased with Bernini's design for this little church, built out of pale pink marble, that it became in effect the chapel of the Quirinal palace across the road. It is designed to create a sense of grandeur in such a tiny space. The star turn is a plaster St Andrew floating through a broken pediment on his way to heaven.

Scuderie Papali al Quirinale

Via XXIV Maggio 16 (06 696 270/ bookings 06 3996 7500/www.scuderie quirinale.it). **Open** during exhibitions only 10am-8pm Mon-Thur, Sun; 10am-10.30pm Fri, Sat. **Admission** varies. **Map** p87 D5 ④

The former stables of the Quirinal palace, this space – where exhibitions are generally excellent – was reworked a decade ago by architect Gae Aulenti, who took care to preserve the original features. There is a breathtaking view of Rome's skyline from the rear staircase as you leave. Credit cards accepted for phone bookings only.

Trevi Fountain

Piazza di Trevi. **Map** p86 C4 ⑮

Anita Ekberg plunged into this fountain wearing a strapless black evening dress in Fellini's classic *La dolce vita*. Now, wading is strictly forbidden. Moreover, the sparkling water is full of chlorine (there's a chlorine-free spout hidden at the back of the fountain to the right). The *acqua vergine* was the finest water in the city, brought by Emperor Agrippa's 25km (15.5-mile) aqueduct to the foot of the Quirinal hill. The fountain as we know it was designed by Nicolo Salvi in 1762. It's a rococo extravaganza of sea horses, conch-blowing tritons, craggy rocks and flimsy trees. Nobody can quite remember when the custom started of tossing coins in to ensure one's return to the Eternal City. The money goes to charity.

Eating & drinking

See also **Il Gelato di San Crispino** (p82).

Al Presidente

Via in Arcione 95 (06 679 7342/www. alpresidente.it). **Meals served** 1-3.30pm, 8-11pm Tue-Sun. Closed 2wks Jan, 2wks Aug. **€€€€. Italian. Map** p87 D4 ⑰

This restaurant under the walls of the Quirinal palace is one of the few really reliable addresses in this *menu turistico*-dominated area. The creative Italian menu is strong on fish: among the *primi* is a delicious asparagus and squid soup, while one of the highlights of the *secondi* is the fish and vegetable millefeuille. There's a light lunch menu (€€) and outside tables too.

Antica Birreria Peroni

Via San Marcello 19 (06 679 5310/ www.anticabirreriaperoni.it). **Meals served** noon-midnight Mon-Sat. Closed 2wks Aug. **€-€€. Bar/ Italian. Map** p86 C5 ⑱

This long-running *birreria* is the perfect place for a quick lunch or dinner. Service is rough-and-Roman but friendly, and the food is good and relatively cheap. Sausage is the main act, with three types of German-style *Wurstel* on offer.

Da Michele

Via dell'Umiltà 31 (349 252 5347/ www.michelepizza.it). **Open** 8am-6pm Mon-Thur, Sun; 10am-3pm Fri, Sun. Closed Jewish holidays; 10 days Pesach (Passover). **€**. No credit cards. **Takeaway pizza. Map** p86 C5 ⑲

Relocated in 2006 from the Ghetto, Da Michele (ex-Zi' Fenizia) does over 50 types of takeaway pizza, all dairy-free. Open till 10pm in summer.

Arts & leisure

Kamispa

NEW *Via degli Avignonesi 11-12 (06 4201 0039/www.kamispa.com)*. **Open** 10am-10pm Mon-Thur, Sun; 10am-midnight Fri, Sat. **Map** p87 E3 ⑳

Massages, scrubs and a wide selection of beauty treatments are available in this gloriously spice-scented haven of minimalist Oriental decor. There's a small swimming pool and a shop. Booking is recommended.

Heading north

North from Villa Borghese, well-heeled suburbs fill the area that stretches between the **Villa Torlonia** and Villa Ada public parks. By the river, a vibrant sport and arts hub is springing to life: rugby is played in the Stadio Flaminio, and football across the Tiber at the **Stadio Olimpico**; while the new **Auditorium** seethes with music-related activity.

ROME BY AREA

Sights & museums

MACRO

NEW *Via Reggio Emilia 54 (06 6710 70400/www.macro.roma.museum).*
Open 9am-7pm Tue-Sun. **Admission** free. No credit cards. **Map** off p87 F1 **51**

Rome's contemporary art scene was given a boost in the 1990s with the opening of this gallery in a converted brewery. The space grew to cover 10,000sq m, thanks to an extension by architect Odile Decq, inaugurated in spring 2009. Shows spill over into MACRO-Future in the Mattatoio in Testaccio.

MAXXI

NEW *Via Guido Reni 2F (06 321 0181/ www.maxxi.darc.beniculturali.it).* Open scheduled to reopen spring 2010. **Map** off p97 A1 **52**
See box p38.

Villa Torlonia

Via Nomentana 70 (06 0608/www.musei villatorlonia.it). **Open** *Park* dawn-sunset daily. *Museums* 9am-one hr before sunset daily. **Admission** €6.50; €3 reductions; extra charge for exhibitions. No credit cards. **Map** off p87 F1 **53**

With its lush park and scattered attractions, Villa Torlonia is a pleasant place to pass a hot day. Once home of the Torlonia family, and wartime residence of Mussolini, it was bought by the council 30 years ago and has been *in restauro* since. Open to the public are the art nouveau *Casina della civette* with its collection of stained glass; the *Casino nobile* with its frescoes; the *Casino dei principi*, housing exhibitions; the faux-medieval villa, home to the Technotown centre; and the Limonaia restaurant/tea room.

Arts & leisure

Auditorium – Parco della Musica

Via P de Coubertin 15 (information 06 8024 1281/bookings Santa Cecilia 06 808 2058/bookings other concerts 199 109783/www.auditorium.com).
Map off p97 A1 **54**

This huge facility is the world's second-most high-profile performing arts centre (after New York's Lincoln Centre), thanks to an eclectic programme and reasonable prices. Guided tours of the complex cost €9 (€5 reductions; Sat & Sun, no credit cards): times change frequently so call ahead (06 8024 1281).
Event highlights Rome's Film Festival will be held here and at other venues on 15-23 Oct 2009 and 29 Oct-6 Nov 2010.

Foro Italico & Stadio Olimpico

Piazza de Bosis/via del Foro Italico.
Map off p97 A1 **55**

An obelisk 36m (120ft) high, with the words *Mussolini Dux* carved on it, greets visitors to the Foro Italico, a sports complex conceived in the late 1920s. The avenue leading west of the obelisk is paved with mosaics of good Fascists doing sporty Fascist things. The same avenue is now trampled on by the hordes that visit the Stadio Olimpico to watch Roma and Lazio football teams. For information on tickets, see p33.

Auditorium – Parco della Musica

Palazzo delle Esposizioni p105

Esquilino, Celio & San Lorenzo

Esquiline & Monti

If you've come to Rome on a budget package, there's a fairly good chance that you'll end up in a hotel on the Esquiline hill, around Termini railway station. It may not be quite what you expected.

In ancient times, and right up until the 1870s when the developers moved in, this was where the rich and powerful had their gardens and villas. Nowadays, municipal authorities try hard to convince us that a 'renaissance' is under way here, but there's no escaping the fact that Esquilino's *palazzi* are grimy and its after-dark denizens can be dodgy. Despite this, the area has charms and attractions.

Piazza Vittorio Emanuele II – the city's biggest square and known simply as piazza Vittorio – was given a new lease of life in the 1980s by a revamp of the central gardens and the arrival of a multi-ethnic community; the food market in a nearby ex-barracks (via Lamarmora) bursts with exotic produce and smells. Then there are vast basilicas (**Santa Maria Maggiore**), intimate mosaic-encrusted churches (**Santa Prassede**), Roman artefacts (**Palazzo Massimo**) and a magnificent post-war railway station building at Termini.

Via Nazionale is a traffic artery lined by carbon-copy high street shops; half way down, the huge **Palazzo delle Esposizioni** showcase reopened in late 2007 after lengthy restoration; the pretty **Villa Aldobrandini** park, up a flight of steps at the south-western end, has wonderful views over the city.

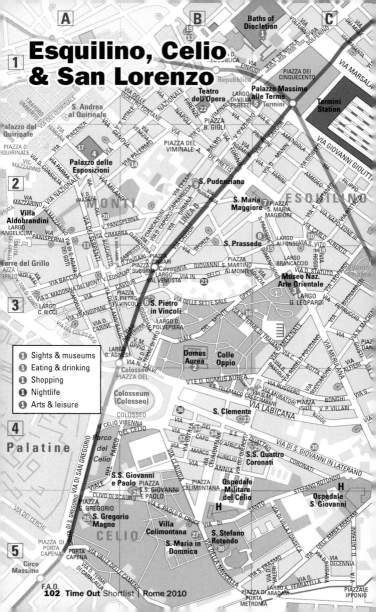

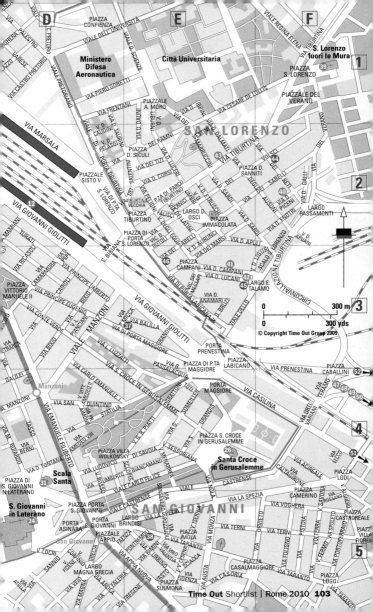

Livia's Villa in Palazzo
Massimo alle Terme

Present-day Monti was the giant Suburra slum where streets ran with effluent and inhabitants died of insomnia.

Nowadays, the alleyways of Monti – north-east of the Forum, between *vie* Nazionale and Cavour – are still noisy and bustling, the difference being that this area is seriously hip.

To the south, on Colle Oppio, Nero fiddled in his **Domus Aurea**, entertaining his guests with his Imperial twanging. Nowadays, this stretch of green is peopled by Roman mums and their offspring during the day, and some very dubious characters after-dark.

Sights & museums

Baths of Diocletian

Viale Enrico de Nicola 78 (06 3996 7700). **Open** 9am-7.45pm Tue-Sun. **Admission** €7; €3.50 reductions; extra charge during exhibitions. No credit cards. **Map** p102 C1 ❶

Diocletian's baths were the largest in Rome when they were built in AD 298-306, covering over a hectare and able to

accommodate 3,000 people. A convent complex, designed by Michelangelo, was built around the largest surviving chunk of the baths in the 1560s. It now contains a collection of stone inscriptions that is sufficiently low-key to allow you to focus on the massive bath buildings themselves and on Michelangelo's 16th-century restoration of the place, including its splendid cloister. (The church of Santa Maria degli Angeli in piazza della Repubblica, and the Aula Ottagona at via Romita 8, were also part of the structure.)

Domus Aurea

Via della Domus Aurea 1 (06 3996 7700). **Open** by appointment only for guided tours 10am-4pm Tue-Fri. **Map** p102 B3 ❷

Note: though crumbling masonry shut the Domus down in 2005, guided tours (€4.50) now allow visitors to view the frescoes and plaster mouldings from restorers' scaffolding. The monument is due to reopen fully in spring 2010.

In the summer of AD 64, fire devastated a large part of central Rome. Afterwards, anything unsinged east of the Forum was knocked down to make way for Emperor Nero's Domus Aurea (Golden House). Its main façade faced south and was entirely clad in gold; inside, every inch not inlaid with gems was frescoed by Nero's pet aesthete Fabullus. The moment Nero died in AD 68, however, work was begun to eradicate every vestige of the hated tyrant. So thorough was the cover-up job that for decades after its frescoes were rediscovered in 1480, no one realised it was the Domus Aurea that they had stumbled across.

Museo Nazionale d'Arte Orientale

Via Merulana 248 (06 4697 4832/ www.museorientale.it). **Open** 9am-2pm Tue, Wed, Fri; 9am-7pm Thur, Sat, Sun. **Admission** €6; €3 reductions. No credit cards. **Map** p102 C3 ❸

This impressive collection of oriental art includes artefacts from the Near

East, such as pottery, gold, votive offerings – some from the third millennium BC – painted fans from Tibet, sacred sculptures, and some Chinese pottery from the 15th century.

Palazzo delle Esposizioni

Via Nazionale 194 (06 696 271/ www.palaexpo.it). **Open** 10am-8pm Tue-Thur, Sun; 10am-10.30pm Fri, Sat. **Admission** from €6; €4.50 reductions. **Map** p102 A2 ❹
This imposing purpose-built 19th-century exhibition space reopened in 2008 after a major restoration. Note that the ticket price can go as high as €12.50, depending on how many shows are on. Event highlights Oct 2009-Feb 2010 Alexander Calder.

Palazzo Massimo alle Terme

Largo di Villa Peretti 1 (06 4802 0275/ bookings 06 3996 7700). **Open** 9am-7.45pm Tue-Sun. **Admission** €7; €3.50 reductions; extra charge during exhibitions. No credit cards. **Map** p102 C1 ❺
In the basement of Palazzo Massimo – home to a large chunk of the Museo Nazionale Romano collection – is an extensive collection of coins, Roman luxuries, descriptions of trade routes and audio-visual displays. On the ground and first floors are busts of emperors – including a magnificent Augustus – and lesser mortals. The first floor begins with the age of Vespasian (AD 69-79): his pugilistic bust is in room 1; room 5 has a gracefully crouching Aphrodite from Hadrian's Villa at Tivoli; in room 7 is a peacefully sleeping hermaphrodite, a second-century AD copy of a Greek original. On the second floor, rare wall paintings from assorted villas have been reassembled, including a stunning garden scene from Livia's Villa near Rome. Room 10 contains Botero-like, larger-than-life (megalographic) paintings, and room 11 has dazzlingly bright marble intarsio works.

San Pietro in Vincoli

San Pietro in Vincoli

Piazza di San Pietro in Vincoli 4A (06 9784 4952). **Open** 8am-12.30pm, 3-6pm daily. **Map** p102 B3 ❻
Built in the fifth century but reworked many times since, this church is dominated by the monument to Pope Julius II, with Michelangelo's imposing Moses (1515). Julius wanted a much grander tomb but died too soon to oversee it; his successors were less ambitious. As a result, the mighty Moses (in a bad translation of the Old Testament, the Hebrew word for 'radiant' was mistaken for 'horned') is wildly out of proportion, and infinitely better than the rest, by Michelangelo's students. Pilgrims come here for the chains. Eudoxia, wife of Emperor Valentinian III (425-55), was given a set of chains said to have been used to shackle St Peter in Jerusalem; with others used on the saint in the Mamertine Prison, they are now conserved in a reliquary on the main altar.

Santa Maria Maggiore

Piazza Santa Maria Maggiore (06 6988 6800). **Open** *Church* 7am-7pm daily. *Museum* (06 6988 6802) 8.30am-6.30pm daily. *Loggia* (guided tours only; booking obligatory) 9am & 1pm Mon-Sat. **Admission** *Church* free. *Museum* €4. *Loggia* €5. No credit cards. **Map** p102 C2 **7**

Local tradition says a church was built on this spot in around AD 366; documents place it almost 100 years later. The church was extended in the 13th and 18th centuries. Inside, above the columns of the nave, restored fifth-century mosaics show scenes from the Old Testament. In the apse, 13th-century mosaics show Christ crowning Mary Queen of Heaven. The Virgin theme continues in fifth-century mosaics on the triumphal arch. The ceiling in the main nave is said to have been made from the first shipment of gold from the Americas. In the 16th and 17th centuries two chapels were added: the first was the Cappella Sistina (last on the right of the nave), designed by Domenico Fontana for Sixtus V (1585-90); directly opposite is the Cappella Paolina, a Greek-cross chapel, designed in 1611 by Flaminio Ponzio for Paul V to house a ninth-century icon of the Madonna on its altar. To the right of the main altar, a plaque marks the burial place of Baroque genius Gian Lorenzo Bernini. In the loggia, high up on the front of the church (tours leave from the baptistry), are glorious 13th-century mosaics that decorated the façade of the old basilica, showing the legend of the foundation of Santa Maria Maggiore.

Santa Prassede

Via Santa Prassede 9A (06 488 2456). **Open** 7.30am-noon, 4-6.30pm daily. **Map** p102 C2 **8**

This church is a ninth-century scale copy of the original St Peter's. Artists from Byzantium made the rich mosaics. In the apse, Christ is being introduced to St Praxedes by St Paul on the right, while St Peter is doing the honours on the left for her sister St Pudenziana. The mosaic on the triumphal arch shows the heavenly Jerusalem, with palm-toting martyrs. Off the right-hand side of the

Santa Maria in Domnica p112

nave is the chapel of San Zeno, a dazzling swirl of blue and gold mosaics, punctuated with saints, animals and depictions of Christ and his mother. The wall and ceiling mosaics are ninth century; Mary in the niche above the altar is 13th century. In a room to the right is a portion of column said to be the one that Jesus was tied to for scourging. Visitors are asked to avoid disturbing masses on Sunday morning.

Santa Pudenziana

Via Urbana 160 (06 481 4622). **Open** 9am-noon, 3-6pm daily. **Map** p102 B2 **9**

The mosaic in the apse of Santa Pudenziana dates from the fourth century and is a remarkable example of the continuity between pagan and Christian art, depicting Christ and the apostles as wealthy Roman citizens wearing togas, against an ancient Roman cityscape.

Eating & drinking

Agata e Romeo

Via Carlo Alberto 45 (06 446 6115/ www.agataeromeo.it). **Meals served**

12.30-2.30pm, 7.30-10.30pm Mon-Fri. Closed 3wks Aug 2wks Jan. €€€€. **Map** p102 C2 ⑩

Agata Parisella was the first chef to demonstrate that Roman cuisine could be refined without sacrificing its wholesome essence. The ravioli stuffed with oxtail, for example, is a tribute to the traditional use of less prestigious cuts of meat. Agata's husband, Romeo Caraccio, presides over the dining room and extensive wine list. The decor is elegant but welcoming; the bill is often steep.

Al Vino al Vino

Via dei Serpenti 19 (06 485 803). **Open** 10.30am-2.30pm, 5.30pm-12.30am Mon-Thur; 10.30am-2.30pm, 5.30pm-1.30am Fri, Sat. Closed 2wks Aug. **Map** p102 A3 ⑪

This friendly hostelry offers some 500 wines, with more than 25 available by the glass. But its speciality is *distillati*: grappas, whiskys and other strong spirits. There's Sicilian-inspired food to soak it all up.

Convoglia

NEW *Via Giolitti 36 (06 9970 1300/ www.convoglia.com).* **Open** *Café* 7.30am-11.30pm daily. *Wine bar* noon-11.30pm daily. *Pizzeria/osteria* 11.30am-3pm, 7-10.45pm daily. €€-€€€. **Map** p103 D2 ⑫

A fantastic setting, with the immense extractor of the former railway workers' canteen dominating this hyper-design multi-purpose space. And it's very handy, right inside the long southern flank of Termini railway station. But Convoglia still has to iron out some teething problems with staff and timing. As this guide went to press, the upstairs restaurant was due to open any day.

Dagnino

Galleria Esedra, via VE Orlando 75 (06 481 8660/www.pasticceriadagnino. com). **Open** 7am-11pm daily. **Map** p102 B1 ⑬

Genuine 1950s decor sets the scene for this café-*pasticceria* that is a corner

of Sicily in Rome. If it's Sicilian and edible, it's here: ice-cream in buns, crisp *cannoli siciliani* filled with ricotta cheese, and shiny green-iced *cassata*.

Doozo

Via Palermo 51-53 (06 481 5655/www. doozo.it). **Meals served** 12.30-3pm, 8-11.30pm Tue-Sat; 8-11.30pm Sun. Closed 2wks Aug. €€. **Map** p102 B2 ⑭

This Japanese restaurant on a quiet street parallel to via Nazionale is spacious and cultured, with tables spilling into a gallery, bookshop and a lovely little Zen garden. There's good sushi, sashimi, tempura and karaage chicken served in bento boxes. The tea room is open 4-6.30pm Mon-Sat.

Hang Zhou

Via San Martino ai Monti 33 (06 487 2732). **Meals served** noon-3pm, 7-11.30pm daily. Closed Aug. €€. **Map** p102 C3 ⑮

Hang Zhou rises above most of Rome's dull Chinese eateries, not so much for the food – which is however quite acceptable – but because

Indian Fast Food p108

Ex-Piazza Vittorio market

it's colourful, friendly and incredibly good value. No bookings are taken, so be prepared to queue.

Indian Fast Food

Via Mamiani 11 (06 446 0792).
Open 11am-4pm, 5-10.30pm Mon-Sat; noon-4pm, 5-10.30pm Sun. **€**. No credit cards. **Map** p103 D3 ⑯
This Indian takeaway is just off piazza Vittorio. You can eat in too, accompanied by Indian music videos.

Open Colonna

NEW *Scalinata di via Milano 9A (06 4782 2641).* **Open** noon-midnight Tue-Sun. **€-€€€**. **Map** p102 A2 ⑰
Michelin-starred chef Antonello Colonna closed his restaurant in the Roman countryside in 2009 to dedicate himself to this bar-restaurant on the roof of the Palazzo delle Esposizioni (p105). At lunchtime, a buffet (€15) has pasta dishes, salads and a range of deserts; the limited-choice à la carte menu costs the same, while a salad or toasted sandwich munched in the comfy bar chairs or outside on the terrace costs even less. In the evening, Open goes upmarket: many of the ingredients for Colonna's mod-Med creations are sourced from his own organic farm.

Trattoria Monti

Via di San Vito 13A (06 446 6573).
Meals served 12.45-2.45pm, 7.45-10.45pm Tue-Sat; 12.45-2.30pm Sun. Closed 1wk Easter, 3wks Aug, 1wk Christmas. **€€€**. **Map** p102 C3 ⑱
The cuisine, like the family that runs this simply chic eaterie, is from the Marches region – so meat, fish and game all feature on an interesting menu. Vegetarians are well served by a range of *tortini* (pastry-less pies). Make sure you book in the evening. The place is at the lower end of this price bracket.

Shopping

The Monday-Saturday morning food market once known simply as 'piazza Vittorio' has moved into more salubrious premises in via Lamarmora: stalls stock the usual Italian fresh produce, cheese and meats, supplemented by halal meat and spices, as well as some exotic fabrics and household goods.

Feltrinelli International

Via VE Orlando 84 (06 482 7878).
Open 9am-8pm Mon-Sat; 10.30am-1.30pm, 4-8pm Sun. **Map** p102 B1 ⑲

An excellent range of fiction, non-fiction, magazines and guidebooks in English and other languages.

Le Gallinelle

Via del Boschetto 76 (06 488 1017/ *www.legallinelle.it).* **Open** 4-7.30pm Mon; 10am-2pm, 4-7.30pm Tue-Sat. Closed 2wks Aug. **Map** p102 A2 ⑳
Vintage and ethnic garments are reworked by Wilma Silvestri and her daughter Giorgia in their funky shop. There are also classic linen suits for men and women.

Nightlife

Hangar

Via in Selci 69 (06 488 1397/www. *hangaronline.it).* **Open** 10.30pm-2.30am Mon, Wed-Sun. Closed 3wks Aug. No credit cards. **Map** p102 B3 ㉑
American John Moss has been at the helm of Rome's oldest gay bar since it opened in 1984. Hangar maintains its friendly but sexy atmosphere whether half full (occasionally midweek) or packed (at weekends and for porn video Monday and striptease Thursday). The venue also boasts a small dark area.

Arts & leisure

Teatro dell'Opera di Roma-Teatro Costanzi

Piazza B Gigli 1 (06 4816 0255/ *www.operaroma.it).* **Map** p102 B1 ㉒
The lavish late 19th-century *teatro all' italiana* interior is quite a surprise after the Mussolini-era angular grey façade and its esplanade with tacky potted palms. The acoustics vary considerably: the higher (cheaper) seats aren't great, so splash out on a box.

Celio & San Giovanni

After Emperor Constantine legalised Christianity in the fourth century, he donated land on which the basilica of **San Giovanni in Laterano** was built. This was a groundbreaking move in the sense that it brought the new religion out into the open; but was fence-sitting in the sense that, at the time, this neighbourhood was about as far as you could get from the city's centre of power.

If the San Giovanni area fell prey to property developers in the late 19th century, the Celio – a haven for an elite of a bucolic bent in ancient times – remains lush and unkempt. It gives a glimpse of what ancient, early Christian and medieval Rome were like. From the remains of ancient aqueducts near the verdant and lovely **Villa Celimontana** park, to frescoes of martyrs in the church of **Santo Stefano Rotondo**, this area has a bit of everything.

Around Villa Celimontana is a slew of ancient churches, including **Santi Giovanni e Paolo**, with its excavated Roman houses beneath.

The tight grid of streets south-east of the Colosseum is home to the fascinating church of **San Clemente**, and **Santi Quattro Coronati**, which is blessed with several extraordinary frescoes.

Also here is Rewind Rome (via Capo d'Africa 5, 06 7707 6627, www.3drewind.com) an extraordinary 3D representation of fourth-century Rome in which tigers will leap at you when you don your 3D glasses and dodge gladiators fighting in the Colosseum (see box p88).

Further east, amid traffic, smog and drab post-Unification apartment buildings are some of Christianity's most important churches – including Vatican-owned San Giovanni itself – and a host of fascinating minor ancient remains.

To the south of the basilica are the sunken brick remains of the Porta Asinaria, an ancient gate in the third-century AD Aurelian Wall. A park follows the ancient wall north to **Santa Croce in Gerusalemme** which is surrounded by a panoply of easily-visible Roman ruins: through the opening in the Aurelian Walls to the right of the church is the Amphitheatrum Castrum (now home to the monks' vegetable garden; see p112), and part of the Circus Varianus; the Baths of Helena, of which you can see only the cistern; and the monumental travertine archway built by Emperor Claudius in the first century AD to mark the triumphal entrance of the aqueducts into the city.

Sights & museums

San Clemente

Via San Giovanni in Laterano (06 774 0021). **Open** 9am-12.30pm, 3-6pm Mon-Sat; noon-6pm Sun. **Admission** *Church* free. *Excavations* €5; €3 reductions. No credit cards. **Map** p102 B4 ㉓

This 12th-century basilica is a 3D time line. In the main church, the *schola cantorum* (choir), with its exquisite carving and mosaic decorations, survives from the fourth-century structure. The apse mosaic is 12th century: from the drops of Christ's blood springs the vine representing the Church, which swirls around peasants in their daily tasks, Doctors of the Church and a host of animals. In the chapel of St Catherine of Alexandria, frescoes by Masolino (c1430) show the saint praying as her torturers prepare the wheel on which she was stretched to death (later giving her name to a firework). From the sacristy, steps lead down to the fourth-century basilica. From there, a stairway descends to an ancient Roman alley. On one side is a second-century Roman *insula* (apartment building) containing a site where the Persian god Mithras was worshipped. On the other side are rooms of a Roman house used for meetings by early Christians.

San Giovanni in Laterano

Piazza San Giovanni in Laterano 4 (06 6988 6433). **Open** *Church* 7am-6.30pm daily. *Baptistry* 7.30am-12pm, 4-7pm daily. *Cloister* 9am-6pm daily. *Lateran Museum (06 6988 6376)* 9am-noon Mon-Sat. **Admission** *Church* free. *Cloister* €2. *Museum* €4. No credit cards. **Map** p103 D5 ㉔

San Giovanni and the Lateran palace were the papal headquarters until they were moved across the river to the Vatican in the 15th century. Constantine gave the plot of land to Pope Melchiades to build the church in 313. Little remains of the original basilica. The interior was revamped by Borromini in 1646. The façade, with its huge statues of Christ, the two Johns (Baptist and Evangelist) and Doctors of the Church, was added in 1735. A few treasures from earlier times survive: a 13th-century mosaic in the apse, a fragment of a fresco attributed to Giotto (behind the first column on the right) showing Pope Boniface VIII announcing the first Holy Year in 1300, and the Gothic *baldacchino* over the main altar. Off the left aisle is the 13th-century cloister; a small museum contains vestments and some original manuscripts of music by Palestrina. The north façade was designed in 1586 by Domenico Fontana, who also placed Rome's tallest Egyptian obelisk outside. Also on this side is the octagonal baptistry that Constantine had built. The four chapels surrounding the font have mosaics from the fifth and seventh centuries.

San Gregorio Magno

Piazza di San Gregorio 1 (06 700 8227). **Open** 9am-noon, 3-6.30pm daily. **Map** p102 A5 ㉕

This Baroque church stands on the site of the home of one of the most remarkable popes, Gregory I (the Great; 590-604), who spent his 14-year pontificate vigorously reorganising the Church. In a chapel on the right is

Sampietrini

Rome's controversial cobblestones.

Motorcyclists and tottering fashionistas don't, as a rule, agree about much. But both groups break out in a rash at the mere mention of Rome's bike-busting, stiletto-snapping cobblestones called *sampietrini*. They're shoe-wrecking instruments of torture, say tottering Roman *signore*. They're life-threateningly slippery when wet, say bikers (aka *centauri*: half man, half cycle).

Enthusiasts, on the other hand, say that these blocks of flint (quarried from a millennia-old lava flow from the Alban Hills and along the Appian way) or porphyry (imported from China when the local stone became economically unviable) are hardwearing, ecological and 100 per cent natural. Moreover, water from Rome's surprisingly frequent downpours disappears down the cracks between the stones like magic. They're beautiful and historic, traditionalists argue,

pointing out that the name comes from paving laid in the revamped St Peter's square in 1585.

City fathers look at the bottom line: these 12x12cm blocks, laid by hand with a long pyramid-shaped 'root' bedded into sand, need constant maintenance. Asphalt, on the other hand is cheap and long-lasting, and so it was this that was put down in 2007 when the cobbles were dug up along via Nazionale, the choked artery leading from Termini railway station to piazza Venezia. Press campaigns and a new mayor in city hall brought a change of heart, however, and *sampietrini* are back – cost be damned! – again along via Nazionale.

And it looks, for the time being, like *sampietrini* will remain fixtures in historically 'sensitive' streets and *piazze* (note the patterns of smaller 6x6cm stones in piazza Navona) and in the Tridente, where pedestrian areas are to be extended. But busy thoroughfares, like the riverside *lungotevere*, are already lost causes.

Asphalt smells dreadful, say *sampietrini* fans, suspiciously sniffing the noxious fumes rising from steaming summer streets. Lovely flat surfaces, say the bikers, roaring down the embankments. In moments of weakness, fashionistas admit to mixed feelings: of course it's bliss to be able to totter out of one's palazzo in six-inch heels without risking life and limb (or one's dignity) on the cobbles. But *sampietrini*: so stylish my dear, and so inimitably Roman.

Santa Croce in Gerusalemme

a marble chair dating from the first century BC, said to have been used by Gregory as his papal throne. Also here is the tomb of Tudor diplomat Sir Edward Carne, who visited Rome several times to persuade the pope to annul the marriage of Henry VIII and Catherine of Aragon, so that the king could marry Anne Boleyn. Outside stand three small chapels (open 10am-noon Tue, Thur, Sat, Sun; closed 2wks Dec-Jan, 1wk Easter, Aug), behind which are the remains of shops that lined this ancient road, the *clivus scauri*.

Santa Croce in Gerusalemme

Piazza Santa Croce in Gerusalemme 12 (06 701 4769/www.basilicasanta croce.com). **Open** *Church* 7am-1pm, 2-7.30pm daily. *Chapel of the Relics* 8am-12.30pm, 2.30-6.30pm daily.
Map p103 E4 ㉖

Founded in 320 by St Helena, mother of Emperor Constantine (who legalised Christianity in 313), this church was rebuilt in the 12th century, and again in 1743-44. Helena had her church constructed to house relics she brought

back from the Holy Land: three chunks of Christ's cross, a nail, two thorns from his crown and the finger of St Thomas – allegedly, the very one that the doubting saint stuck into Christ's wound. All of these are displayed in a chapel at the end of a Fascist-era hall at the left side of the nave. The vegetable garden, kept by the monks of the adjoining monastery, can be visited by appointment. The garden gates were designed by Jannis Kounellis and mounted in 2007.

Santa Maria in Domnica

Via della Navicella 10 (06 7720 2685). **Open** 9am-noon, 4.30-7pm daily.
Map p102 B5 ㉗

The carved wood ceiling and porticoed façade date from the 16th century but Santa Maria in Domnica – known as the *navicella* (little ship), after the Roman statue that stands outside – is a ninth-century structure containing one of Rome's most charming apse mosaics. What sets this lovely design in rich colours apart is that Mary and Jesus look cheerful: the cherry-red daubs of blush on their cheeks give them a healthy glow.

Santi Giovanni e Paolo

*Piazza Santi Giovanni e Paolo 13
(church 06 700 5745/excavations 06
7045 4544/www.caseromane.it)*. **Open**
Church 8.30am-noon, 3.30-6pm daily.
Excavations (reservation obligatory)
10am-1pm, 3-6pm Mon, Thur-Sun.
Admission *Church* free. *Excavations*
€6; €4 reductions. No credit cards.
Map p102 B5 ㉓

Traces of the original fourth-century
church can still be seen in the
12th-century façade on piazza Santi
Giovanni e Paolo, which is overlooked
by a 12th-century bell tower. An 18th-
century revamp left the church's interi-
or looking like a banqueting hall.
Around the corner in Clivo di Scauro,
steps lead down to labyrinthine excavations: from four different buildings –
including the house of fourth-century
martyrs John and Paul – and dating
from the first century AD on, the 20-odd
excavated rooms include some evi-
dently used for secret Christian worship. Call ahead for tours in English.

Santi Quattro Coronati

*Via dei Santi Quattro 20 (06 7047
5427)*. **Open** 9.45am-11.45, 4-5.45pm
daily. **Map** p102 C4 ㉙

A fourth-century church here was
rebuilt as a fortified monastery in the
11th century; the outsized apse is from
the original church. The church has an
upper-level *matronium*, where women
sat during religious functions. There
is a beautiful cloister (from the early
13th century). In the oratory next to
the church (ring the bell and ask for
the key) are frescoes, also painted in
the 13th century as a defence of the
popes' temporal power. They show a
pox-ridden Constantine being healed
by Pope Sylvester, crowning him
with a tiara and giving him a cap to
symbolise the pope's spiritual and
earthly authority.

Santo Stefano Rotondo

*Via di Santo Stefano Rotondo 7
(06 421 191)*. **Open** 9.30am-12.30pm,

2-5pm Tue-Sat; 9.30am-12.30pm
Sun. **Map** p102 B5 ㉚

One of the very few round churches
in Rome, Santo Stefano dates from
the fifth century. The church is
exceptionally beautiful, with its
Byzantine-inspired simplicity. The
34 horrifically graphic 16th-century
frescoes of martyrs being boiled,
stretched and slashed disturb the
atmosphere somewhat.

Scala Santa & Sancta Sanctorum

*Piazza di San Giovanni in Laterano
(06 772 6641)*. **Open** *Scala Santa*
6.30-noon, 3.30-6pm daily. *Sancta
Sanctorum* (booking obligatory) 10.30-
11.30am, 3-4.30pm Mon, Tue, Thur-Sat;
3.30-4.30pm Wed. **Admission** *Scala
Santa* free. *Sancta Sanctorum & St
Silvester chapel* €5. No credit cards.
Map p103 D4 ㉛

Tradition says that these are the stairs
that Jesus climbed in Pontius Pilate's
house before being sent to his crucifixion. They were brought to Rome in
the fourth century by St Helena,
mother of the Emperor Constantine. A
crawl up the Scala Santa has been a
fixture on every serious pilgrim's list
ever since. At the top of the Holy
Stairs (but also accessible by non-holy
stairs to the left) is the pope's private
chapel, the Sancta Sanctorum. In a
glass case on the left wall is a fragment of the table on which the Last
Supper was supposedly served. The
exquisite 13th-century frescoes in the
lunettes and on the ceiling are attributed to Cimabue. Freshly restored, the
San Silvestro chapel area of the Sancta
Sanctorum is now also on view.

Eating & drinking

Il Bocconcino

*Via Ostilia 23 (06 7707 9175/www.
ilbocconcino.com)*. **Meals served**
12.30-3.30pm, 7.30-11.30pm Mon,
Tue, Thur-Sun. Closed 2wks Aug.
€€. **Map** p102 B4 ㉜

ROME BY AREA

This trattoria near the Colosseum looks like it's been around for generations but it's a fairly recent addition, with a friendly welcome, good renditions of Roman favourites and a small, well-priced wine list. Service can be very slow.

Café Café

Via dei Santi Quattro 44 (06 700 8743/ www.cafecafebistrot.it). **Open** 11am-1am daily. Closed 2wks Aug. **€**. **Map** p102 B4 ➌➌

A café, yes, but also a perfect spot for lunch – with soups, salads and pasta dishes – after a stomp around the Colosseum. There's a brunch buffet from 11.30am to 4pm on Sundays.

Luzzi

Via San Giovanni in Laterano 88 (06 709 6332). **Meals served** noon-3pm, 7pm-midnight Mon, Tue, Thur-Sun. Closed 2wks Aug. **€€**. **Map** p102 B4 ➌➍

On busy nights (and most are) this neighbourhood trattoria is the loudest and most crowded 40 square metres in Rome. Perfectly decent pizzas, pasta dishes and *secondi* are served, all strictly in the Roman tradition. Outside tables operate all year round.

Shopping

Immediately outside the Roman walls by the basilica of San Giovanni, via Sannio is home each weekday morning and all-day Saturday to stalls piled high with cheapo new and second-hand clothes.

Soul Food

Via San Giovanni in Laterano 192-194 (06 7045 2025). **Open** 10.30am-1.30pm, 3.30-8pm Tue-Sat. Closed 2wks Aug. **Map** p102 C4 ➌➎

This vintage record shop is a vinyl-collector's heaven, with indie-rock, punk, beat music, exotica, lounge, rockabilly and more.

Nightlife

Coming Out

Via San Giovanni in Laterano 8 (06 700 9871/www.comingout.it). **Open** 11am-2am daily. **Map** p102 B4 ➌➏

This hugely popular pub offers beers, cocktails and a reasonably wide range of snacks to a predominantly youthful crowd of gay men and women, who spill out of the venue and onto the street most evenings. There's live music on Thursdays.

Micca Club

Via Pietro Micca 7A (06 8744 0079/ www.miccaclub.com). **Open** 10pm-4am Thur-Sat; 6pm-2am Sun. Closed May-mid Sept. **Admission** free Thur, Sun; €10 pre-booked on the website, €15 on the door Fri, Sat. **Map** p103 E3 ➌➐

A huge spiral staircase leads down to this cavernous underground venue with one of Rome's most eclectic nightlife programmes, ranging from live acts and international DJ sets to serious jazz. There's a music-fuelled Sunday vintage market from 6pm, and *aperitivi* with a generous buffet from 7pm each evening.

Skyline

Via Pontremoli 36 (06 700 9431/ www.skylineclub.it). **Open** 10.30pm-4am daily. **Map** p103 E5 ➌➑

At this ever-popular gay club the crowd is relaxed and mixed, with constant movement between the bar areas, the video parlour and the cruisy cubicle and dark areas. It hosts naked parties on Mondays.

San Lorenzo

San Lorenzo has a history of rebellion. It was planned in the 1880s as a working-class ghetto, with few public services or amenities. Unsurprisingly, it soon developed into Rome's most politically radical district.

Santa Maria in Domnica p112

This basilica was donated by Constantine to house the remains of St Lawrence after the saint met his fiery end on a griddle. Rebuilt in the sixth century, it was later united with a neighbouring church. Bombs plunged through the roof in 1943, making San Lorenzo the only Roman church to suffer war damage, but it was painstakingly reconstructed by 1949. On the right side of the 13th-century portico are frescoes from the same period, showing scenes from the life of St Lawrence. Inside the triumphal arch are sixth-century mosaics. Behind the church is Rome's major cemetery.

Eating & drinking

Bar à Book
Via dei Piceni 23 (06 4544 5438/ www.barabook.it). **Open** 4pm-midnight Tue-Thur; 4pm-2am Fri, Sat; 11am-8pm Sun. Closed Aug. **Map** p103 F2 ⑩

With its long wooden central table and shelves piled high with books, this café in artsy San Lorenzo looks like the design-conscious study of an eccentric 1960s-loving academic. In fact, it's the latest creation of the people who own Tram Tram, a restaurant just round the corner (via dei Reti 44, closed Mon, €€) that serves excellent creative Roman and Puglian specialities. In the bar, *aperitivi* come with a DJ on Saturdays from 7.30pm.

Cribbio!
Via dei Campani 65 (06 490 217/ www.ristorantecribbio.com). **Meals served** 8.30pm-midnight Tue-Sun. Closed 2wks Aug. €€. **Map** p103 E3 ⑪

A recent addition to San Lorenzo's thriving eating scene, Cribbio! serves interesting versions of some local favourites, including a great *tonnarelli cacio e pepe* (pasta with cheese and pepper) and a wonderful tuna tartare. Service can be a little frosty.

These days it retains some of its threadbare, jerry-built, working-class character. But it's more radical-chic than just plain radical: a constant influx of artists and students mingles with the few surviving salt-of-the-earth locals.

Along the north-east side is the vast Verano cemetery, with the basilica of **San Lorenzo fuori le Mura** by its entrance.

To the north-west, the **Città universitaria** (the main campus of Europe's biggest university, La Sapienza), with buildings designed in the 1930s by Marcello Piacentini and Arnaldo Foschini, shows the Fascist take on the architecture of higher education.

Sights & museums

San Lorenzo fuori le Mura
Piazzale del Verano 3 (06 491 511). **Open** 8am-noon, 4-6.30pm daily. **Map** p103 F1 ㊴

ROME BY AREA

Marcello

Via dei Campani 12 (06 446 3311).
Meals served 7.30-11.30pm Mon-Fri.
Closed 3wks Aug. €. No credit cards.
Map p103 E3 ㊷
Inside this anonymous-looking trat
hordes of hungry students wolf food
down at old wooden tables. Alongside
offal specialities like tripe and *pajata*
(calf intestines) are light and more creative dishes such as *straccetti ai carciofi* (strips of veal with artichokes).

Said

*Via Tiburtina 135 (06 446
9204/www.said.it).* **Open** 12.30pm-
midnight Mon-Sat. Closed 2wks Aug.
Map p103 E2 ㊸
Said has been producing exquisite
chocolate in this factory in San Lorenzo
since 1923; you can purchase it in the
shop at the same address from 10am-
8am. But its industrial-chic tea room-
restaurant, with a fireplace, comfy
armchairs and glassed-over courtyard,
is a recent addition. Chocolate pops up
in unexpected places on the lunch menu
(€€); dinner is served from 7.30pm.

Nightlife

Dimmidisì

*Via dei Volsci 126B (06 446 1855/
www.dimmidisiroma.it).* **Open** 7pm-
2am Tue-Sun. Closed July-Sept.
Map p103 F2 ㊹
From its *aperitivo* hour, often accompanied by live bands, until into the early
hours, this pared-back space hosts live
acts and top DJs from Italy and abroad.

Locanda Atlantide

*Via dei Lucani 22B (06 4470 4540/
www.locandatlantide.it).* **Open** 9pm-
2am Tue-Sun. Closed mid June-mid
Sept. **Admission** free-€10. No credit
cards. **Map** p103 E3 ㊺
An unpretentious venue hosting an
array of events that range from
concerts and DJ acts to theatrical
performances. It pulls an alternative
crowd. Extra charge for concerts.

Skyline p114

Mads

NEW *Via dei Sabelli 2 (328 641 8983/
www.mads-project.it).* **Open** 10pm-
2am Tue-Sat. Closed July & Aug.
Admission free-€5. No credit cards.
Map p103 E3 ㊻
The cavernous space of this laid-back
venue in San Lorenzo hosts regular concerts, plus themed parties, women-only
nights and excellent DJ sets. Some special events are held on Sundays. Check
the website for events in outdoor venues
during the summer closure.

Heading south

Beyond San Lorenzo and San
Giovanni lie the endless, ugly
suburbs that sprung up, largely
unplanned, to house the influx
of workers to the capital in the
economic boom of the 1960s and
'70s. The average visitor to Rome
is unlikely to venture this far. But
those who do will find an attraction
or two to make the trek worthwhile.
   Squeezed between via Casilina
and via Prenestina, the Pigneto
district has recently achieved that

critical mass of bars, restaurants and trendsters that turns a below-the-radar district hip. Heavily bombed in World War II and rebuilt piecemeal, the anarchic, bohemian feel of the place attracted arty types like Pier Paolo Pasolini (much of his first film, *Accattone*, was shot here). Today, partly-pedestrianised via del Pigneto is home to a morning market (Mon-Sat) and some cool restaurants and bars.

Eating & drinking

Bar Necci
Via Fanfulla da Lodi 68 (06 9760 1552/ www.necci1924.com). **Open** 8am-1am daily. Closed 2wks Aug. €€. **Map** p103 F4 ⓸⓻
The victim of a devastating arson attack in March 2009, this former old blokes' bar (used by Pasolini as his HQ when filming Accattone nearby), will resume its more recent role as a shabby-chic brunch/lunch/dinner place with marvellous 1960s-style decor as swiftly as possible, says co-owner and chef Ben Hirst, who is responsible for the quality mod-Med cuisine. Tables outside.

Primo
Via del Pigneto 46 (06 701 3827/ www.primoalpigneto.it). **Meals served** 7pm-midnight Tue-Sat; 12.45-3pm, 7pm-midnight Sun. Closed 1wk Aug. €€. **Map** p103 F4 ⓸⓼
Slow Food-inspired Primo is warehouse-cool in design and eclectic in its culinary offerings, which are usually (though not consistently) good. The vibe is laid-back, with staff clad in matching t-shirts and an endless stream of keen customers coming for Roman classics or dishes with a creative twist. Doors stay open till 1am or later for drinks and tapas.

Il Tiaso
Via Perugia 20 (333 284 5283/ www.iltiaso.com). **Open** 6pm-2am Mon-Sat. Closed 2wks Aug. **Map** p103 F4 ⓸⓽

This book-lined wine bar in vibrant Pigneto is as unpretentious and laid-back as they come.

Tiger Tandoori
NEW *Via del Pigneto 193 (06 9761 0172/www.tigertandoori.com).* **Open** noon-2am Mon, Wed-Sun. €€. **Map** p103 F4 ⓹⓪
Just the far side of the railway cutting that slices though Pigneto, this teeny weeny takeaway place – an extravaganza of Bollywood movie posters and Peter Sellars tributes – serves up excellent korma, balti and (of course) tandoori dishes, plus dhosas – a rarity in Rome. There are a couple of tables for perching.

Nightlife

Circolo degli Artisti
Via Casilina Vecchia 42 (06 7030 5684/ www.circoloartisti.it). **Open** 9.30pm-1am Tue-Thur for concerts only; 9pm-4.30am Fri, Sat; 7pm-midnight Sun. Closed Aug. **Admission** from €6, depending on event. No credit cards. **Map** off p103 F4 ⓹⓵
This is Rome's most popular venue for small- and medium-scale bands from international alternative music circuits. There's a popular gay night on Fridays. On Saturdays (admission €5 after midnight), 'Screamadelica' offers top-quality concerts by some of Europe's best alternative artists and emerging Italian bands.

Qube
Via di Portonaccio 212 (06 438 5445/www.qubedisco.com/www. muccassina.com). **Open** 11.30pm-5am Thur-Sat. Closed May-Oct. **Admission** free-€20. **Map** off p103 F1 ⓹⓶
Thursday means rock and Saturday brings sets by well-known DJs, but it's on Friday that this cavernous space explodes, when it's taken over by the Muccassina crew for their wildly extravagant gay event.

The Aventine & Testaccio

ROME BY AREA

Aventine & Caracalla

There's an air of moneyed calm on the leafy Aventine hill, which was first colonised by King Ancius Marcius in the seventh century BC. At first, foreigners and other undesirables drifted up here from the river port below. But they were driven out when the hill was set aside for plebeians in 456 BC. And here the *plebs* remained, building their temples and villas.

It's a lovely place for a stroll. The delightful Parco Savello – still surrounded by the crenellated walls of a 12th-century fortress of the Savello family – has dozens of orange trees and a spectacular view over the city, especially at sunset. In nearby piazza Cavalieri di Malta, peek through the keyhole of the priory of the Knights of Malta to

enjoy the surprise designed by Gian Battista Piranesi: a telescopic view of the dome of St Peter's.

Across busy viale Aventino is the similarly well-heeled San Saba district and, beyond the white cuboids of the UN's Food and Agricultural Organisation, the giant **Baths of Caracalla**.

Sights & museums

Baths of Caracalla

Viale delle Terme di Caracalla 52 (06 3996 7700). **Open** 9am-2pm Mon; 9am-1hr before sunset Tue-Sun. **Admission** €6 (includes Tomb of Cecilia Metella & Villa dei Quintili); €3 reductions. No credit cards. **Map** p120 D2 ❶
The high-vaulted ruins of the Terme di Caracalla are peaceful today, but were anything but tranquil in their heyday, when up to 1,600 Romans could sweat

it out in the baths and gyms. You can get some idea of their original splendour from the fragments of mosaic and statuary that litter the site.

The baths were built between AD 213 and 216. The two cavernous rooms down the sides were the gymnasia, where Romans engaged in such strenuous sports as toss-the-beanbag. There was also a large open-air *natatio* (pool), saunas and baths, as well as a library, a garden, shops and stalls. Underneath it all was a network of tunnels where slaves trod the giant wheels that pumped clean water up to bathers. Caracalla's baths were in use until 537, when the Visigoths sacked Rome and severed the city's aqueducts.

Santa Sabina

Piazza Pietro d'Illiria 1 (06 57 941).
Open 7am-11.30pm, 3.30-6.30pm daily.
Admission free. **Map** p120 B1 ❷
Santa Sabina was built in the fifth century over an early Christian place of worship; the bit of mosaic floor visible through a grate at the entrance is all that remains of the earlier building. It underwent a merciless restoration in the 1930s, being restored back to its fifth to ninth-century appearance, and is now arguably the closest thing to an unadulterated ancient basilica in Rome. The fifth-century cypress doors are carved with biblical scenes. The nave's Corinthian columns support an arcade decorated with ninth-century marble inlay work; the choir dates from the same period. Selenite has been placed in the windows as it would have been in the ninth century. A window in the entrance porch looks on to the place where St Dominic is said to have planted an orange tree brought from Spain in 1220. The lovely cloister dates from the 13th century.

Eating & drinking

Il Gelato

NEW *Viale Aventino 59 (no phone).*
Open 10.30am-10pm Tue-Sun.
Ice-cream. **Map** p120 C2 ❸

Finally, there's no need to schlep out to the EUR district to experience Claudio Torcè's extraordinary ice-cream. See box p124.

Testaccio & Ostiense

Testaccio is bustling, noisy, workaday and still populated by brusquely salt-of-the-earth long-term residents. But this close to the *centro storico*, the district couldn't remain exclusively working class for long: an influx of young(ish) professionals has upped property prices and turned Testaccio into a very desirable area.

Locals of all stripes mix contendedly in the gardens of piazza Santa Maria Liberatrice on warm evenings, linked by an almost universal devotion to the AS Roma football team and an indulgent fondness for the elderly

Protestant Cemetery p123

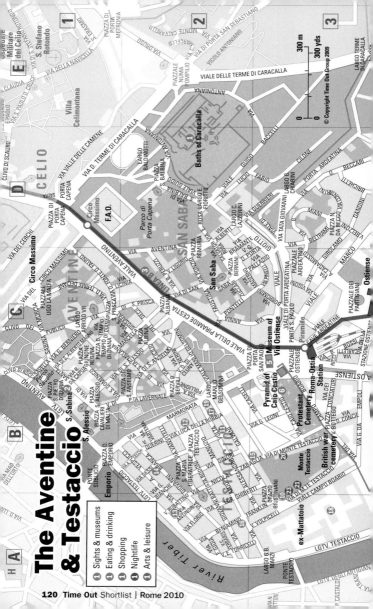

The Aventine & Testaccio

Legend:
- Sights & museums
- Eating & drinking
- Shopping
- Nightlife
- Arts & leisure

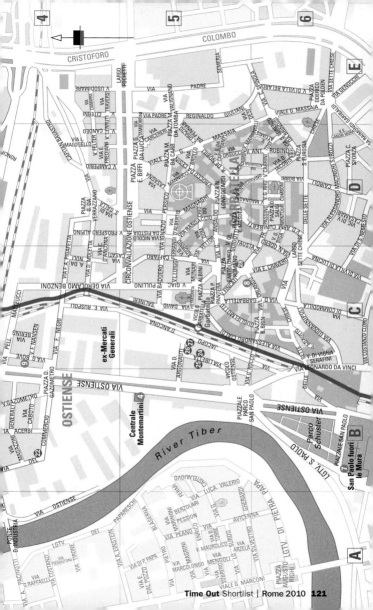

Centrale Montemartini

ladies who still traipse to the market in their slippers of a morning.

There are no major monuments here, just traces of Testaccio's hard-working past: an ancient river port, a rubbish tip composed of discarded potsherds (Monte Testaccio) and an abandoned abattoir slowly being made over into an arts centre-cum-alternative marketplace. Testaccio is also home to Rome's most happening nightlife.

Further south, via Ostiense slices through once run-down suburbs earmarked for some interesting development: Dutch architectural superstar Rem Koolhaas is turning the former wholesale fruit and vegetable market into a complex of youth-oriented exhibition spaces, sports centres and shopping centres – what the authorities describe as 'Rome's Covent Garden'.

However, the signs of change and renewal have been visible for a while – ever since the **Centrale Montemartini** power station was converted into one of the capital's most striking museums, the **Teatro Palladium** reopened (revamped and with a fascinating programme), and Testaccio's vibrant after-hours activity began seeping south.

Sights & museums

Centrale Montemartini

Via Ostiense 106 (06 574 8042/ www.centralemontemartini.org).
Open 9am-7pm Tue-Sun. **Admission** €4.50; €2.50 reductions; extra charge during exhibitions. No credit cards.
Map p121 B5 ④
Centrale Montemartini contains the leftover ancient statuary from the Capitoline Museums – but the dregs are pretty impressive, and the setting itself is worth a visit. Fauns and Minervas, bacchic revellers and Apollos are starkly white but oddly at home in this former generating station.

Museum of Via Ostiense

Via R Persichetti 3 (06 574 3193).
Open 9.30am-1.30pm, 2.30-4.30pm

San Paolo fuori le Mura

Tue, Thur; 9.30am-1.30pm Wed, Fri, Sat, 1st & 3rd Sun of mth. **Admission** free. **Map** p120 C3 **⑤**

This third-century AD gatehouse, called Porta Ostiensis in antiquity and Porta San Paolo today, contains a quaint collection of artefacts and prints describing the history of via Ostiense – the Ostian Way, built in the third century BC to join Rome to its port at Ostia. There's a large-scale model of the ancient port, and you can cross the crenellated walkway for a bird's-eye view of the true finesse of the modern Roman motorist.

Protestant Cemetery

Via Caio Cestio 6 (06 574 1900/ www.protestantcemetery.it). **Open** 9am-5pm Mon-Sat; 9am-1pm Sun. **Admission** free (donation expected). **Map** p120 B3 **⑥**

This heavenly oasis of calm in the midst of a ruckus of traffic has been the resting place for foreigners who have passed on to a better place since 1784. Officially the 'non-Catholic' cemetery, this charmingly old-world corner of the city accommodates Buddhists, Russian Orthodox Christians and atheists. In the older sector you'll find the grave of John Keats, who coughed his last in Rome at the age of 26. Close by is the tomb of Shelley, who died a year after Keats in a boating accident.

San Paolo fuori le Mura

Via Ostiense 184 (06 4543 5574/ www.abbaziasanpaolo.net). **Open** *Basilica* 7am-7pm daily. *Cloister* 9am-1pm, 3-6pm daily. **Map** p121 B6 **⑦**

Constantine founded this basilica to commemorate the martyrdom of St Paul nearby. The church has been rebuilt several times; most of the present church is only 150 years old. Features to have survived include 11th-century doors; a strange 12th-century Easter candlestick featuring human-, lion- and goat-headed beasts spewing the vine of life from their mouths; and a 13th-century canopy above the altar, by Arnolfo di Cambio. In the nave are mosaic portraits of all the popes from Peter to the present incumbent. There are only seven spaces left; once they're filled, the world, apparently, will end. In the confessio beneath the altar is the tomb of St Paul, topped by a

Gelato wizards

Ice-cream makers who continue to raise the standards.

Il Gelato

In the beginning was **Il Gelato di San Crispino** (p82). In 1992, the Alongi brothers – fanatical ice-cream purists – began whipping up something completely new in their first outlet in the southern suburbs. Ice-cream made from scratch (even good *gelatai* resort to industrially made ice-cream bases), with flavours provided by the finest pistacchios from Bronte in Sicily, 20-year-old marsala (*zabaione*) and seasonal fruit so fresh it's like tasting the original, whipped up and frozen.

This sudden eruption on to a Roman scene where *gelato* was good but never truly great forced others to pull themselves up by their bootstraps and unleashed a new wave of copycat gourmet *gelaterie*, some of which were not bad at all but none of which truly rivalled the original.

The past few years, though, have seen more aggressive competitors for the Alongi's unofficial title of manufacturers of some of the best ice-cream, anywhere.

Applying the same strict standards to their methods, the new generation have allowed their imaginations to run free with experimental flavours and textures.

At **Gelateria Il Teatro** (p82), Stefano and his wife Silvia draw from a past as pastry chefs to create surprises such as *cannolo*- and *panettone*-flavoured *gelato*. Their chocolate – 80 per cent pure cocoa – is exquisite, as is the caramel and pear with sesame.

Claudio Torcè began his ice-cream career with a suburban outlet – called, simply, **Il Gelato** (p119) – which became a word-of-mouth mecca for *gelato* lovers. Nowadays, you can experience his product in the Aventine district. Torcè's flavours are even more outlandish than those of Il Teatro, with cream of capsicum, ricotta cheese with orange peel, and tomato with rice on the menu of around 100 varieties. His peanut ice-cream is superb, as is the wide range of chocolate flavours: 80 per cent cocoa with ginger is sublime.

stone slab pierced with holes through which devotees stuff bits of cloth to imbue them with the apostle's holiness. Monks chant vespers at 5pm daily.

Eating & drinking

See also **Città dell'Altra Economia** (p127), **Volpetti** (p127).

Al Ristoro degli Angeli

Via Luigi Orlando 2 (06 5143 6020/ www.ristorodegliangeli.it). **Meals served** 8-11.30pm Mon-Sat. Closed Aug, 2wks Sept. **€€€**. **Italian**. Map p121 C5 ❽

Rather off the beaten track in the charming 1920s workers' suburb of Garbatella, the Ristoro's vibe is old-style French bistro but the excellent food is all Italian. Many organic products go into dishes such as pasta with fresh tuna, capers and wild fennel, or beef millefeuille with radicchio and smoked provola cheese. There are always fish and vegetarian options. The wine list is small but interesting,

the homemade desserts are luscious and there are tables outside.

Andreotti

Via Ostiense 54B (06 575 0773). **Open** 7.30am-9.30pm daily. Closed 2wks Aug. **Café/bar**. Map p121 C4 ❾

The Andreotti family claims to serve up 700 cups of its excellent coffee every day – and that was before a recent overhaul doubled the space and lengthened the counter. This has allowed even more scope for sampling this historic bar's excellent breakfast *cornetti*, cakes, light lunchtime snacks and evening *aperitivi* with nibbles.

Checchino dal 1887

Via di Monte Testaccio 30 (06 574 6318/www.checchino-dal-1887.com). **Meals served** 12.30-3pm, 8pm-midnight Tue-Sat. Closed Aug; 1wk Dec. **€€€€**. **Roman**. Map p120 A3 ❿

Imagine a pie shop becoming a top-class restaurant, and the odd mix of humble decor, elegant service, hearty food and huge cellar falls into place. Vegetarians should give the Mariani

Al Ristoro degli Angeli

Testaccio

family's restaurant a wide berth: offal is the speciality. Pasta dishes like the *bucatini all'amatriciana* are delicious.

Da Felice
Via Mastro Giorgio 29 (06 574 6800/ www.feliceatestaccio.com). **Meals served** 12.30-3pm, 8-11.30pm Mon-Sat; 12.30-2.45pm Sun. Closed 3wks Aug. €€€. **Roman**. Map p120 B2 ⑪
This former spit-and-sawdust trat has had an industrial-chic makeover but its high-quality traditional fare – including classics such as *tonnarelli cacio e pepe* and *abbacchio al forno con patate* (baked lamb with potatoes) – remains good. The wine list is impressive. Be sure to book.

L'Oasi della Birra
Piazza Testaccio 38 (06 574 6122/ www.oasidellabirra.com). **Open** 7pm-12.30am Mon-Sat; 7pm-12.30am Sun. Closed 2wks Aug. **Wine bar**. Map p120 B2 ⑫
An off-licence and speciality food shop, the 'Oasis of Beer' becomes an *apertivo* haunt in the evening, with more than 500 brews on offer, including beers from award-winning Italian micro-breweries. The selection of wines by the bottle is almost as impressive, and the *aperitivo* buffet (from 7pm)

delicious. Full-scale meals (€€) with a Teutonic slant are also served. There are tables outside.

Piccolo Alpino
Via Orazio Antinori 5 (06 574 1386). **Meals served** 12.30-2.30pm, 6-11pm Tue-Sun. Closed 1wk Aug. €. No credit cards. €€. **Italian/pizzeria**. Map p120 A2 ⑬
There are no frills in this very cheap, very cheerful eatery, where the pizzas are good and some of the pasta dishes – the *spaghetti con le vongole* stands out – are perfectly acceptable too (though these will push the bill into the €€ bracket).

Remo
Piazza Santa Maria Liberatrice 44 (06 574 6270). **Meals served** 7pm-1am Mon-Sat. Closed 3wks Aug. €. **Pizzeria**. Map p120 B2 ⑭
This pizzeria is a Testaccio institution. You can choose to sit at wonky tables on the pavement, or in the deafening interior. The thin-crust Roman pizzas are excellent, as are the *bruschette al pomodoro*.

Il Seme e la Foglia
Via Galvani 18 (06 574 3008). **Open** 8am-2am Mon-Sat. Closed

3wks Aug. No credit cards.

Café/bar. Map p120 B3 🟡

This lively daytime snack bar and evening pre-club stop is always packed out with students from the music school opposite. At midday, there's generally a pasta dish, plus large salads (€6-€7) and a selection of creative filled rolls.

Tallusa

Via Beniamino Franklin 11 (333 752 3506). **Open** 11am-4pm, 5pm-1.30am daily. **€**. **Mediterranean**. Map p120 A2 🟡

Always packed, this tiny eat-in or takeaway joint specialises in southern and eastern Mediterranean cuisine – dishes range from Sicilian specialities to falafel and a full range of Lebanese-style mezedes. It's very friendly and very cheap but rather erratic in its opening times.

Tuttifrutti

Via Luca della Robbia 3A (06 575 7902). **Meals served** 7.30-11.30pm Mon-Sat. Closed 3wks Aug. **€€€**. **Italian**. Map p120 B2 🟡

Behind an anonymous glass door, this trattoria is Testaccio's best-value dining experience, at the lower end of this price bracket. Michele guides you through a changing menu of creative fare. There is usually a veggie option and the wine is excellently priced.

Shopping

The produce market (Mon-Sat, mornings) in piazza Testaccio is an excellent place to pick up the wherewithal for a picnic or to stock your fridge if you're self-catering. Nearby streets, and the north-western aisle of the market itself, have been colonised by vendors of shoes of every description, including bargains on last season's models. For men's shoes, stop by the market on Saturday.

Città dell'Altra Economia

Largo Dino Frisullo (06 5730 0419/ www.cittadellaltraeconomia.org). **Open** 10am-1.30pm, 2.30-8pm Tue-Sat; 10am-8pm Sun. Map p120 A3 🟡

Extremely difficult to find, this 'city of alternative economy' comprises a wonderful organic food shop selling mostly local products, a fair trade store, advisors on ethical banking and solar heating, plus a welcoming bar and a wholesome restaurant (€€), both serving exclusively organic products. And it's all inside a gloriously restored pavilion of the former municipal slaughterhouse, with a huge open area outside, overlooked by Monte Testaccio (p122), where you can let kids loose for a runabout on sunny days. Opening hours change frequently.

Volpetti

Via Marmorata 47 (06 574 2352/ www.fooditaly.com). **Open** 8am-2pm, 5-8.15pm Mon-Sat. Map p120 B2 🟡

This is one of the best delis in Rome. It's hard to get away without one of the jolly assistants loading you up with samples – pleasant, but painful on the wallet. Around the corner is Volpetti Più (via A Volta 8-10, 06 574 4306, open 10.30am-3.30pm, 5.30-9.30pm Mon-Sat), a self-service restaurant where you can taste the deli's delicious cured meats and cheeses, along with pizza, salads and more.

Nightlife

Akab

Via di Monte Testaccio 68-69 (06 5725 0585/www.akabcave.com). **Open** midnight-5am Wed-Sat. Closed Aug. **Admission** (incl 1 drink) €10-€20. Map p120 B3 🟡

This long-term fixture of the Testaccio scene has an underground cellar and a street-level room, plus a garden for warmer months. Tuesday L-Ektrica sessions feature international DJs. There's retro on Wednesday, R&B on Thursday and house on Friday and Saturday.

ROME BY AREA

L'Alibi

Via di Monte Testaccio 40-44 (06 574 3448/www.lalibi.it). **Open** 11.30pm-5am Thur-Sun. **Admission** (incl 1 drink) €10-€15. **Map** p120 B3 ㉑
Rome's original gay club, the Alibi is still, in theory, a great place to dance away, with a well-oiled sound system. But it's showing its age. And a new straight-friendly approach and Friday hetero night have proved something of a turn-off all round.

Alpheus

Via del Commercio 36 (06 574 7826/ www.alpheus.it). **Open** 10.30pm-4am Fri-Sun; other days vary. Closed mid June-mid Sept. **Admission** varies. **Map** p121 B4 ㉒
An eclectic club with a varied crowd, the Alpheus has four halls for live gigs, music festivals, theatre and cabaret, all followed by a disco. The music changes nightly and from room to room: rock, chart R&B and Latin alongside world music, retro and happy trash. Watch out for the regular *Gorgeous I Am* gay events.

Caruso-Café de Oriente

Via di Monte Testaccio 36 (06 574 5019/www.carusocafedeoriente.com). **Open** 10pm-4am Tue-Sun. Closed mid June-mid Sept. **Admission** (incl 1 drink) €8-€10; free Sun. No credit cards. **Map** p120 B3 ㉓
A must for lovers of salsa, this club offers Latin American tunes every night apart from Saturday (anything from reggae to hip hop), and live acts almost daily. There's a roof terrace.

Classico Village

Via Libetta 3 (349 596 2398/www. classico.it). **Open** 9pm-1.30am Mon-Thur; 9pm-4am Fri, Sat. **Admission** €5-€15. **Map** p121 C5 ㉔
This former factory in the trendy neighbourhood of Ostiense is able to offer up to three (mainly rock-based) events simultaneously in its large spaces, all of which face on to a courtyard – a heavenly spot to chill out in on warm evenings. DJ sets usually follow the shows.

Goa

Via Libetta 13 (06 574 8277). **Open** midnight-4am Thur-Sat. Closed mid May-mid Sept. **Admission** (incl 1 drink) €10-€25. **Map** p121 C5 ㉕
One of the best of Rome's fashionable clubs, Goa is a techno-ethno fantasy of iron and steel with oriental-style statues and colours. Thursday's Ultrabeat night brings in Europe's top electronic music DJs. Goa also opens some Sundays (5pm-4am); there's a women-only event on the last Sunday of the month.

Rashomon

Via degli Argonauti 16 (347 340 5710). **Open** 11pm-4am Wed-Sun. Closed July & Aug. **Admission** free-€10. No credit cards. **Map** p121 C5 ㉖
Run by afficionados of alternative clubs in London and Berlin, Rashomon offers electro-rock, indie, electronica and new wave. There are often live acts, including emerging locals.

La Saponeria

Via degli Argonauti 20 (06 574 6999/ www.saponeriaclub.it). **Open** 11.30pm-5am Fri, Sat. Closed mid May-mid Sept. **Admission** €5-€15. **Map** p121 C5 ㉗
One of the liveliest clubs in Ostiense, this stylish, curvy, white space gets hopelessly packed on weekends. Friday is techno and electronic, Saturday is hip hop and R&B.

Arts & leisure

Teatro Palladium

Piazza Bartolomeo Romano 8 (06 5733 2768/www.teatro-palladium.it). **Map** p121 C5 ㉘
This beautiful 1920s theatre in Garbatella offers a mix of top-quality electronic music acts, cutting-edge theatre, art performances and, oddly, university seminars on diverse topics.

Piazza Sant'Egidio

Trastevere & the Gianicolo

Trastevere

With its picturesque alleyways and colour-washed *palazzi*, Trastevere has long been a tourist mecca. These days, local residents are up in arms about the extent to which this lovely area on the Tiber's right bank is becoming one big wine bar and *birreria*. But as you wander its ivy- and washing-draped streets, this is unlikely to bother you.

Trastevere is the Rome of your romantic dreams. It's quaint but buzzing, historical but without the imposing ruins and galleries you feel you have to 'do' on the other side of the river.

Here – across the Tiber: *trans Tiberim* – your main tasks will include rambling through narrow cobbled streets, soaking up the rustic charm, basking in the laid-back feel of the place and selecting the likeliest-looking of those over-abundant bars for *aperitivi*.

Trasteverini claim descent from slave stock. Through the Imperial period, much of the *trans Tiberim* area was agricultural, with farms, vineyards, country villas and gardens laid out for the pleasure of the Caesars. Trastevere was a working-class district in papal Rome and remained so until well after Unification.

Viale Trastevere slices the district in two. At the hub of the much-visited western part is piazza **Santa Maria in Trastevere** with its eponymous church. Fewer tourists make it to the warren of cobbled alleys in the eastern half, where craftsmen still ply their trades around the lovely church of **Santa Cecilia in Trastevere**.

Further upriver, Ponte Sisto provides handy pedestrian access back across to the *centro storico*.

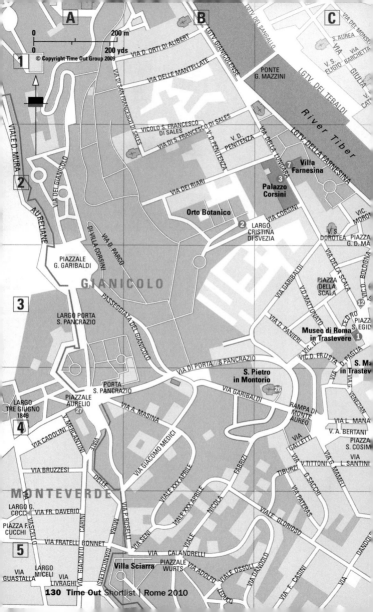

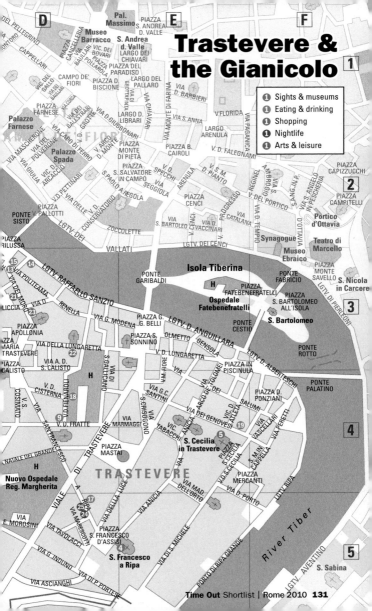

Trastevere & the Gianicolo

- **1** Sights & museums
- **1** Eating & drinking
- **1** Shopping
- **1** Nightlife
- **1** Arts & leisure

Orto botanico

fountains and fish ponds, creating luxuriant hidden corners disturbed only by frolicking children.

Palazzo Corsini – Galleria Nazionale d'Arte Antica

Via della Lungara 10 (06 6880 2323/ www.galleriaborghese.it). **Open** 9am-7pm Tue-Sun. **Admission** €4; €2 reductions. No credit cards. **Map** p130 C2 ❸

A 17th-century convert to Catholicism, Sweden's Queen Christina established her glittering court here in 1662. The stout monarch smoked a pipe, wore trousers and entertained female and (ordained) male lovers here. Today, her home houses part of the national art collection, with scores of Madonnas and Children (the most memorable is a Madonna by Van Dyck). Other works include a pair of Annunciations by Guercino; two St Sebastians (one by Rubens, one by Annibale Carracci); Caravaggio's *St John the Baptist*; and a triptych by Fra Angelico. There's also a melancholy *Salome* by Guido Reni.

San Francesco a Ripa

Piazza San Francesco d'Assisi 88 (06 581 9020). **Open** 7am-noon, 4-7pm Mon-Sat; 7am-1pm, 4-7.30pm Sun. **Map** p131 E5 ❹

This church stands on the site of the hospice where St Francis of Assisi stayed when he visited Rome in 1219; a near-contemporary portrait hangs in the cell where the saint slept. The original 13th-century church was rebuilt in the 1680s. It contains Bernini's sculpture of the Beata Ludovica Albertoni (1674), showing the aristocratic Franciscan nun dying in an agonised, sexually ambiguous Baroque ecstasy.

Santa Cecilia in Trastevere

Piazza Santa Cecilia 22 (06 589 9289). **Open** *Church & excavations* 9.30am-12.30pm, 4-6.30pm daily. *Cavallini frescoes* 10.15am-12.15pm Mon-Sat,

ROME BY AREA

Sights & museums

Museo di Roma in Trastevere

Piazza Sant'Egidio 1B (06 581 6563/ www.museodiromaintrastevere.it). **Open** 10am-8pm Tue-Sun. **Admission** €3; €1.50 reductions; extra charge during exhibitions. No credit cards. **Map** p130 C3 ❶

This rather dusty folklore museum, housed in a 17th-century convent, has a series of watercolours of 19th-century Rome and some whiskery waxwork tableaux evoking the life of 18th- and 19th-century *trasteverini.*

Orto botanico (Botanical Garden)

Largo Cristina di Svezia 24 (06 4991 7107). **Open** 9am-5.30pm Tue-Sat. **Admission** €4; €2 reductions. No credit cards. **Map** p130 B2 ❷

Established in 1883, Rome's Botanical Gardens are a welcome haven from the rigours of a dusty, hot city: plants tumble over steps and into

Tidying up the Tiber

San Francesco a Ripa

The lower banks of the River Tiber are paved with all kinds of good intentions. But despite (half-hearted) cycle paths and the occasional flurry of activity around a few ferry docks, they have remained very much the domain of tramps under bridges and some threatening mangy dogs. These broad expanses of riverside walkway are, all in all, a wasted opportunity.

Until the late 19th century, the Tiber was very much a part of Roman life: people traded along it, washed in it, drank from it, contracted nasty diseases from it and had their lives turned upside down by it during frequent devastating floods. After Rome became the capital of united Italy, city fathers put an end to this state of affairs by constructing the massive embankments we see today: perfect for holding back floodwaters, but sadly isolating Old Father Tiber from the city.

The latest initiative to change this state of affairs comes from the ruling council of Lazio, the region of which Rome is capital. A €4million scheme to clean up riverbanks and build jetties along the Tiber's course to the north and south-west of town, including stops – complete with bike-hire racks – in some of the region's natural reserves, aims to entice Romans and visitors alike back down to the Tevere (as it's known in Italian). It now remains to be seen whether good intentions (and hefty funding) will reap results.

11am-12.15pm Sun. **Admission** *Frescoes* €2.50. *Excavations* €2.50. No credit cards. **Map** p131 E4 ⑤

This church stands on the site of a fifth-century building that was itself built over an older Roman house, part of which can be visited. According to legend it was the home of the martyr Cecilia: after an attempt to suffocate her in her bath, her persecutors tried to behead her with three strokes of an axe (the maximum permitted). She sang for the several days it took her to die, and so became the patron saint of music. Her tomb was opened in 1599, revealing her undecayed body. It disintegrated, but not before a sketch was made, on which Stefano Maderno based the sculpture below the high altar. Her sarcophagus is in the crypt. In the upstairs gallery is a small fragment of what must have been one of the world's greatest frescoes. In this 13th-century *Last Judgement*, Pietro Cavallini flooded the apostles with a totally new kind of light – the same that was to reappear in Giotto's work.

Freni e Frizioni p136

Santa Maria in Trastevere

Piazza Santa Maria in Trastevere (06 589 7332/www.santamariain trastevere.org). **Open** 7.30am-8pm daily. **Map** p130 C3 ⑥

Legend has it that a miraculous well of oil sprang from the ground where Santa Maria now stands the moment that Christ was born, and flowed to the Tiber all day. The first church on this site was begun in the early fourth century; the present building was erected in the 12th, and has wonderful mosaics. Those on the façade, from the 12th and 13th centuries, show Mary breastfeeding Christ, and ten women with crowns and lanterns (they may represent the parable of the wise and foolish virgins). Inside, the apse has a 12th-century mosaic of Jesus and his mother. Lower down, between the windows, there are beautiful 13th-century mosaics showing scenes from the life of the Virgin by Pietro Cavallini. The Madonna and Child with rainbow overhead is also by Cavallini. In the chapel to the left of the high altar is a very rare sixth-century painting on wood of the Madonna.

Villa Farnesina

Via della Lungara 230 (06 6802 7268/ www.lincei.it). **Open** 9am-1pm Mon-Sat. **Admission** €5; €4 reductions. No credit cards. **Map** p130 C2 ⑦

Built in 1508-11 for rich papal banker Agostino Chigi, this palazzo became the property of the powerful Farnese family in 1577. Chigi was one of Raphael's principal patrons. The stunning frescoes in the ground-floor Loggia of Psyche were designed by Raphael but executed by his followers while the master dallied with his mistress. The Grace with her back turned, to the right of the door, is attributed to him. Around the corner, in the Loggia of Galatea, Raphael himself created the victorious goddess in her seashell chariot.

Eating & drinking

See also **Lettere Caffè** (p138).

Alberto Ciarla

Piazza San Cosimato 40 (06 581 6068/www.albertociarla.com). **Open** *Bottiglieria* noon-midnight Mon-Sat. **Meals served** *Restaurant* 8.30pm-midnight Mon-Sat. Closed 1wk Jan, 1wk Aug. €€-€€€€. **Seafood**. **Map** p130 C4 ⑧

This mirrors-and-glitz time warp of a restaurant serves some of Rome's best fish dishes, with the emphasis on raw seafood. If the (hefty) bill worries you, go for one of the taster menus (from €50) or check out Alberto's stylish wine bar, La Bottiglieria di Alberto Ciarla, where seafood is given a creative twist and offered along with a daunting choice of excellent wines. Here you can perch and nibble or go for a full meal; either way, the price tag will be considerably lower.

Alle Fratte di Trastevere

Via delle Fratte di Trastevere 49-50 (06 583 5775/www.allefratteditrastevere.com). **Meals served** noon-3pm, 6.30-11pm Mon, Tue, Thur-Sat; 6.30-11pm Sun. Closed 2wks Aug. €€. **Roman/ Neapolitan**. **Map** p131 D4 ⑨

Libreria del Cinema p136

The cheerful Alle Fratte does honest Roman trattoria fare with Neapolitan influences. Service is friendly, attentive and bilingual. First courses come in generous portions. *Secondi* include roast sea bream and veal escalopes in marsala. Post-prandial *digestivi* flow freely.

Bir & Fud

NEW *Via Benedetta 23 (06 589 4016/ birefud.blogspot.com).* **Meals served** 7.30pm-midnight daily. Closed 2wks Aug. €€. **Pizzeria/Roman**. **Map** p131 D3 ⑩

Narrow and buzzing, Bir & Fud serves exactly what the name says: interesting beers from lesser-known breweries, plus food that's all super-fresh and additive free: excellent pizza, bruschetta, mixed salads and some very Roman offal. The venue opens at 6.30pm for *aperitivi* and stays open until 1am on Saturday.

Cioccolata e Vino

Vicolo del Cinque 11A (06 5830 1868/ www.cioccolataevino.com). **Open** 8pm-2am Mon; 2pm-2am Tue-Sun. **Bar/shop**. **Map** p130 C3 ⑪

Half-shop, half-bar, this choc-box-sized Trastevere emporium is a non-stop mecca: for hot chocolate, a delicious espresso with a piece of bitter chocolate in the bottom of your tiny cup, a tasting of handmade chocs or a glass of wine from a small but interesting selection. (For dieting teetotallers, there are secondhand books downstairs in the cellars.)

Dar Poeta

Vicolo del Bologna 45 (06 588 0516/ www.darpoeta.com). **Meals served** 7.30pm-midnight daily. €€. **Pizzeria**. **Map** p130 C3 ⑫

Dar Poeta does high-quality pizza with creative toppings, such as the house pizza (with courgettes, sausage and spicy pepper). The varied *bruschette* are first-rate, and healthy salads offer a break from all those carbs. Be prepared to queue, as bookings aren't taken.

Enoteca Ferrara

Piazza Trilussa 41 (06 580 3769/www. enotecaferrara.it). **Open** *Wine bar & shop* 5pm-2am Mon; 12.30pm-2am Tue-Sun. **Wine bar**. **Map** p131 D3 ⑬

Via dei Fienaroli

This warren of a place may also be a restaurant (8-11.30pm daily, €€€€), but we recommend sticking to the comfortable, dimly lit wine bar with its good choice of wines by the glass, and an encyclopaedic (though rather expensive) bottle menu. From 6pm to 2am you can graze through an appetising selection of bar snacks for €7-€9.

Freni e Frizioni

Via del Politeama 4-6 (06 5833 4210/ www.freniefrizioni.com). **Open** 6pm-2am daily. **Bar**. Map p131 D3 ⑭

Housed in a former mechanic's workshop, this shabby-chic temple to the *aperitivo* cult is mobbed by crowds of hipsters hitting the generous (free) snack table (from 7pm) then spilling out of 'Brakes and Clutches' and across the square, glass and plate in hand. As this guide went to press, F&F's 12.30pm opening for delicious light lunches on pavement tables had been suspended, but the situation may change.

Friends Art Café

Piazza Trilussa 34 (06 581 6111/ www.cafefriends.it). **Open** 7am-2am

Mon-Sat; 6pm-2am Sun.
Bar/café. **Map** p131 D3 ⑮

Habitués meet in this lively bar for everything from breakfast to after-dinner cocktails. The chrome detailing and brightly coloured plastic chairs lend the place a retro-1980s funhouse feel. Lunch and dinner menus offer *bruschette*, salads and pastas at reasonable prices. There's an equally lively branch near piazza Navona in via della Scrofa 60.

Glass Hostaria

Vicolo del Cinque 58 (06 5833 5903/ www.glasshostaria.it). **Meals served** 8pm-11.30pm Tue-Sun. Closed 2wks Jan, 2wks July. €€€. **Italian**. Map p130 C3 ⑯

Ultra-modern Glass kicks against the trad Trastevere dining scene, with unusual creative pan-Italian dishes... most of which work. Service is mostly friendly, the wine list is interesting and it's not bad value, given the setting.

Jaipur

Via di San Francesco a Ripa 56 (06 580 3992/www.ristorantejaipur.it). **Meals served** 7pm-midnight Mon; noon-3pm, 7-11.30pm Tue-Sun. €€. **Indian**. Map p131 D5 ⑰

Jaipur does some of Rome's best Indian food (not that there's much competition), and it's good value too – which helps make up for the rather garish lighting and colour scheme. The menu ranges from basic starters to an extensive selection of tandoori specials, curries and murghs, plus a range of vegetarian dishes.

Libreria del Cinema

Via dei Fienaroli 31D (06 581 7724/ www.libreriadelcinema.roma.it). **Open** 3-10pm Mon; 11am-10pm Tue-Fri; 11am-11pm Sun. Closed 2wks Aug. **Café**. **Map** p131 D4 ⑱

This bookshop is heaven for movie buffs, with its vast stock of cinema-related material and its busy events programme. At the intimate little café,

Porta Portese flea market

aficionados swap cinema tales over light lunches (€€) and *aperitivi*; the café opens at 11am.

Le Mani in Pasta

Via de' Genovesi 37 (06 581 6017/ www.lemaniinpasta.com). **Meals served** 12.30-3pm, 7.30-11pm Tue-Sun. Closed 3wks Aug, 10 days Dec. **€€€.** **Italian**. Map p131 E4 ⑲
This relative newcomer offers decent, creative home cooking, big portions, friendly service and great value for money, all of which make it popular, so book ahead. Antipasti such as the chargrilled vegetables or sautéed clams and mussels, and huge mountains of pasta, such as the spaghetti with cuttlefish and artichokes, may mean you never get as far as good main courses like fillet steak with green peppercorns.

Ombre Rosse

Piazza Sant'Egidio 12 (06 588 4155). **Open** 7.30am-2am Mon-Sat; 10am-2am Sun. **Café/bar**. Map p130 C3 ⑳
In the heart of Trastevere, this café is a meeting spot day and night. Food (€€) is served throughout the day but Ombre Rosse is best for people-

watching: snagging a table outside is a coup after dark, when they fill to bursting. Service is slow but friendly.

Shopping

See also **Cioccolata e Vino** (p135), **Libreria del Cinema** (p136).
Piazza San Cosimato is home to a produce market (early to about 2pm Mon-Sat) that manages to retain a local feel in this tourist-heavy area. On Sunday mornings, the Porta Portese flea market engulfs via Portuense and surrounding streets: watch out for pickpockets as you root through bootleg CDs, clothes, bags and fake designer gear.

Almost Corner Bookshop

Via del Moro 45 (06 583 6942). **Open** 10am-1.30pm, 3.30-8pm Mon-Sat; 11am-1.30pm, 3.30-8pm Sun. Map p131 D3 ㉑
This English-language bookshop is packed to the rafters with fiction, plus books on history, art, archaeology and lots more. Charming owner Dermot O'Connell is unfailingly help-ful. Check the noticeboard if you're

ROME BY AREA

Almost Corner Bookshop p137

Big Mama

Vicolo San Francesco a Ripa 18 (06 581 2551/www.bigmama.it). **Open** 9pm-1.30am Tue-Sat. Closed June-mid Sept. **Admission** free with membership (annual €13, monthly €8); extra charge (€8-€22) for big acts. **Map** p131 D5 ㉔

Rome's blues temple, where an array of respected Italian and international artists play regularly, guaranteeing a quality night out for live-music aficionados. There's jazz too. Food is served: book to ensure you get a table.

Lettere Caffè

Via di San Francesco a Ripa 100-101 (339 439 4913/www.letterecaffe.org). **Open** 4pm-2am daily. Closed 3wks Aug. **Map** p131 D5 ㉕

Poetry slams and readings compete with live concerts – from rockabilly to jazz beginning at 10.30pm – and DJ sets in this bookish bar where well-priced wines and spirits and yummy home-made cakes complete the picture.

Gianicolo & Monteverde

The Gianicolo is the highest of central Rome's hills, though not one of the official seven. The view from the summit over the red roofs of the *centro storico* is quite quite lovely. It's leafy up here and – apart from the occasional car whizzing around the equestian statue of Unification hero Giuseppe Garibaldi – a calm place for a stroll. Only the portrait busts lining the paths, and the cannon fired each day at noon, serve as reminders of the bloody battle fought here between Unification forces and the French in 1849.

To the south, tortuous via Garibaldi passes by the Baroque Fontana Paola, a fountain made in 1612 to celebrate the reopening of an ancient Roman aqueduct; the columns come from the original St

seeking work, lodgings or Italian lessons. Closed on Sunday in August.

Roma – Store

Via della Lungaretta 63 (06 581 8789/ www.romastoreprofumi.com). **Open** 10am-8pm daily. **Map** p131 D3 ㉒

This blissful sanctuary of lotions and potions stocks an array of gorgeous scents: old-school Floris, Creed and Penhaligon's rub shoulders with modern classics such as home-grown Acqua di Parma and Lorenzo Villoresi. Staff can be very abrupt, however.

Valzani

Via del Moro 37A/B (06 580 3792/ www.valzani.it). **Open** 2-8pm Mon, Tue; 10am-8pm Wed-Sun. Closed July, Aug. **Map** p131 D3 ㉓

Sachertorte and spicy, nutty *pangiallo* are the specialities in this Trastevere institution, but they are the tip of a sweet-toothed iceberg.

Nightlife

See also **Freni e Frizioni** (p136), **Friends Art Café** (p136) and **Ombre Rosse** (p137).

Peter's. Between the fountain and the church of **San Pietro in Montorio** – with the exquisite **Tempietto** in its courtyard – stands the unlikely Fascist-era Ossario Garibaldino (open 9am-1pm Tue-Sun), containing the remains of heroes of the Risorgimento, Italy's struggle for Unification.

West of here stretches the leafy well-heeled suburb of Monteverde, home to vast, green expanses of the Villa Pamphili park. Rome's largest public green space, it's a wonderful place to stroll of a summer evening.

Nearby is the smaller but equally lovely Villa Sciarra garden, with rose arbours, a children's play area and a miniature big dipper.

Sights & museums

Tempietto di Bramante & San Pietro in Montorio

Piazza San Pietro in Montorio 2 (06 581 3940). **Open** *Tempietto* 9.30am-12.30pm, 2-4pm Tue-Sun. Closed on Sun afternoons in Aug. *Church* 8.30am-noon, 3-4pm Mon-Sat; 8.30am-noon Sun. **Map** p130 C4 ❷⁵
High up on the Gianicolo, on one of the spots where St Peter was said to have been crucified (St Peter's is another), San

Pietro in Montorio conceals an architectural gem in its courtyard: the Tempietto, designed by Donato Bramante in 1508. This round construction, with its Doric columns, was the first modern building to follow exactly the proportions of one of the classical orders. In 1628, Bernini added the staircase down to the crypt. The 15th-century church has a chapel by Bernini (the second on the left). Paintings include a Sebastiano del Piombo and a Guido Reni.

Eating & drinking

Antico Arco

Piazzale Aurelio 7 (06 581 5274/ www.anticoarco.it). **Meals served** 7.30-11.30pm daily. Closed 2wks Aug. €€€€. **Italian**. **Map** p130 A4 ❷⁷
A 2007 refit gave the Antico Arco a minimalist-but-warm new interior, served up with some interesting innovations in the kitchen. But the old favourites are still there too, from the amazing onion flan with grana cheese sauce, to *primi* like risotto with castelmagno cheese. There is a range of delicious *secondi*, and the desserts are fantastic. Sommelier Maurizio will steer you through an extensive, well-priced wine list. Book at least a couple of days in advance. The wine bar opens at 6pm.

ROME BY AREA

Antico Arco

Swiss Guard

The Vatican & Prati

The Vatican & Borgo

The St Peter's we see today was consecrated in 1626; the previous basilica on this spot was consecrated in the early years of the fourth century. The link between this area and Christianity, however, predates even that earlier church.

In AD 54, Emperor Nero built a circus in the *campus vaticanus*, a marshy area across the river from the city centre. Ten years later, when fire destroyed two-thirds of Rome, Nero blamed the Christians, and the persecution of this new cult began, with much of the Christian-persecuting taking place in Nero's circus. Top apostle Peter is believed to have been crucified here and buried on the spot where, in 326, Emperor Constantine built the first church of St Peter.

Not all of the following popes resided in the Vatican but, throughout the Christian era, pilgrims have flocked to the tomb of the founder of the Roman Church.

Around it, the Borgo district grew up to service the burgeoning Dark Age tourist industry. Pope Leo IV (847-55) enclosed Borgo with the 12-metre-high (40-foot) Leonine Wall. Pope Nicholas III (1277-80) extended the walls and provided a papal escape route, linking the Vatican to the huge, impregnable Castel Sant'Angelo by way of a long *passetto* or covered walkway.

After the Sack of Rome in 1527, Pope Paul III got Michelangelo to build bigger, better walls but the popes moved to the Lateran, then the Quirinal, palaces. Only in 1870, with the Unification of Italy, were they forced back across the Tiber once more. Until 1929, the pope pronounced the Italian state to be sacrilegious. But on 11 February 1929, Pius XII and Mussolini signed the Lateran Pacts, awarding the Church a huge cash payment, tax-free status and a constitutional role that led to an important and continuing moral influence over legislation on social issues.

The Vatican City occupies an area of less than half a square kilometre, making it the world's smallest state. Despite having fewer than 800 residents, it has its own diplomatic service, postal service, army (the Swiss Guard), heliport, station, supermarket, and radio and TV stations. It has observer status at the UN, and issues its own stamps and currency. Outside in Borgo, locals mingle with off-duty Swiss Guards and priests from the Vatican Curia (administration).

Vatican tips

■ **On-line information**: the website www.vatican.va contains information on church matters. For information on the monuments, attractions and institutions of the Vatican state, see www.vaticanstate.va.

■ **Dress code**: the Vatican enforces its dress code strictly, both in St Peter's and in the Vatican Museums. Anyone wearing shorts or a short skirt, or with bare shoulders or midriff, will be turned away.

■ **Timing**: the queues to visit both St Peter's and the Vatican Museums (15 minutes' brisk walk between the two) are usually huge. Factor in an hour or more of waiting time for each.

■ **Papal audiences**: when in Rome, the pope addresses crowds in St Peter's Square at noon on Sunday. On Wednesday mornings at 10.30, he holds a general audience in St Peter's Square, if the weather is fine, otherwise in the modern Sala Nervi audience hall. Though it's possible to join the crowd at the back of the piazza for outside audiences (there are big screens to bring the action closer), you'll need tickets for audiences in the Sala Nervi or for seats close to the pontiff in St Peter's Square. If you want tickets, make your request well in advance by fax to the

Prefettura della Casa Pontificia (06 6988 4857, fax 06 6988 5863).

■ **Vatican Gardens**: the Vatican walls surround splendid formal gardens, which can be visited on Tuesday, Thursday and Saturday – weather permitting – on guided tours (€18, €14 reductions). Call 06 6988 4676 to book several days in advance.

Sights & museums

Castel Sant'Angelo

Lungotevere Castello 50 (06 681 9111/ www.castelsantangelo.com). **Open** 9am-7.30pm Tue-Sun. **Admission** €5; €2.50 reductions. Extra charge during exhibitions. No credit cards. **Map** p143 D4 ❶
Begun by Emperor Hadrian in AD 135 as his mausoleum, Castel Sant'Angelo has been a fortress, prison and papal residence. It now plays host to temporary art shows, although the real pleasure of

Castel Sant'Angelo

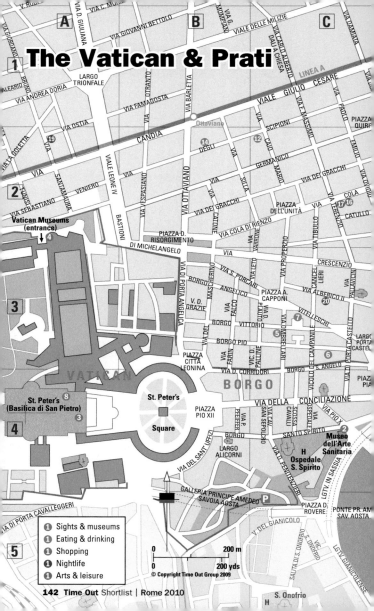

The Vatican & Prati

Vatican Museums (entrance)

St. Peter's (Basilica di San Pietro)

St. Peter's Square

VATICAN

BORGO

PIAZZA PIO XII

PIAZZA CITTÀ LEONINA

Museo dell'Arte Sanitaria

H Ospedale S. Spirito

GALLERIA PRINCIPE AMEDEO SAVOIA AOSTA

S. Onofrio

- ● Sights & museums
- ● Eating & drinking
- ● Shopping
- ● Nightlife
- ● Arts & leisure

0   200 m
0   200 yds

© Copyright Time Out Group 2009

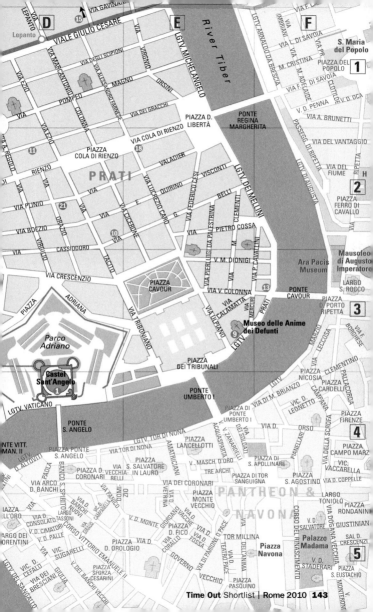

D

VIA GAVINANA

VIA LEPANTO

Lepanto

VIALE GIULIO CESARE

E

VIA MICHELANGELO

River Tiber

F

VIA L. DI SAVOIA

S. Maria del Popolo

PIAZZA DEL POPOLO **1**

VIA DEGLI SCIPIONI

VIA MARCANTONIO

VIA EZIO

VIA ALESSANDRO FARNESE

VIA VIRGINIO

VIA ORSINI

VIA DELLE PENNA

VIA A. BRUNETTI

VIA DEL VANTAGGIO

POMPEO

COLONNA

MAGNO

VIA DEI GRACCHI

PIAZZA D. LIBERTÀ

PONTE REGINA MARGHERITA

PASSEGG. DI RIPETTA

VIA DEL FIUME

H

VIA COLA DI RIENZO

PIAZZA COLA DI RIENZO

VALADIER

VISCONTI

LGTV DEI MELLINI

2

PIAZZA FERRO DI CAVALLO

P R A T I

RIENZO

VIA

QUIRINO

BELLI

VIA

VIA PIETRO COSSA

VIA PLINIO

VIA

VIA

CICERONE

VIA

VIA M. DIONIGI

VIA BOEZIO

VIA ORAZIO

VIA

CASSIODORO

VIA

VIA PIER LUIGI DA PALESTRINA

VIA P. CAVALLINI

Ara Pacis Museum

Mausoleo di Augusto Imperatore

LARGO S. ROCCO

VIA VIRGILIO

TACITO

VIA V. COLONNA

VIA CALAMATTA

PONTE CAVOUR

PIAZZA D. PORTO DI RIPETTA

3

VIA CRESCENZIO

PIAZZA CAVOUR

VIA TRIBONIANO

VIA ULPIANO

VIA MERCURI

LGTV

Museo delle Anime dei Defunti

PIAZZA ADRIANA

Parco Adriano

Castel Sant'Angelo

PIAZZA DEI TRIBUNALI

PONTE UMBERTO I

PIAZZA DI PONTE UMBERTO I

VIA DI M. BRIANZO

PIAZZA NICOSIA

CLEMENTINO

VIA DELLA SCROFA

PIAZZA CARDELLI

PIAZZA FIRENZE

4

LGTV VATICANO

PONTE S. ANGELO

LGTV TOR DI NONA

VIA DELL'ARCO DI NONA

PIAZZA LANCELLOTTI

VIA DEI SOLDATI

VIC. D. LEONETTO

ORSO

PIANELLARI

PIAZZA CAMPO MARZ

NTE VITT. MAN. II

PIAZZA PONTE S. ANGELO

VIA TOR DI NONA

AMATRICIANI

VIA S. SALVATORE IN LAURO

VIA MASCH. D'ORO

PIAZZA DI S. APOLLINARE

VIA D. COPPELLE

VIC. VACCARELLA

IAZZA LL'ORO

BANCO S. SPIRITO

PIAZZA D. VECCHIA CORONARI

BELLI

TRE ARCHI

PIAZZA DI TOR SANGUIGNA

PIAZZA S. AGOSTINO

LARGO TONIOLO

PIAZZA RONDANINI

5

LARGO DEI FIORENTINI

VIA DEI CORONARI

VIA D. VETRINA

P A N T H E O N &

VIA DELLA DOGANA VECCHIA

GIUSTINIAN

VIC. D. CEFALO

CORSO VITTORIO EMANUELE II

LARGO CONSOLATO TASSONI

V.D. CIMATORI

V.D. PALLE

PIAZZA D. FICO

VIA D. FOSSA

VIA D. CORALLO

VIA DEL PARIONE

N A V O N A

V.D. SALVATORE CORSO DEL RINASCIMENTO

Palazzo Madama

SAL D. CRESCENZI

IAZZA DEI BRESCIANI

VIA GIULIA

VICOLO SUGARELLI

PIAZZA SFORZA CESARINI

PIAZZA DI D. OROLOGIO

GOVERNO

TOR MILLINA

VIA D. TEATRO PACE

DELL'ANIMA

Piazza Navona

V.D. STADERARI

PIAZZA S. EUSTACHIO

PIAZZA DEI BANCHI VECCHI

VIA D. BANCHI VECCHI

PIAZZA PASQUINO

St Peter's (Basilica di San Pietro)

a visit lies in wandering from Hadrian's original spiralling ramp entrance to the upper terraces, with their superb views over the city. Between, there is much to see: lavish Renaissance salons, decorated with spectacular frescoes and trompe l'oeils; the glorious chapel in the *Cortile d'Onore* designed by Michelangelo; and, halfway up an easily missed staircase, Clement VII's tiny bathroom, painted by Giulio Romano.

Museo Storico Nazionale dell'Arte Sanitaria

Lungotevere in Sassia 3 (06 689 3051). **Open** 10am-noon Mon, Wed, Fri. Closed Aug. **Admission** €5. No credit cards. **Map** p142 C4 ❷
A hostel and church were established here in around 726 by King Ine of Wessex to cater for weary pilgrims from the north. Known as the *burgus saxonum* or 'in Sassia', this became the nucleus of the world's first purpose-built hospital. British funds for the hostel were cut off with the Norman invasion of England in 1066, after which it passed into papal hands and thence to the Templar knight Guy de Montpellier,

who founded the Order of the Holy Spirit. A few rooms of the modern hospital here house a gruesome collection of medical artefacts. Two massive 15th-century frescoed wards were emptied not all that long ago of their beds to provide space for itinerant exhibitions.

St Peter's (Basilica di San Pietro)

Piazza San Pietro (06 6988 1662/ 06 6988 5518). No credit cards. Map p142 A4 ❸
Basilica Open *Oct-Mar* 7am-6pm daily. *Apr-Sept* 7am-7pm daily. **Admission** free.
Dome Open *Oct-Mar* 8am-5pm daily. *Apr-Sept* 8am-6pm daily. **Admission** €5; €7 with lift.
Grottoes Open *Oct-Mar* 7am-5pm daily. *Apr-Sept* 7am-6pm daily. **Admission** free.
Necropolis Apply at the Excavations Office (fax 06 6987 3017/scavi@fsp.va). **Open** *Guided tours* 9am-5pm Mon-Sat. **Admission** €10.
Treasury Museum Open *Oct-Mar* 9am-5.15pm daily. *Apr-Sept* 9am-6.15pm daily. **Admission** €6; €4 reductions.

The current St Peter's was consecrated on 18 November 1626 by Urban VIII, exactly 1,300 years after the consecration of the first basilica on the site. By the mid 15th century, the south wall of the original basilica was collapsing. Pope Nicholas V had 2,500 wagonloads of masonry from the Colosseum carted here, just for running repairs. It took the arrogance of Pope Julius II and his pet architect Donato Bramante to knock the millennia-old basilica down, in 1506.

Following Bramante's death in 1514, Raphael took over the work. In 1547, he was replaced by Michelangelo; he died in 1564, aged 87, after coming up with a plan for a massive dome. Completed in 1590, this was the largest brick dome ever constructed, and is still the tallest building in Rome. In 1607, Carlo Maderno designed a new façade, crowned by enormous statues of Christ and the apostles.

After Maderno's death Bernini took over and became the hero of the hour with his sumptuous baldachin and elliptical piazza. This latter was built between 1656 and 1667; the oval measures 340 by 240m (1,115 by 787ft), and is punctuated by the central Egyptian obelisk and two symmetrical fountains by Maderno and Bernini. The 284-column, 88-pillar colonnade is topped by 140 statues of saints.

In the portico (1612), opposite the main portal, is a mosaic by Giotto (c1298), from the original basilica. Five doors lead into the basilica: the central ones come from the earlier church, while the others are all 20th century. The last door on the right is opened only in Holy Years by the pope himself. Inside, a series of brass lines in the floor show the lengths of other churches around the world that are not as big. Bernini's vast *baldacchino* (1633), cast from bronze purloined from the Pantheon, hovering over the high altar, is the real focal point. Below the altar, two flights of stairs lead to the *confessio*, where a niche contains a ninth-century mosaic of Christ, the only

thing from old St Peter's that stayed in its original place. Far below lies the site of what is believed to be St Peter's tomb, discovered during excavations in 1951.

Pilgrims head straight for the last pilaster on the right before the main altar, to kiss the big toe of Arnolfo da Cambio's statue of St Peter (c1296), or to say a prayer by the crystal casket containing the mummified remains of Pope John XXIII, who was beatified in 2002. Tourists make a beeline for the first chapel on the right, where Michelangelo's *Pietà* (1499) is found. Following an anti-clockwise direction, the third chapel has a tabernacle and two angels by Bernini, plus St Peter's only remaining painting: a *Trinity* by Pietro da Cortona (the others have been replaced by mosaic copies).

Bernini's Throne of St Peter (1665) stands at the far end of the nave. Encased in it is a wood and ivory chair, probably dating from the ninth century but for many years believed to have belonged to Peter himself. To the right of the throne is Bernini's 1644 monument to his patron Urban VIII.

On the pillars supporting the main dome are venerated relics, including a chip off the True Cross. In the left aisle, beyond the pilaster with St Veronica holding the cloth with which she wiped Christ's face, Bernini's tomb for Pope Alexander VII shows the pope shrouded with a cloth of reddish marble, from beneath which struggles a skeleton clutching an hourglass. Near the portico end of the left aisle is a group of monuments to the Old Pretender James Edward Stuart and family.

Beneath the basilica are the Vatican grottoes – Renaissance crypts containing papal tombs. The Necropolis, where St Peter is said to be buried, lies under the grottoes. The small treasury museum off the left nave of the basilica contains stunning liturgical relics. The dome, reached via hundreds of stairs (there's a cramped lift as far as the basilica roof, then 320 steps to climb to get to the very top), offers fabulous views.

Vatican Museums

Viale del Vaticano (06 6988 3860/ www.vatican.va). **Open** 8.30am-6pm Mon-Sat (ticket office closes 2hrs before). *Year-round* last Sun of mth 9am-12.30pm. Closed Catholic holidays. **Admission** €14; €8 reductions; free last Sun of mth. No credit cards. **Map** p142 A2 ❹

Begun by Pope Julius II in 1503, this immense collection represents the accumulated fancies and obsessions of a long line of strong, often contradictory personalities. The signposted routes cater for anything from a dash to the Sistine Chapel to a five-hour plod. There are also itineraries for wheelchair users. Wheelchairs can be borrowed at the museum: you warn them you'll be needing one by faxing 06 6988 5433.

Borgia Rooms

This six-room suite was adapted for the Borgia Pope Alexander VI (1492-1503) and decorated by Pinturicchio with a series of frescoes on biblical and classical themes.

Galleria Chiaramonte

Founded by Pius VII in the early 19th century, this is an eclectic collection of Roman statues, reliefs and busts.

Gallerie dei Candelabri & degli Arazzi

The long gallery, which is studded with candelabra, contains Roman statues, while the next gallery has ten huge tapestries (*arazzi*), woven by Flemish master Pieter van Aelst from cartoons by Raphael.

Galleria delle Carte Geografiche

A 120m-long (394ft) gallery, with the Tower of the Winds observation point at the north end. Ignazio Danti drew the extraordinarily precise maps of Italian regions and cities.

Egyptian Museum

Founded in 1839, this selection of ancient Egyptian art from 3,000 BC to 600 BC includes statues of a baboon god, painted mummy cases, real mummies and a marble statue of Antinous, Emperor Hadrian's lover.

Etruscan Museum

This collection contains Greek and Roman art as well as Etruscan masterpieces, including the contents of the Regolini-Galassi Tomb (c650 BC).

Museo Paolino

Highlights of this collection of Roman and neo-Attic sculpture include a beautifully draped statue of Greek tragedian Sophocles and a trompe l'oeil mosaic of an unswept floor.

Museo Pio-Clementino

The world's largest collection of classical statues fills 16 rooms. Don't miss the first-century BC *Belvedere Torso* by Apollonius of Athens, the Roman copy of the bronze *Lizard Killer* by Praxiteles and, in the octagonal Belvedere Courtyard, the exquisite *Belvedere Apollo* and *Laocoön*.

Pinacoteca

The Pinacoteca (picture gallery) holds many of the pictures that the Vatican managed to recover from France after Napoleon whipped them in the early 19th century. The collection ranges from Byzantine school works and Italian primitives to 18th-century Dutch and French old masters, and includes Giotto's *Stefaneschi Triptych*; a *Pietà* by Lucas Cranach the Elder; several delicate Madonnas by Fra Filippo Lippi, Fra Angelico, Raphael and Titian; Raphael's last work, *The Transfiguration*; Caravaggio's *Entombment*; and a chiaroscuro *St Jerome* by Leonardo da Vinci.

Sistine Chapel

The world's most famous frescoes cover the ceiling and one immense wall of the *Cappella Sistina*, built by Sixtus IV in 1473-84. For centuries it has been used for popes' private prayers and

Clericus Cup

Teams in the Vatican football league play to win.

Pope Benedict XV is a keen football supporter (Bayern Munich is his team) but as yet he hasn't been glimpsed at the San Pietro Oratory pitches, cheering on the teams of the fledgling Vatican football league. It can only be a matter of time. It's clear that the support for the project comes right from the top, with even the highest-ranking prelates turning up: Scottish Cardinal Keith O'Brien was spotted at a key match played by the trainee priests of the British Colleges United team.

There's little to set the Clericus Cup apart from any other league. Matches are noisy affairs: trumpets, rattles, drums and raucous chanting in Latin so disturbed residents in the area around this sports club close to the Vatican walls, that instruments and ghetto blasters have had to be banned. And the 16 teams competing for the Clericus Cup play to win, to the point where a worrying flurry of blue temporary expulsion cards was handed out in the 2008-9 season, and send-offs were commonplace. The 2008 finals, which began with prayers, were marked by controversy over a player diving in the area at a key moment.

Parish playgrounds the world over hum to the sound of boys kicking balls, but some of those boys who have stuck with the Church – especially the Latin American seminarians – are of near-professional standard. The pontifical universities take the league extremely seriously, as do international seminaries (such as the north American 'Martyrs', see www.pnac.org/clericus/index.htm), the Benedictines and the Legionaries of Christ. The Swiss Guard and Vatican security staff also field teams. Vatican secretary of state Cardinal Tarcisio Bertone, a fervid Juventus supporter, may not have been joking recently when he floated the idea of a Vatican team donning the white and gold colours of the Holy See to compete in top-level international fixtures.

Football, says Pope Benedict, should promote 'honesty, solidarity and fraternity'... which presumably means not throwing your shirt at the referee, as happened during one match. This unholy offence saw the player's team banned from the rest of the championship.
■ www.csi-net.it

ROME BY AREA

Vatican crunch

It was Pope John Paul II who decided, in 1981, that the balance sheet of the Holy See should be made public, to dispel 'myths' about the Church's immense wealth. Since then, year-end figures have wavered considerably (mostly in the black to 1999; four bad years from 2000-3; in the clear again in 2004 and 2005; back in the red in 2006-7).

Despite some reported fancy financial footwork – like cashing in shares for gold – well before deep gloom hit the markets, the credit crunch of late 2008 hit the Vatican too: the Holy See's financiers predicted a balance sheet in even worse shape than its 2007 €9 million deficit (€13.5 million for the state as a whole).

The greatest dead weight on the Holy See's finances in 2007 was the Vatican Radio and the Osservatore Romano daily. And as the credit crunch bit in 2008, the strength of the euro against the dollar further deepened the Holy See's woes.

But however bad things get, it's unlikely that the Holy See will have to go begging for aid. For a state that doesn't even cover one square kilometre, its assets are considerable, from the €19 million worth of gold ingots stashed away, to currency reserves of €340 million and bonds and shares worth €520 million at the end of 2007. Moreover, the value of Vatican-owned real estate is set at €424 million. No value has been set on its artistic holdings.

papal elections. In the 1980s and '90s, the 930sq m (10,000sq ft) of *Creation* (on the ceiling) and the *Last Judgement* (on the wall behind the altar) were subjected to a controversial restoration.

In 1508, Michelangelo was commissioned to paint some undemanding decoration on the ceiling of the chapel. He offered to do far more than that, and embarked upon his massive venture alone, spending the next four-and-a-half years standing (only Charlton Heston lay down) on 18m-high (60ft) scaffolding. A sequence of biblical scenes, from the Creation to the Flood, begins at the *Last Judgement* end; they are framed by monumental figures of Old Testament prophets and classical sibyls.

In 1535, aged 60, Michelangelo returned. Between the completion of the ceiling and the beginning of the wall, Rome had suffered. From 1517, the Protestant Reformation threatened the power of the popes, and the sack of the city in 1527 by Imperial troops was seen by Michelangelo as the wrath of God. The *Last Judgement* dramatically reflects this gloomy atmosphere. In among the larger-than-life figures, Michelangelo painted his own miserable face on the human skin held by St Bartholomew, below and to the right of the powerful figure of Christ.

Before Michelangelo set foot in the chapel, the stars of the 1480s – Perugino, Cosimo Roselli, Botticelli, Ghirlandaio – had created the paintings on the walls.

Raphael Rooms

Pope Julius II gave 26-year-old Raphael carte blanche to redesign four rooms of the Papal Suite. The Study (Stanza della Segnatura, 1508-11) covers philosophical and spiritual themes. The star-packed *School of Athens* fresco has contemporary artists as classical figures: Plato is Leonardo; the glum thinker on the steps at the front – Heraclitus – is Michelangelo; Euclid is Bramante; and Raphael himself is on the far right-hand side behind a man in white. Raphael next turned to the Stanza di Eliodoro

(1512-14), where the portra-yal of God saving the temple in Jerusalem from the thieving Heliodorus was intended to highlight the divine protection enjoyed by Pope Julius. The Dining Room (Stanza dell'Incendio; 1514-17) is dedicated to Pope Leo X (the most obese of the popes, he died from gout aged 38). The room is named for the *Fire in the Borgo*, which Leo IV apparently stopped with the sign of the cross. The Reception Room (Sala di Constantino, 1517-24) was completed by Giulio Romano after Raphael's death in 1520, and tells the legend of Emperor Constantine's miraculous conversion. The Loggia di Raffaello (usually closed) has a beautiful view over Rome; started by Bramante in 1513, and finished by Raphael, it has 52 small paintings on biblical themes, and leads into the Sala dei Chiaroscuri. The adjacent Chapel of Nicholas V has scenes from the lives of saints Lawrence and Stephen by Fra Angelico (1448-50).

Eating & drinking

Enoteca Nuvolari

Via degli Ombrellari 10 (06 6880 3018). **Open** 6.30pm-2am Mon-Sat. Closed Aug. No credit cards. **Enoteca**. **Map** p142 C3 ❺

The younger denizens of Borgo hang out in this welcoming *enoteca*. The *aperitivo* hour (6.30-8.30pm) is accompanied by a free buffet; more filling soups and pâtés are on offer next door (8pm-midnight, €€) in the dining room.

Paninoteca da Guido

Borgo Pio 13 (06 687 5491). **Open** 8am-4pm Mon-Sat. Closed 3wks Aug. €. No credit cards. **Snack bar**. **Map** p142 C3 ❻

This hole-in-the-wall joint is one of the best places to grab a snack in the Vatican area. Guido does filled rolls, made up while you wait: ham, mozzarella, rocket, olive paste, etc. There are also a couple of pasta dishes. You'll have to fight for one of the few outside tables, though.

Re Calamaro!

🟦 NEW *Piazza delle Vaschette 14A (06 6476 0299/www.recalamaro.it).* **Open** noon-3.30pm, 6-10pm Tue-Fri, Sun; noon-11pm Sat. €. **Seafood**. **Map** p142 C3 ❼

If your energy is flagging after a trawl round the Vatican Museums, the array of freshly fried fish and vegetable goodies in this delightful boat-themed snack bar will replenish those missing calories nicely. Squid or octopus rings and potato wedges, and delicious artichoke hearts are available, from €3 a serving.

Il Ristoro

Basilica di San Pietro (06 6988 3376). **Open** *Oct-Mar* 8.30am-5pm Mon-Sat. *Apr-Sept* 8.30am-6pm Mon-Sat. No credit cards. **Café**. **Map** p142 A4 ❽

Take the St Peter's dome lift for Rome's most unlikely 'cappuccino with a view' – on the roof of the basilica. There's nothing but water, coffee, soft drinks and a dull selection of ice-creams on the menu, but the wonder of being up here between those giant marble saints will make you feel light-headed anyway.

Prati

The Prati district was a provocation. Built over meadows (*prati*) soon after Rome became capital of the newly unified Italian state in 1871, its grand *palazzi* housed the staff of the ministries and parliament. But its broad avenues were named after historic figures who had fought against the power of the Papal States, and the largest of its *piazze* – nestling beneath the Vatican walls – was named after the Risorgimento, the movement that had destroyed the papacy's hold on Italy.

A solidly bourgeois district, Prati has a main drag – via Cola di Rienzo – that provides ample opportunities for retail therapy. Imposing military barracks line viale delle Milizie, and the bombastic Palazzo di Giustizia (popularly known as *il palazzaccio*,

Settembrini

'the big ugly building') sits between piazza Cavour and the Tiber. On the riverbank is one of Catholic Rome's truly weird experiences: the **Museo delle Anime dei Defunti**.

Sights & museums

Museo delle Anime dei Defunti

Lungotevere Prati 12 (06 6880 6517). **Open** 7.30-11am, 4.30-7pm Mon-Sat; 8.30am-1pm, 4.30-8pm Sun. **Map** p143 E3 ❾

This macabre collection, attached to the church of Sacro Cuore di Gesù in Prati, contains hand- and fingerprints left on the prayer books and clothes of the living by dead loved ones, to request masses to release their souls from purgatory. Shuts earlier in summer.

Eating & drinking

L'Arcangelo

Via GG Belli 59-61 (06 321 0992/ www.ristorantidiroma.com/arcangelo). **Meals served** 12.30-2.30pm, 8-11.30pm Mon-Fri; 8-11pm Sat. Closed 2wks Aug. €€€. **Creative Italian**. **Map** p143 D2 ❿

The sombre L'Arcangelo has dark wood panelling below tobacco-sponged walls, linen tablecloths and a jazz soundtrack. The seasonal dishes are impressive: a tartlet of octopus and potato with olive oil is simple but delicious, and potato gnocchi with lamb and artichokes is a worthy follow-up. *Secondi*, like tripe with mint and pecorino, are clever variations on the Roman tradition.

Art Studio Café

NEW *Via dei Gracchi 187A (06 3260 9104/www.artstudiocafe.it).* **Open** 7.30am-9.30pm Mon-Sat. Closed 2wks Aug. €-€€. **Café/snack bar**. **Map** p143 D2 ⓫

There's an arty theme to this bright, café where you can munch your creative lunchtime salad (€6.50) or pasta dish while leafing through chic magazines or art-related tomes. A boutique has attractive handmade jewellery, silk scarves and household objects. There's an *aperitivo* buffet from 6-9pm plus lectures and all kinds of arty crafty courses.

Del Frate

Via degli Scipioni 118 (06 323 6437/ www.enotecadelfrate.it). **Meals served** 1-3pm, 6.30pm-midnight Mon-Fri; 6.30pm-1.30am Sat. Closed 3wks Aug. €€€. **Wine bar/Italian**. **Map** p142 C2 ⓬

This venerable bottle shop expanded into a wine bar annexe a few years back. Tables often spill over into the *enoteca* itself. The oven-baked ravioli with salmon and courgette sauce is a good demonstration of the modern approach; seconds might include a scallop of sea bass with pan-fried cicoria. The only off-note is the steep mark-up on wines.

Gran Caffè Esperia

Lungotevere dei Mellini 1 (06 3211 0016). **Open** Oct-Apr 7am-9.30pm daily. May-Sept 7am-midnight daily. **Café/bar**. **Map** p143 F3 ⓭

The pavement tables at this newly restored café are hotly contested when the sun shines on them in the morning. Work on your tan while eating toasted *cornetti* with ham and cheese, or smoked salmon sandwiches. The coffee's great.

Isola della Pizza

Via degli Scipioni 43, 45, 47 (06 3973 3483/www.isoladellapizza.com). **Meals served** 12.30-3pm, 7.30pm-midnight Mon, Tue, Thur-Sun. Closed 3wks Aug. **€-€€€**. **Pizzeria/Italian**. **Map** p142 B2 ⑭
This huge Island of Pizza is a throbbing eating factory, with noisy, hungry hordes digging into immense pizzas (served at lunch too, a rarity in Rome), a range of good pasta dishes or great hunks of meat slung on an open fire.

Settembrini

Via Luigi Settembrini 25 (06 323 2617/ www.ristorantesettembrini.it). **Meals served** 12.30-3pm, 8-11pm Mon-Fri; 8-11pm Sat. Closed 2wks Aug. **€€€**. **Creative Italian**. **Map** off p143 D1 ⑮
Settembrini mixes design and tradition both in its warmly minimalist decor and its menu. In chef Luigi Nastri's Italo fusion approach, flavours of southern Italy are prominent and ingredients are sourced with a strong regard for quality. *Aperitivi* are served from 6pm to 8pm.

Shopping

Castroni

Via Cola di Rienzo 196 (06 687 4383). **Open** 8am-8pm Mon-Sat. **Map** p142 C2 ⑯
Not only does this deli have specialities from all over Italy and foreign staples (vegemite? real Indian pickles?) that are notoriously difficult to find in Rome, it also serves (and sells) excellent coffee, and the ice-cream isn't bad either.

Franchi

Via Cola di Rienzo 200 (06 687 4651/ www.franchi.it). **Open** 9am-8.30pm Mon-Sat. **Map** p142 C2 ⑰

This dream of a deli has just about anything you could ever want to eat: cheeses from everywhere, cured meat and fresh, ready-to-eat seafood dishes.

Iron G

Via Cola di Rienzo 50 (06 321 6798/ www.iron-g.com). **Open** 10.30am-7.30pm daily. Closed 2wks Aug. **Map** p143 E2 ⑱
This boutique supplies clubwear for the fashion victims of this well-heeled neighbourhood. Hip labels mix with ethnic and local accessories.

Nightlife

Alexanderplatz

Via Ostia 9 (06 3974 2171/www. alexanderplatz.it). **Open** 8pm-1.30am daily. Closed June-Sept. **Admission** free with monthly (€10) membership. **Map** p142 A2 ⑲
Rome's pioneering jazz club offers nightly concerts with famous names from Italy and beyond. In summer, Alexanderplatz shifts to Villa Celimontana for the park's eponymous Jazz Festival (p40).

The Place

Via Alberico II 27-29 (06 6830 7137/ www.theplace.it). **Open** 7.30pm-2.30am Tue-Sun. Closed mid June-mid Sept. **Admission** €5-€15. **Map** p142 C3 ⑳
A vibrant jazz club with a stage for live acts, the Place draws a thirty- to fortysomething crowd for mostly Italian jazz bands, plus DJs at the weekend. The restaurant serves from 7.30pm, during the 'Sound Check' rehearsal session.

Arts & leisure

El Spa

Via Plinio 15C/D (06 6819 2869/ www.elspa.it). **Open** 10am-9pm Mon-Thur, Sun; 10am-10pm Fri, Sat. Closed 1wk Aug. **Map** p143 D2 ㉑
Decorated in Middle Eastern style, this spa focuses on holistic treatments. Try the *mandi lulur*, an ancient Indonesian treatment that leaves skin silky-soft.

Ostia Antica excavations p157

Out of Town

The Appian Way

Striking out from ancient Rome like so many spokes in a massive wheel were the great consular roads. These carried men and weapons and goods and travellers to all corners of the Empire. The first and greatest of these was the via Appia Antica, known as the *Regina viarum* – the 'queen of roads'.

Built in the fourth century BC by statesman and censor Appius Claudius Caecus, the Appia went first to the strategic city of Capua, near Naples, and was then extended to link *Caput mundi* with the Adriatic at Brindisi in 121 BC.

By the time it reached Brindisi, the Appia was the Romans' main route to their eastern Empire, a perfect thoroughfare for speeding troops and supplies to where they were most needed. In 71 BC, 6,600 followers of rebellious gladiator-slave Spartacus were crucified along the Appia as a warning to other underlings with ideas above their station. But well-to-do Romans chose to end their days here too, building their family mausoleums alongside the road, which was soon lined with tombs, vaults and sarcophagi.

Today, only a fraction of this magnificent funerary decoration remains, but it suffices to make this the most fascinating, and the most picturesque, of the ancient roads.

Christians also began burying their dead here (burial was always performed outside a sacred city boundary known as the *pomerium*), initially in necropoli and later underground, creating the 300-kilometre (200-mile) network of tunnels known as the **catacombs**. This system wasn't used for secret worship, as was once thought: authorities were perfectly aware of their existence. A Jewish catacomb still exists at via Appia Antica 119.

Via Appia Antica suffered at the hands of marauding Goths and Normans; successive popes did as much damage, grabbing any good pieces of statuary or marble that remained and reducing the ancient monuments to unrecognisable stumps. But this is still a wonderful place to spend a day, preferably a Sunday or holiday when all but local traffic is banned.

The www.parcoappiaantica.org website provides exhaustive information for visitors.

You can explore the area more extensively by renting a bike at the **Punto Informativo** (via Appia Antica 58-60, 06 513 5316, €10 per day, open daily); at the **Catacombs of San Sebastiano** (below, €9 per day, closed Sun); or at the Appia Antica Café at via Appia 175 (338 346 5440, closed Mon in Nov-Mar).

Another ancient route lies nearby: the great Roman aqueduct that brought fresh water from the hills near Tivoli dominates the **Parco degli Acquedotti**, accessible from viale Appio Claudio.

Getting there

You can take the hop-on, hop-off **Archeobus** (tickets €13, €8 reductions), which leaves from Termini railway station about every 20 minutes between 9am and 4pm, and stops by most major sights. Alternatively, the following regular bus services ply part of the way:
118 from viale Aventino (Circo Massimo metro) to the catacombs of San Callisto and San Sebastiano.
218 from piazza San Giovanni to Porta San Sebastiano, down the Appia to the Domine Quo Vadis? church, then along via Ardeatina.
660 from Colli Albani metro station to the Circus of Maxentius and Tomb of Cecilia Metella.

Sights & museums

Catacombs of San Callisto
Via Appia Antica 110 (06 5130 1580/ www.catacombe.roma.it). **Open** 9am-noon, 2-5pm Mon, Tue, Thur-Sun. Closed late Jan-late Feb. **Admission** €6; €3 reductions.
This is Rome's largest underground burial site. Buried in the 20km (12 miles) of tunnels are 16 popes, dozens of martyrs and thousands of Christians. They are stacked down, with the oldest on the top. Named after third-century Pope Callixtus, the area became the first official cemetery of the Church of Rome. The crypt of St Cecilia is the spot

The Appian Way p152

where this patron saint of music is believed to have been buried, before she was transferred to her eponymous church in Trastevere.

Catacombs of San Sebastiano

Via Appia Antica 136 (06 785 0350/ www.catacombe.org). **Open** 9am-noon, 2-5pm Mon-Sat. Closed mid Nov-mid Dec. **Admission** €6; €3 reductions.

The name 'catacomb' originated here, where a complex of underground burial sites situated near a tufa quarry was described as being *kata kymbas* – 'near the quarry'. The guided tour will take you into the crypt of St Sebastian, the martyr always depicted nastily pierced by a hail of arrows (though this was just one of several unpleasant forms of torture), who was buried here in the late third century. Above, the fourth-century basilica of San Sebastiano was originally called Basilica Apostolorum, because the remains of Saints Peter and Paul were hidden here. On display is the marble slab in which Christ left his footprints during his miraculous apparition at the spot on the via Appia where the Domine Quo Vadis church (open 7-12.30pm, 2.30-6pm daily) now stands.

Circus of Maxentius

Via Appia Antica 153 (06 780 1324/ www.villadimassenzio.it). **Open** 9am-1.30pm Tue-Sun. **Admission** €3; €1.50 reductions. No credit cards.

This area of lovely green countryside contains one of the best-preserved Roman circuses. It was built by Emperor Maxentius for his private use, before his defeat and death at the hands of co-ruler Constantine in AD 312. Remains of the Imperial palace are perched above the track, at its northern end. Also found on this part of the site is the mausoleum Maxentius built for his beloved son Romulus.

Museo delle Mura

Via di Porta San Sebastiano 18 (06 7047 5284/www.museodellemura roma.it). **Open** 9am-2pm Tue-Sun. **Admission** €3; €1.50 reductions. No credit cards.

Housed inside the San Sebastiano gate, at the head of the Appian Way, this delightful museum not only charts the history of Rome's walls, but allows visitors to hike along the top of them for 350m (1,150 ft). As this guide went to press, the walkway was closed to the public, with no date set for reopening.

Tomb of Cecilia Metella

Via Appia Antica 161 (06 780 0093). **Open** 9am-4.30pm Tue-Sun. **Admission** €6 (includes Baths of Caracalla & Villa dei Quintili); €3 reductions. No credit cards.
Note opening hours are erratic.
This colossal cylinder of travertine is the final resting place of a woman from the wealthy Metella family in the first century BC. During the 14th century, the powerful Caetani family incorporated the tomb into a fortress, adding the crenellations to the top of the structure. The spot where Cecilia was buried is a fine example of brick dome-making. Downstairs, pieces of the volcanic rock used in the construction of via Appia Antica can be seen.

Villa dei Quintili

Via Appia Nuova 1092 (06 712 9121). **Open** 9am-4.30pm Tue-Sun. **Admission** €6 (includes Baths of Caracalla & Tomb of Cecilia Metella); €3 reductions. No credit cards.
Magnificently situated between the ancient and the modern *vie* Appia (but accessible only from the latter), this sumptuous second-century AD villa was owned by the influential Quintili brothers, who were murdered by the Emperor Commodus. The villa closes one hour before sunset throughout the summer months.

EUR

Italian Fascism was at once monstrous and absurd, but out of it came some of 20th-century Europe's most fascinating architecture and urban planning. (See also pp44-46 The Ideal City)

In the early 1930s, Rome's governor Giuseppe Bottai – the leading arbiter of taste among the Fascists – had the idea of expanding landbound Rome along via Ostiense towards the sea, some 20 kilometres (12.5 miles) away. Using as an excuse the universal exhibition

Palazzo della Civiltà del Lavoro

pencilled in for 1942, he intended to combine cultural and exhibition spaces with a monument to the regime: buildings such as the Palazzo dei Congressi and the Palazzo della Civiltà del Lavoro are fine examples.

Architect Marcello Piacentini was charged with co-ordinating the ambitious project, but the planning committee became so bogged down in argument that very little had been achieved by the outbreak of World War II. After the war, work resumed in an entirely different spirit. Still known as EUR (*Esposizione universale romana*), it's now a business district, where unrelieved planes of icy travertine and reinterpretations of classical monuments let you know you're not in Kansas any more.

Several didactic museums – like the **Museo dell'Alto Medioevo**, **Museo della Civiltà Romana** (now containing an astronomy museum), and the **Museo Preistorico ed Etnografico L Pigorini** – allow visitors a glimpse inside these monuments to the hubris of Italian Fascism.

ROME BY AREA

Village of Ostia Antica

Getting there

Take metro B to EUR Fermi
or EUR Palasport, or buses
30Exp, 170, 714.

Sights & museums

Abbazia delle Tre Fontane

Via Acque Salvie 1 (06 540 1655/
www.abbaziatrefontane.com). **Open**
Santi Vincenzo e Anastasio 6.45am-
12.30pm, 3-8.45pm daily. *Other*
churches 8am-1pm, 3-6pm daily.
Shop 9.30am-1pm, 3.30-7pm daily.
Admission free.
North-east of EUR centre (and reach-
able by bus 767) lies a haven of
ancient, eucalyptus-scented green,
with three churches commemorating
the points where St Paul's head supposedly bounced after it was severed
in AD 67. (Being a Roman citizen,
Paul was eligible for the relatively
quick head-chop, as opposed to the
long, drawn-out crucifixion.) These
are the grounds of the Trappist
monastery of Tre Fontane, where

water has gurgled and birds have
sung since the fifth century. The
church of San Paolo delle Tre Fontane
is said to be built on the spot where
the apostle was executed; apart from
a column to which Paul is supposed
to have been tied, all traces of the
fifth-century church were destroyed
in 1599 by architect Giacomo della
Porta, who was also responsible for
the two other churches. Monks planted the eucalyptus trees in the 1860s,
believing they would drive away the
malarial mosquitoes; a liqueur is now
brewed from the trees and sold in a
little shop along with chocolate and
remedies for all ills.

Museo dell'Alto Medioevo

Viale Lincoln 3 (06 5422 8199). **Open**
9am-2pm Tue-Sun. **Admission** €2;
€1 reductions. No credit cards.
Focusing on the decorative arts from the
period between the fall of the Roman
Empire and the Renaissance, this museum has gold- and silver-decorated
swords, buckles and horse tackle, plus
more mundane objects: ceramic bead

jewellery and the metal frames of what may be Europe's earliest folding chairs.

Museo della Civiltà Romana

Piazza G Agnelli 10 (06 5422 0919/ www.museociviltaromana.it). **Open** *Museum* 9am-2pm Tue-Sat; 9am-1.30pm Sun. *Planetarium* 9am-2pm Tue-Fri; 9am-7pm Sat, Sun. **Admission** *Museum* €6.50; €4.50 reductions. *Planetarium* (booking obligatory 06 0608) €6.50; €4.50 reductions. *Joint ticket* €8.50; €6.50 reductions. No credit cards.

With its blank white walls and lofty, echoing corridors, this building, from 1937, is Fascist-classical at its most grandiloquent. There's a fascinating cutaway model of the Colosseum's maze of tunnels and lifts, as well as casts of the intricate reliefs on Trajan's column. The centrepiece is a giant model of Rome in the fourth century AD, which puts the city's scattered fragments and artefacts into context. The palazzo also contains the Museo dell'Astrologia and a planetarium (www.planetarioroma.it).

Museo Preistorico ed Etnografico L Pigorini

Piazzale G Marconi 14 (06 549 521/ www.pignorini.art.beniculturali.it). **Open** 9am-2pm Tue-Sun. **Admission** €6; €3 reductions. No credit cards.

Prehistoric Italian artefacts together with material from a range of world cultures are on display here. The lobby contains a reconstruction of the prehistoric Guattari cave near Monte Circeo, south of Rome, with a genuine Neanderthal skull. The ethnological collection is on the first floor; the second floor has archaeological finds from digs all over Italy.

Ostia Antica

A new high-speed train service means that Pompeii is just over two hours from Rome. But you can save yourself the stress and expense with a jaunt to ancient Rome's port instead. There's no looming volcano or carbonised bodies, but the excavated ruins (*scavi*) of Ostia Antica convey

Viterbo, medieval miracle

The Christian hey-day of the out-of-the-way town.

It was only briefly, and only in the 13th century, that Viterbo became the nerve centre of the Christian world. But this short burst of glory explains the unexpected medieval magnificence of this sleepy city north of Rome.

Transport links back then were good: Viterbo straddled the much-trodden via Francigena (www.via francigena.com) pilgrim route from Canterbury to Rome. Nowadays, a single-track railway line from San Pietro or Ostiense stations (€9 return) takes you there, past the pointy extinct volcanoes and perfectly circular lakes of the Roman *campagna*.

While *Caput mundi* shuddered from one wave of anarchy to another, the 100km (62 miles) that separated it from Viterbo made popes feel safe there… until 1305 when they gave up on Italy completely, and removed the seat of the papacy to Avignon.

The walled city was built to last, in massive dark grey blocks of volcanic tufa. Some of the earliest masonry is still visible in piazza del Palazzo dei Papi, where it formed the foundations of the Roman temple of Hercules. This main square looks like a film set, with its crenellated loggia and the vast conclave hall (five popes were elected in Viterbo in 1266-81), plus its stripey two-tone belltower and its Romanesque cathedral, which was given a fashionable new façade in the 16th century.

A second wave of money poured into the city under Renaissance Pope Sixtus IV: you can see the oak-tree coat of arms of his Della Rovere family on the magnificent Palazzo dei Priori in piazza del Plebiscito, the town hall. The city boasts 100 impressive fountains, and many fine early churches, like the tiny jewel-like San Sisto, Santa Maria Nuova (a treasure house of early art), San Francesco alla Rocca (with two intricate cosmatesque papal tombs), and the cloistered monastery buildings of Santa Maria in Gradi (now part of the Tuscia University) where St Thomas Aquinas preached and wrote.

Since then, Viterbo has been very much a backwater, which makes its wonderful state of preservation a surprise. In fact, it wasn't until the Allies' carpet bombing of railway yards on two sides of the city in World War II that Viterbo suffered much damage or underwent any change.
■ Ufficio turistico, via Ascenzi 4, 0761 325 992.

the everyday life of a working Roman town every bit as well as Pompeii does.

Five minutes' walk from the entrance to the excavations, the medieval village of Ostia Antica has a castle (built in 1483-86 for the bishop of Ostia, the future Pope Julius II) and picturesque cottages, which were inhabited by the people who worked in the nearby salt pans.

Getting there

Ostia Antica is a 20-minute train ride from Roma-Lido station, next to Piramide metro.

Sights & museums

Scavi di Ostia Antica

Viale dei Romagnoli 717, Ostia Antica (06 5635 8099/www.itnw.roma.it/ ostia/scavi). **Open** *Nov-Feb* 8.30am-4pm Tue-Sun. **Admission** €6.50; €3.25 reductions. No credit cards.
Legend has it that Ostia was founded by Ancus Martius, the fourth king of Rome, in the seventh century BC, although the oldest remains date from 'only' c330 BC. Ostia was Rome's main port for more than 600 years.

Abandoned after sackings by barbarians in the fifth century, the town was gradually buried by river mud. Over the centuries, the coastline has receded, leaving Ostia landlocked and obsolete. Visit on a sunny weekday and bring a picnic (not actually allowed but keep a low profile and you probably won't be ejected). It's open until 7.30pm in summer.

The *decumanus maximus* (high street) runs from the Porta Romana for almost a kilometre (half a mile), past the theatre and forum, before forking left to what used to be the seashore. The right fork, via della Foce, leads to the Tiber. Either side of these main arteries lies a network of intersecting lanes where the best discoveries can be made.

Behind the theatre is one of Ostia's most interesting features: the Forum of the Corporations. Here the trade guilds had their offices, and mosaics on the floor of shops that ring the open square refer to the products each guild dealt in – shipowners had ships on the floor, ivory dealers had elephants. Further along on the right is the old mill, where the furrows ploughed by the blindfolded donkeys that turned them are still visible. In the tangle of streets between the decumanus and the museum, don't miss the *thermopolium* – an ancient Roman bar. Located off the forum to the south-east are the forum baths and nearby is the *forica*, or ancient public latrine. Off via della Foce, the House of Cupid and Psyche is an elegant fourth-century construction; the House of the Dioscuri has beautiful mosaics; the Insula of the Charioteers still has many of its frescoes.

A dusty old museum (same hours) contains bits of statuary etc from the digs, plus there's a shiny new café and bookshop... though mangy dogs may bar your path as you approach.

Tivoli

Just 20 kilometres (12.5 miles) from Rome, Tivoli (ancient Tibur) is home to two UNESCO World Heritage Sites – **Villa d'Este**, in Tivoli itself, and **Hadrian's Villa**, five kilometres (three miles) down the hill – which make it an ideal destination for a day trip.

Getting there

Take the COTRAL bus from Ponte Mammolo metro station; note that the bus marked *autostrada* is a quicker service. If you're travelling by bus, visit Tivoli town first (the regular service is marked 'via Tiburtina' and takes about 45mins to Tivoli) and get off at the main square

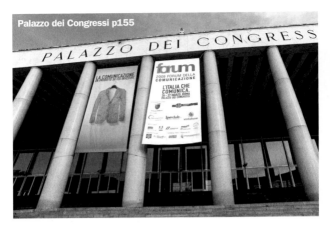

(piazza Garibaldi) for Villa d'Este. From the bus stop in front of the tourist office in piazza Garibaldi, frequent orange (local) buses serve Villa Adriana (10 mins) down the hill. From Villa Adriana, both local and COTRAL buses travel to Rome.

Local trains go to Tivoli from Tiburtina station; bus 4 goes from Tivoli station to the centre of town for the Villa d'Este.

Sights & museums

Hadrian's Villa (Villa Adriana)

Via di Villa Adriana, Villa Adriana (0774 382 733). **Open** 9am-5pm daily. **Admission** €6.50; €3.25 reductions; extra charge during exhibitions. No credit cards.

Villa Adriana, the retreat of Emperor Hadrian, is strewn across a gentle slope. Built from AD 118 to 134, it has some fascinating architectural spaces and water features.

Hadrian was an amateur architect and it is believed that he designed many of the elements in his magnificent villa himself. In the centuries following the fall of the Roman Empire, the villa became a luxury quarry for treasure-hunters. At least 500 pieces of statuary in collections around the world have been identified as coming from this site. The restored remains lie amid olive groves and cypresses and are magnificently impressive. The model in the pavilion up the hill from the entrance gives an idea of the villa's original size.

Where the original entrance to the villa lay is still uncertain; today the first space you'll encounter after climbing the road from the ticket office is the *pecile* (or *poikile*), a large pool that was once surrounded by a portico with high walls, of which only one remains. Directly east of the *poikile*, the *Teatro marittimo* (Maritime Theatre) is one of the most delightful inventions in the whole villa. A circular brick wall, 45m (150ft) in diameter, encloses a moat, at the centre of which is an island of columns and brickwork; today a cement bridge crosses the moat, but originally there would have been wooden bridges, which could be removed.

Beneath the building called the winter palace, visitors can walk along the perfectly preserved *cryptoporticus* (covered corridor).

ROME BY AREA

In the valley below is the lovely *canopus*: a long, narrow pool, framed on three sides by columns and statues, including a marble crocodile. At the far (southern) end of the pool is a structure called the *serapeum*, used for lavish entertaining. Summer guests enjoyed an innovative form of air-conditioning – a sheet of water poured from the roof over the open face of the building, enclosing diners.

Villa d'Este

Piazza Trento 1, Tivoli (0774 332 920/www.villadestetivoli.info). **Open** 8.30am-1hr before sunset Tue-Sun. **Admission** €6.50; €3.25 reductions. No credit cards.

Dominating the town of Tivoli is the Villa d'Este, a lavish pleasure palace built in 1550 for Cardinal Ippolito d'Este, son of Lucrezia Borgia, to a design by architect Pirro Ligorio. Inside the villa there are frescoes and paintings by Correggio, Da Volterra and Perin Del Vaga (including views of the villa shortly after its construction). But the gardens are the main attraction. Ligorio developed a complex 'hydraulic machine' that channelled water from the River Aniene (still the source today) through a series of canals under the garden. Using know-how borrowed from the Romans, he created 51 fountains spread around the terraced gardens. The sibyls (pagan high-priestesses) are a recurring theme – it was at Tivoli that the Tiburtine sibyl foretold the birth of Christ – and the grottoes of the sibyls behind the vast fountain of Neptune echo with thundering artificial waterfalls.

Technological gimmickry was also a big feature; the Owl Fountain (operates every two hours from 10am) imitated an owl's song using a hydraulic mechanism, while the *Fontana dell'organo idraulico* (restored and in operation every two hours from 10.30am) used water pressure to compress air and play tunes.

Electric carts are provided free for disabled visitors to tour the gardens; booking is essential (0774 335 850).

Low cost relocation

Anyone who's run the gauntlet of Rome's Ciampino airport (p180) will understand that international transit through the Italian capital was badly in need of a shake-up. However, a September 2008 decision to relocate low-cost flights to Viterbo (p158) – its airport brought up to scratch with a €700 million cash injection – by 2013 has prompted protests from all sides, not least from Ryanair, which announced it would boycott the new airport.

Ciampino was Rome's main airport until Fiumicino (p180) took over the role in the 1960s; the former then became a small military and charter hub. Lack of space to expand meant little could be added in the way of facilities to handle traffic, which, after the advent of low-cost carriers, had grown to 5.4 million passengers a year by 2007.

But despite Ciampino's inadequacies, this airport does offer advantages over Viterbo: most importantly, it's 15km from Rome centre, and though there's no good train link, buses run fairly swiftly into town.

The 65km (40-mile) run into Rome from Viterbo, on the other hand, is covered by the log-jammed via Cassia, and by a commuter railway line that can barely cope with current passenger levels. And promises by local authorities to provide new transport links by 2013 have been met with disbelief: building infrastructure in Italy is always a painfully slow process.

MOZART
Hotel & Suites
R O M A
Via dei Greci 23\b - 00187 Roma

www.hotelmozart.com - info@hotelmozart.com - tel.+39 06 36001915

Essentials

Casa Montani p172

Hotels

Rome is no city for hotel bargains: despite a drop-off in tourist numbers in 2007-8, it remains a seller's market, and, with a few exceptions – both on the positive side and the negative – you will get what you pay for.

There are four- and five-star options aplenty, with generous lashings of high concept design. And cheap, though not always salubrious, backpacking options abound around the Termini station area. The gap in the centre where charming two- and three-stars should cater to more demanding travellers with lower credit limits is slowly filling out.

Greater competition over the past few years from the boutique hotels popping up around the *centro storico* means that older-style hotels and *pensioni* are being forced to upgrade both amenities and decor if they want to stay in business. The appearance on the scene of such small gems as **Casa Montani** (p172) will help this process along.

It's only at the lower end that Rome is still lagging behind: in all but a few notable cases – for example, the **Beehive** (p175) and the **Okapi Rooms** (p175) – the gulf in standards between rock bottom and the lower edge of moderate is immense: in Rome, it's worth paying just that little bit more. Either that, or go out on a limb, for example with a very un-Roman camping experience.

Location

There are three five-star hotels close to Termini station, but the vast majority of hotels in this area – the **Esquilino** – are cheap *pensioni* swarming with backpackers. It's not Rome's most picturesque corner, and almost certainly not what you dreamt of for your Roman holiday. It's definitely worth considering looking further afield.

A room in the *centro storico* offers many advantages, not least of which are a shower between

ESSENTIALS

sightseeing and dinner, and a pleasant stroll (rather than a bus) back to the hotel afterwards. The area around **campo de' Fiori** offers mid-priced hotels with lots of character, and a central piazza that is a lively market by day and a hip Roman hangout by night (though don't stay too late, as it gets rowdy as the evening wears on); the area around the **Pantheon** and **piazza Navona** is generally a bit pricier. Moving distinctly up the price range, Rome's top-end hotels have traditionally clustered around **via Veneto**; it's nothing like as lively as it was in its *dolce vita* heyday, and there's a strong whiff of expense accounts in the air. But brave efforts are underway to relaunch this famous street, and it definitely has a certain grandeur. The **Tridente** area near the Spanish Steps, hub of designer shopping, is full of elegant hotels at the upper end of the price scale.

If you're looking for some peace, the **Celio**, just beyond the Colosseum, offers a break from the frantic activity of the *centro storico*, as does another of Rome's seven hills: the **Aventine**, an exclusive residential outpost no distance at all from the *centro*.

Heading across the river, the characterful **Trastevere** district is a pleasant place to stay, with good bus and tram connections to the major sights; in recent years it has blossomed from hotel-desert to hotel-bonanza, offering an array of price options. Just north of here, the medieval alleys around the **Vatican** give on to the busy retail thoroughfares of **Prati**: it's lively during the day but hushed at night.

Booking a room

Always reserve a room well in advance, especially at peak times, which now means most of the year,

SHORTLIST

Newcomers
- Casa Montani (p172)
- Crossing Condotti (p169)
- Donna Camilla Savelli (p179)
- Leon's Place (p177)
- Residenza Santa Maria (p179)

Utter luxury
- De Russie (p173)
- Exedra (p177)
- Hassler Villa Medici (p173)
- St Regis Grand (p178)
- Westin Excelsior (p175)

Great cooking
- Baby at Hotel Aldrovandi (box p166)
- Filippo la Mantia at Hotel Majestic (box p166)
- La Pergola at Rome Cavalieri (box p166)

Cool pools
- Exedra (p177)
- Radisson SAS es. Hotel (p178)

Chic & cheap
- The Beehive (p175)
- Daphne Inn (p172)
- Relais Palazzo Taverna (p171)

Bargain hotels & hostels
- Foresteria Orsa Maggiore (p179)
- Pensione Paradise (p179)

Stunning suites
- La Cupola at the Westin Excelsior (p175)
- Garden Suite at the Inn at the Roman Forum (p177)
- Grand Suite at the Exedra (p177)
- Pompeian suite at the Hotel Celio (p177)
- Royal Suite at the St Regis Grand (p178)

ESSENTIALS

Hotel meals

Imàgo

Perhaps because of the wealth of great food on offer out in the streets of Rome, the city's hotels have never (with one exception) cut the mustard on the culinary front.

But top-ranking chefs have, of late, come round to the concept of hotel cuisine, and four of Rome's top eateries are now in hotels.

La Pergola (Rome Cavalieri, via Cadlolo 101, 06 35 091, www.romecavalieri.it, dinner for two €400 plus wine) is a Rome classic, and the only restaurant in this city of food to boast three Michelin stars. Given the position – high up on Monte Mario – you might think people go for the view. But with food like this on your plate, the view pales. German chef Heinz Beck creates an ever-changing menu of daring perfection. Utterly fresh, utterly flavoursome, it also has an award-winning cellarful of wine.

Alfonso Iaccarino's **baby** (Aldrovandi Palace, via U Aldrovandi 15, 06 321 6126, www.aldrovandi.com, dinner for two €220 plus wine), the pool-side restaurant inside Hotel Aldrovandi, brings all the wondrous flavours of the chef's southern Campania region to the capital. Iaccarino's

Don Alfonso restaurant above the Amalfi Coast has two Michelin stars; in 2009, baby got one too. Organic ingredients from his farms are on the plate at both places.

Chef Francesco Apreda began his cooking career very young at the Hassler hotel but experienced kitchens in London (Le Gavroche) and Tokyo before returning to the Hassler as executive chef, and overseeing the rebirth of its rooftop restaurant as **Imàgo** (Hassler, piazza Trinità dei Monti 6, 06 6993 4726, www.imago restaurant.com, dinner for two €190 plus wine) in 2006. Apreda's dishes abound with the freshest of vegetables, and his travels tell on this Italian menu with a difference.

Bursting on to the hotel-food scene in spring 2009 with his irrepressible Sicilian ebullience, news photographer turned chef **Filippo La Mantia** left his post at the successful Trattoria restaurant in the *centro storico* to take up his pots and pans in the kitchen of the Hotel Majestic (via V Veneto 50, 06 421 441, www.rome-hotels-majestic.com, dinner for two €150 plus wine). La Mantia's delicate, onion-free, citrus-perfumed touch is the keynote here.

with lulls during winter (January to March) and in the dog days of August. If you're coming at the same time as a major Christian holiday (Christmas or Easter) it's recommended to book weeks, or even months, ahead.

Booking is almost always via hotel websites, but smaller places may asked for a fax confirming a booking, with a credit card number as deposit. The www. venere.com booking service offers many hotels in all price ranges. The **Hotel Reservation** (www. hotelreservation.it/06 699 1000) service, which has desks at Fiumicino airport, Ciampino airport and at Termini station, offers a free booking service.

Avoid the touts that hang around Termini: you're likely to end up paying more than you should for a very grotty hotel.

Standards & prices

Italian hotels are classified on a star system, from one to five. One star usually indicates *pensioni*, which are cheap but have very few facilities; you may have to share a bathroom. The more stars, the more facilities a hotel will have, but bear in mind that a higher rating offers no guarantee of friendliness, cleanliness or decent service.

Prices generally rise by a relentless ten per cent a year in Rome, but it's worth keeping an eye out for good deals on hotel websites: many now operate a booking system similar to low-cost airlines, with room prices determined by demand in any given period. If you're staying in a group or for a longish period, ask about discounts.

If you're visiting with children, most hotels will be happy to squeeze a cot or camp bed into a room, but they will probably charge 30 to 50 per cent extra for the privilege.

Alternative accommodation

If you're travelling with children and/or staying for a while, you might prefer to opt for an apartment rental. Websites like www.myhomeyourhome.it, www.romanreference.com and www.flatinrome.com have many on their books. London-based www.aplaceinrome.com has a delightful few. For B&B accommodation, check out www.bbitalia.it or www.b-b.rm.it.

Flaminio Village (via Flaminia Nuova 821, 06 333 2604/06 3322 0505, www.villageflaminio.it) offers a place to pitch your tent, as well as bungalows to rent in landscaped gardens with a large swimming pool and good facilities.

Some religious institutes offer cheap (though not always cheerful) accommodation. Find them through www.monasterystays.com, www.santasusanna.org or www.hospites.it.

Our choice

The hotels listed in this guide have been chosen for their location, because they offer value for money, or simply because they have true Roman character. Unless stated, rates are for rooms with bathrooms, and include breakfast. Our price categories refer to standard double rooms in high season; at quieter times, many hotels slash prices by as much as 50 per cent.

In the deluxe category (€€€€) the emphasis is on luxury; a standard double will cost over €400. Those in mid- to upper-price ranges are smaller, many in old *palazzi*, with pretty, though often small, bedrooms. Expect to pay €120 to €250 for a moderately priced hotel (€€), and anywhere from €250 to €400 for an expensive room (€€€).

ESSENTIALS

Albergo Cesàri

since 1787

★ ★ ★

Your three stars in the heart of Rome

Established in 1787, the Albergo Cesàri remains an island of peaceful elegance in the heart of Rome, ideally situated between the Fontana di Trevi and the Pantheon.

The hotel was built during the first half of the 18th century, and has accommodated many famous figures, including Stendhal and Gregorovius.

Completely refurbished in 2007, the hotel now features 47 sound-proof guestrooms including new 10 superior rooms. All rooms are equipped with satellite television and pay-per-view, air conditioning, mini-bar, in room safe, hairdryer, direct-dial telephone and complimentary coffee and tea making facilities. Additional amenities include DSL Internet station, Wi-Fi connection free of charge in rooms and throughout the hotel, buffet breakfast and a private garage near the hotel (at extra cost). Non-smoking floors are also available.

The hotel's new Roof Garden has a bar and lounge area with spectacular views of the Eternal City.

A tourist's dream locale, the hotel is close to Rome's most important theatres, trendy restaurants, and fashionable streets such as Via Condotti, Via Veneto, and Piazza di Spagna - home to Armani, Versace, Valentino and many other famous designer boutiques.

LOCATION

Albergo Cesàri is only a few minutes from the Termini Main Railway Station, the Leonardo train to Fiumicino Airport, and is also a convenient walking distance from bus and metro access stations.

00186 Roma - Via di Pietra, 89/a
Tel. + 39 06 6749701 Fax + 39 06 67497030
info @albergocesari.it - booking @albergocesari.it
www.albergocesari.it

Pensioni are fairly basic, but those listed here are friendly and usually family-run; you'll be very hard pressed to find a half-decent double room for less than €120 per night.

Few Roman hotels – with the exception of the grander ones – have access for the disabled. Though staff are generally very willing to help guests who have mobility difficulties, the real problem is that most places have so many stairs that there's not much they can do. As hotels renovate, they do tend to add a room for the disabled if they can.

A no-smoking law introduced in 2005 applies to hotels' public areas. Some hotels are still fairly laissez-faire when it comes to guests lighting up in the rooms so long as they open a window, but if you can't do without your nicotine, check this before booking

Relais Palazzo Taverna p171

Il Centro

Abruzzi

Piazza della Rotonda 69 (06 9784 1351/ www.hotelabruzzi.it). **€€**.
The location is this hotel's main selling point. Recent renovations have up graded what used to be a dingy establishment. Many rooms have great views of the Pantheon; some are very small.

Campo de' Fiori

Piazza del Biscione 6 (06 6880 6865/ www.hotelcampodefiori.com). **€€**.
Just off busy campo de' Fiori, this hotel underwent a complete renovation in 2006, with impressive results: though not spacious, the rooms are finely fitted out in rich colours. The small but elegant bathrooms have bronze-effect tiles with antique mirrors. The pretty roof terrace has great views.

Crossing Condotti

NEW *Via Mario de' Fiori 28 (06 6992 0633/www.crossingcondotti.com).* **€€€**.
This brand-new five-room hotel is remarkably central: a short stroll from

Prada, Bulgari and other fashion heavyweights. There's free Wi-Fi and antique furniture, but decor is just slightly too conventional. At the lower end of this price range.

Due Torri

Vicolo del Leonetto 23 (06 6880 6956/ www.hotelduetorriroma.com). **€€**.
In a labyrinth of cobbled streets, the Due Torri has a welcoming feel. The 26 rooms are cosy rather than spacious, and kitted out with dark wooden furniture. If you're persistent, you might get one of the rooms with a private terrace overlooking the rooftops.

Pensione Barrett

Largo Argentina 47 (06 686 8481/ www.pensionebarrett.com). **€**.
A bewildering number of antiques and curios decorate this hotel, giving it an eccentric feel. Rooms are a mishmash of faux-classical columns and mouldings, dark wood furniture, wood-beamed ceilings and pastel walls; some have great views over largo

ESSENTIALS

ROME: MEDITERRANEO
MASSIMO D'AZEGLIO
ATLANTICO - NORD
FLORENCE: RELAIS CERTOSA

WWW.BETTOJAHOTELS.IT
TOLL-FREE 800.860004

THE TRADITION OF HOSPITALITY

ROME IN THE HEART OF THE CITY
FLORENCE A VILLA SURROUNDED BY A GARDEN

HB BETTOJA HOTELS
ROME - FLORENCE

Argentina. Breakfast is not included. Poet Elizabeth Barrett Browning stayed in this building in 1848.

Relais Palazzo Taverna & Locanda degli Antiquari

Via dei Gabrielli 92 (06 2039 8064/ www.relaispalazzotaverna.com). €€.
In a 15th-century building, these twin *residenze* have sleek, modern decor. Spacious bedrooms have white-painted wood ceilings, wallpaper with bold graphics and bedlinen in spicy tones. Breakfast is served in the rooms.

Residenza in Farnese

Via del Mascherone 59 (06 6821 0980/ www.residenzafarneseroma.it). €€.
This converted convent in a narrow ivy-lined alley has been refurbished without losing its charm. A chandelier in the lobby lends a sense of opulence; home-made jams for breakfast reflect the homely charm of the place. Rooms run the gamut from basic updated cells with small marble bathrooms to more comfortable pastel-hued rooms with hand-painted furnishings. At the higher end of this price range.

St George Roma

Via Giulia 62 (06 686 611/ www.stgeorgehotel.it). €€€€.
This new five-star on gorgeous via Giulia is a study in coolly elegant designer neutrals and dark wood, with lashings of travertine in public spaces and bathrooms, and the odd deco-inspired detail. There's a spa – with small indoor pool – in the basement, a cigar lounge and a rooftop terrace.

Sole al Pantheon

Piazza della Rotonda 63 (06 678 0441/ www.hotelsolealpantheon.com). €€€.
Dating back to the 15th century, the Sole al Pantheon is one of Europe's oldest hotels. Rooms have a fresh feel, though, with tiles and pretty frescoes. Bathrooms are not luxurious but they do have whirlpool baths. Rooms at the front have great views of the Pantheon.

Book at bedtime

Rabelais, Montaigne and Goethe lodged at the ancient Hostaria dell'Orso (now reinvented as a chic luxury restaurant), while Ludovico Ariosto favoured the Sole al Pantheon, which first opened its doors to guests in 1467 and is still going strong (below, left). Charles Dickens and Henry James were put up at the luxe De Russie (p173). And George Eliot and Thomas Mann stayed at the Hotel Internazionale (but not together).

Rome inspired many writers, but not all could afford to stay at the city's premier establishments. Most – like Keats, Shelley, James Joyce and Walter Scott – rented humble apartments. Others stayed with friends: Gogol dreamed up *Dead Souls* while relaxing in the delicious grottoes of Russian Princess Wolkonsky's magnificent villa – now the British ambassador's residence.

Wherever they stayed – and the city is dotted with plaques recording the visits of novelists and poets – they found inspiration. To keep the tradition alive, a group of Italian hotels has formed the **Golden Book** association (Roman members include the Hotel Celio, p177 and the Sole al Pantheon), which publishes literary volumes for its patrons and also promotes the Eureka! competition. This encourages aspiring writers to produce travel-linked tales. Guests to Rome this year will find a collection of the best tucked under their pillowcases.
■ www.goldenbookhotels.it

ESSENTIALS

Aleph

Teatro di Pompeo

Largo del Pallaro 8 (06 6830 0170/
www.hotelteatrodipompeo.it). €€.
This small, friendly hotel occupies a
palazzo that was built on the site of the
ancient Teatro di Pompeo; its *pièce de
résistance* is its cave-like breakfast
room, tucked away inside the ancient
ruins. The guest rooms are simply decorated in neutral tones, with terracotta
floors and high, wood-beamed ceilings.
Opt for one of the rooms in the main
hotel building rather than those in the
more basic annexe a few streets away.

Teatro Pace 33

Via del Teatro Pace 33 (06 687 9075/
www.hotelteatropace.com). €€.
On a cobbled alley near piazza Navona,
this 17th-century former cardinal's residence has a Baroque spiral staircase
that winds up four floors (there's no lift,
but chairs are provided every couple of
floors so you can catch your breath).
Rooms are spacious and elegantly decorated with wood floors, heavy drapes
and marble bathrooms; all have their
original beamed ceilings. Breakfast is

served in the rooms. Good low-season
deals can be had on the hotel website.

Tridente & Borghese

Aleph

Via di San Basilio 15 (06 422 901/
www.boscolohotels.com). €€€€.
This Adam Tihany-designed hotel with
a theme – heaven and hell – has common
areas in various intensities of devil-red,
and bright, 'heavenly' bedrooms. It's a
world away from the luxe-but-dull decor
of many of via Veneto's mega-hotels,
making it a favourite of the fashion set.
A top-floor terrace bar and restaurant
operate in warmer months; there's a sub-
terranean spa in white and icy blue.
Rooms are modern and luxurious.

Casa Howard

Via Capo le Case 18 (06 6992 4555/
www.casahoward.com). €€.
All rooms in this beautiful *residenza*
near piazza di Spagna have been
designed with an emphasis on quality.
Some rooms have (private) bathrooms
along the hall. There's a Turkish bath
too. The five new (and slightly more
expensive) rooms added around the
corner at via Sistina 149 have ensuite
bathrooms. Massages can be arranged
at both properties.

Casa Montani

NEW *Piazzale Flaminio 9 (06 3260
0421/www.casamontani.it). €€.*
This delightful five-room townhouse
overlooking the Porta del Popolo gate is
a rarity in Rome: charming, exquisitely
decorated, impeccably run... and good
value. A delicious breakfast is served in
the rooms: Wi-Fi internet is free.

Daphne Inn

*Via degli Avignonesi 20; via di
San Basilio 55 (06 4782 3529/
www.daphne-rome.com). €€.*
The Daphne Inn has two locations: one
near the Trevi Fountain, the other off
via Veneto. Each has seven rooms –
some with ensuite baths and some that

share – all of which are fitted out in organic-modern style with terracotta floors, neutral tones and simple framed leaf prints on the walls. Excellent value and a warm welcome.

De Russie

Via del Babuino 9 (06 328 881/ www.roccofortecollection.com). €€€€. The De Russie's modern elegance is a million miles away from the luxury-schmaltz of many hotels on via Veneto. Fabulous gardens and a state-of-the-art health centre make it a star-magnet. Some rooms are smaller and less opulent than you might expect.

Eden

Via Ludovisi 49 (06 478 121/ www.lemeridien.com/eden). €€€€. Elegantly understated, the Eden offers the attentiveness and attention to detail of a top-notch hotel without the stuffiness. Handsome reception rooms, tastefully decorated bedrooms, and a roof terrace with restaurant, piano bar and truly spectacular views are plus points.

Fontanella Borghese

Largo Fontanella Borghese 84 (06 6880 9504/www.fontanella borghese.com). €€. This hotel is elegantly done out in relaxing cream and muted colours. Shopping meccas via del Corso and via Condotti are just around the corner: it's an ideal bolthole when the credit cards start to melt.

Hassler Villa Medici

Piazza Trinità dei Monti 6 (06 699 340/ www.hotelhasslerroma.com). €€€€. This is one of Rome's classic hotels, with all the trimmings you might expect: chandeliers everywhere, polished wood and marble, plush fabrics and grand oil paintings, and a garden out back. The attentiveness of the staff distinguishes the Hassler from the impersonal top chain hotels in Rome. A few steps away, and with a royal box view over the Spanish Steps, is Il Palazzetto (vicolo del

Hotel Art

Bottino 8, www.ilpalazzettoroma.com), an annexe under the same ownership.

Hotel Art

Via Margutta 56 (06 328 711/ www.hotelart.it). €€€. On a street famed for its art studios, this hotel's lobby has white pods serving as check-in and concierge desks. Hallways are in retina-burning shades, but bedrooms have creamy bedlinens and dark wood furniture. There's a small gym.

Inn at the Spanish Steps

Via Condotti 85 (06 6992 5657/ www.atspanishsteps.com). €€€€. The Inn at the Spanish Steps offers luxury boutique-hotel accommodation on one of the world's most famous shopping streets. Rooms are an extravagant mix of plush fabrics and antiques; some of the deluxe rooms have 17th-century frescoes. Just down the road, its sister establishment – View at the Spanish Steps – has more restrained decor, with sober grey and blue fabrics, darkwood floors and black-and-white tiled bathrooms.

ESSENTIALS

Okapi Rooms

*Via della Penna 57 (06 3260 9815/
www.okapirooms.it).* €.
Sticking with the exotic beast theme,
owners of the Pensione Panda (below)
have opened this fresh, bright outpost
a stone's throw from piazza del Popolo.
Though pretty basic and reportedly
noisy at times, Okapi Rooms offers air-
con and internet access, and one room
has a little terrace.

Pensione Panda

*Via della Croce 35 (06 678 0179/
www.hotelpanda.it).* €.
Panda's location, near the piazza di
Spagna, is its main selling point. Its
rooms are clean but very basic; newly
renovated rooms have high, wood-
beamed ceilings and terracotta floors.
There's no lift and no breakfast, but
centro storico bargains are hard to
come by, and Panda is usually booked
solid in high season.

Portrait Suites

*Via Bocca di Leone 23 (06 6938 0742/
reservations 055 2726 4000/
www.lungarnohotels.com).* €€€€.
Stylish Portrait Suites is owned by
fashion designer Salvatore Ferragamo.
Memorabilia from the company
archives decorate the hallways; in the
bedrooms, a black-and-slate colour
scheme is offset with touches of pink
and lime. There are spacious marble
bathrooms, walk-in wardrobes and a
glamorous kitchenette. Breakfast is
served in the rooms or on the spectacular terrace.

Residenza A

*Via Veneto 183 (06 486 700/
www.hotelviaveneto.com).* €€.
On the first floor of an imposing palazzo,
Residenza A is a boutique hotel with
splashy modern art enlivening its
grey and black colour scheme. The
rooms have been luxuriously finished,
with great extras such as flatscreen
computers and free internet, roomy
showers and Bulgari bath products.

Residenza Cellini

*Via Modena 5 (06 4782 5204/
www.residenzacellini.it).* €€.
This luminous and spacious *residenza*
has huge guest rooms decorated with
faux-antique wooden furniture. The
bathrooms have jacuzzis or showers
with hydro-massage. On the floor
that opened in January 2007, three
rooms have balconies and all are decorated in the same classic style; there's
a terrace too.

Westin Excelsior

*Via V Veneto 125 (06 47 081/www.
westin.com/excelsiorrome).* €€€€.
The Excelsior's public spaces are
lavish and its rooms – with marble
bathrooms – are a Hollywood-style fantasy. The Villa La Cupola suite is the
priciest bed in Rome, rumoured to cost
over €20,000 a night.

Esquilino & Celio

The Beehive

*Via Marghera 8 (06 4470 4553/
www.the-beehive.com).* €.
American owners Steve and Linda
Brenner mix their penchant for design-
icon furnishings with reasonable rates
and basic amenities to create a 'youth
hostel meets boutique hotel' vibe.
There's a sunny garden, an all-organic
restaurant and a yoga studio, plus free
internet access. Breakfast not included.

Capo d'Africa

*Via Capo d'Africa 54 (06 772 801/
www.hotelcapodafrica.com).* €€€.
The Capo d'Africa's lobby may be
somewhat hotel-design-by-numbers but
its location, on a quiet street near the
Colosseum, is great. The rooms are spacious and comfortable, if bland; the
rooftop breakfast room has knock-out
views of the Colosseum.

Domus Sessoriana

*Piazza Santa Croce in Gerusalemme
10 (06 706 151/www.domus
sessoriana.it).* €€.

Reminders of this hotel's past – it's set in the monastery attached to the church of Santa Croce in Gerusalemme – are everywhere, from huge religious canvases to the ex-refectory where breakfast is served. Tastefully decorated rooms are divided into two wings; those in the 'Conventual' wing overlooking the vegetable garden are more pleasant.

Exedra

Piazza della Repubblica 47 (06 489 381/ www.boscolohotels.com). €€€€.
From its splendid porticoed exterior to its opulent lobby, the Exedra is very glamorous. The rooms run from plush and utterly comfortable to outrageous. From May to September, the rooftop bar/restaurant and pool offer spectacular views. There's a spa too. The only drawback is the location: it's a little too close to Termini station for comfort.

Hotel Celio

Via dei Santissimi Quattro 35C (06 7049 5333/www.hotelcelio.com). €€.
With its frescos and mosaic floors, this three-star is a tribute to the arts of the city and definitely plusher-looking than hotels in this price range. Rooms – and bathrooms in particular– are on the tiny side, though, and staff can be frosty.

Inn at the Roman Forum

Via degli Ibernesi 30 (06 6919 0970/ www.theinnattheromanforum.com). €€€€.
This boutique hotel's location, on a quiet, picturesque street, gives it an exclusive feel. Rooms are a sumptuous mix of rich fabrics and antiques; the spacious deluxe rooms have canopied beds and marble bathrooms. Breakfast is served on the roof terrace, or in a cosy room with an open fire. The two executive suites can be booked together as the Master Garden Suite, an exclusive apartment with a walled garden.

Lancelot

Via Capo d'Africa 47 (06 7045 0615/ www.lancelothotel.com). €€.

The Beehive p175

This beautifully kept and attractive family-run hotel has elegant mixes of linen, wood and tiles in the bedrooms, some of which have terraces facing the Palatine and the Colosseum. The reception has been given a personal touch with tiled floors and antique furniture, along with some unusual *objets*.

Leon's Place

NEW *Via XX Settembre 90-94 (06 890 871/www.leonsplacerome.com) €€€.*
This brand-new business-orientated hotel is on the cold side of high-concept design, but if you like your (smallish but perfectly comfortable) room monotone and your bar fluorescent, then this hotel a few doors down from the British embassy is for you. Breakfasts are generous.

Nerva

Via Tor de' Conti 3 (06 678 1835/ www.hotelnerva.com). €€.
The family-run Nerva is handy for the Forum, and the rather old-fashioned rooms have all been refurbished. The staff are a friendly bunch.

ESSENTIALS

Donna Camilla Savelli

Radisson SAS es. Hotel
Via F Turati 171 (06 444 841/
www.rome.radissonsas.com). €€€.
Built on the site of an ancient cemetery,
this 'concept' hotel caters for business
clients – who don't baulk at the location,
by the train station – and diehard design
fans. The stunning rooftop has a bar
and a pool. In the all-white rooms, the
bed is on a low platform, divided from
the bathroom by a glass screen.

St Regis Grand
Via VE Orlando 3 (06 47 091/
www.stregis.com/grandrome). €€€€.
The hotel's original chandeliers dazzle
in massive marbled reception rooms,
decorated in opulent gold, beige and red.
Rooms have been individually designed
using rich fabrics, and are filled with
silk-covered Empire and Regency-style
furnishings. There's a gym and a sauna.

Aventine & Testaccio

Sant'Anselmo,
Villa Pio & Aventino
Piazza di Sant'Anselmo 2/via di
Santa Melania 19 (06 570 057/
www.aventinohotels.com). €€-€€€.

The three hotels in this group are within a stone's throw of one another in an
exclusive, leafy residential area. The
more ornate Sant'Anselmo has recently reopened after refurbishment. The
Villa San Pio consists of three separate
buildings that share the same pretty
gardens and an airy breakfast room; it
has a light feel, making it a pleasant
place to stay. The Aventino is less man-
icured. Some rooms have jacuzzis.

Trastevere & the Gianicolo

Arco del Lauro
Via dell'Arco de' Tolomei 27 (06
9784 0350/www.arcodellauro.it). €.
On a picturesque backstreet, Arco del
Lauro has six tasteful rooms decorated in modern, fresh neutrals. Budget
residenze are few and far between in
chichi Trastevere: this one is airy and
spotlessly clean. Breakfast is taken in
a bar in a nearby piazza.

Buonanotte Garibaldi
Via Garibaldi 83 (06 5833 0733/
www.buonanottegaribaldi.com). €€€.

Artist Luisa Longo's three rooms around a courtyard garden act as a showcase for her distinctive creations: wall panels, bedcovers and curtains in hand-painted silk, organza and velvet. Guests are greeted after a day's sightseeing with a restorative glass of wine.

Casa di Santa Francesca Romana

Via dei Vascellari 61 (06 5812 1252/ www.sfromana.it). **€**.

This ex-convent is now a hotel with a noticeably churchy feel. It's popular with businessmen on a budget and with families (for the spacious quad rooms). Breakfast is served in a lovely courtyard.

Donna Camilla Savelli

NEW *Via Garibaldi 27 (06 588 861/ www.alpitourworldhotels.it).* **€€€**.

A few elderly nuns still wonder the corridors of this former convent – designed by Borromini – striking an odd note in this plush hotel from luxury Italian hotel chain Alpitour. Rooms are in the cells where the nuns once slept, and are therefore on the small side. But they have four-star comforts, marble bathrooms and views over the pretty garden.

Foresteria Orsa Maggiore

Via San Francesco di Sales 1A (06 689 3753/www.foresteriaorsa. altervista.org). **€**.

Inside a 16th-century convent that for years has been home to a feminist cultural centre, this women-only hostel offers B&B accommodation in bright, clean single, double and dorm rooms at rock-bottom prices. The right-on complex also has eateries, exhibition spaces, a bookshop and a fairtrade store.

Hotel Santa Maria

Vicolo del Piede 2 (06 589 4626/ www.hotelsantamaria.info). **€€**.

On the site of a 16th-century convent, the Santa Maria has rooms with cool tiled floors, floral print decor and spacious bathrooms. They all open on to a sunny courtyard with orange trees.

Around the corner at via dell'Arco di San Calisto 20 (06 5833 5103/ www.residenzasantamaria.com, €€), the Residenza Santa Maria is this hotel's charming new offshoot.

Residenza Arco de' Tolomei

Via dell'Arco de' Tolomei 27 (06 5832 0819/www.inrome.info). **€€**.

This bijou *residenza* projects a cosy, welcoming feel. There's beautiful wood flooring, plentiful antiques and a sunny breakfast room. All of the bedrooms are individually designed in a whimsical, English country-house style; the three on the upper floor have terraces, the two below are slightly larger.

Vatican & Prati

Bramante

Vicolo delle Palline 24 (06 6880 6426/ www.hotelbramante.com). **€€**.

Once home to 16th-century architect Domenico Fontana, this became an inn in 1873. It has a large, pleasant reception and a little patio for the summer. The 16 rooms of varying sizes are simple yet elegant; most have high-beamed ceilings, some have wrought-iron beds.

Colors Hotel & Hostel

Via Boezio 31 (06 687 4030/ www.colorshotel.com). **€**.

A short walk from St Peter's, Colors has bright, clean dorm and hotel accommodation, plus self-catering kitchen facilities, and a terrace. Superior rooms have breakfast included. All rooms have aircon. Credit cards are accepted for the superior rooms only.

Pensione Paradise

Viale Giulio Cesare 47 (06 3600 4331/ www.pensioneparadise.com). **€**.

Rooms in this budget hotel are on the poky side, but friendly staff and a decent location ensure that backpackers keep on coming. There's no breakfast and no air-con, but if you're willing to rough it a little, you could do far worse.

Getting Around

Arriving & leaving

Airports

Aeroporto Leonardo da Vinci, Fiumicino

Via dell'Aeroporto di Fiumicino (06 65 951/www.adr.it). **Open** 24hrs daily.
There's an express **rail** service between Fiumicino airport and Termini railway station, which takes 31mins and runs every 30mins from 6.36am until 11.36pm daily (5.52am-10.52pm to Fiumicino). A one-way ticket costs €11.

The regular service from Fiumicino takes 25-40mins, and stops at Trastevere, Ostiense, Tuscolana and Tiburtina stations. Trains leave about every 20mins (less often on Sun) between 5.57am and 11.27pm (5.05am-10.33pm to Fiumicino). Tickets cost €5.50.

Tickets for either service can be bought with cash or credit card from ticket booths or self-ticketing machines. Stamp your ticket in the machines at the head of the platform before boarding, or you risk a fine.

Terravision (06 9761 0632, www.terravision.it) runs a coach service from Fiumicino to Termini, which also makes stops in the northern suburbs (along via Aurelia) and at Lepanto (journey time to Termini: 70mins). As this guide went to press, this service for the handful of low-cost airlines using Fiumicino had been suspended. Check the website for latest details.

During the night, a Cotral **bus** service runs between Fiumicino (outside Terminal C) and Termini and Tiburtina railway stations in Rome; tickets cost €4.50. Buses leave Tiburtina at 12.30am, 1.15am, 2.30am and 3.45am, stopping at Termini railway station 10mins later. Departures from Fiumicino are at 1.15am, 2.15am, 3.30am and 5am. Neither Termini nor Tiburtina are attractive places at night, so it's advisable to get a taxi on from there to your final destination.

Aeroporto GB Pastine, Ciampino

Via Appia Nuova 1651 (06 65 951/ www.adr.it). **Open** 24hrs daily.
Though bus services claim to run into the early morning, often they don't. Booking tickets online before you leave home may signal to bus drivers not to pack up early. Taxi drivers at this airport have a reputation for preying on tourists.

On paper at least, the most hassle-free way to get into town from Ciampino is to take a coach. **Terravision** runs services to Termini station (journey time: 40mins). Buses leave from outside the arrivals hall after each arrival. Buses from Termini to Ciampino leave from via Marsala. This is a dedicated service for low-cost airlines, so you'll need to show your ticket or boarding pass to buy a ticket (€8 single, €14 return; €4/€7 reductions), which can be booked online with a discount, or bought (cash only) in Arrivals at Ciampino, at the Terravision office in the Termini forecourt or on the bus.

SIT Bus Shuttle (06 591 6826, www.sitbusshuttle.it) runs a frequent service from Termini (via Marsala) to Ciampino (45 minutes, €6, 4.30am-9.30pm), and Ciampino to Termini (8.45am-11.45pm). Tickets can be bought on the bus or online.

Schiaffini buses (800 700 805, www.schiaffini.it) runs a service between Ciampino and Anagnina metro station every 30-40mins (6am-10.40pm daily), and to Ciampino station (where frequent trains depart for Rome Termini) 5.45am-23.25pm daily; both cost €1. It also runs regular services (€4.50) between the airport and Termini station. Very early morning services cost €1.20 and €5 respectively. Buy tickets on board.

Cotral (www.cotralspa.it) buses run regularly between the airport and Anagnina metro station (€1.20), and between the airport and Ciampino town's railway station (€1).

By bus

There is no central long-distance bus station in Rome. Most coach services terminate outside the following metro stations: Saxa Rubra (routes north); Cornelia, Ponte Mammolo and Tiburtina (north and east); Anagnina and Laurentina (routes south).

By train

Most long-distance trains arrive at Termini station, also the hub of Rome's transport network. Beware of pickpockets. Night trains may arrive at Tiburtina or Ostiense.

For bookings and information on mainline rail services across Italy, call **Trenitalia** (24hrs daily) on 892 021 (06 6847 5475 from abroad) or go to www.trenitalia.it. Tickets can be bought at stations (credit cards accepted over the counter and by ticket machines) or online. Under-12s pay half fare; under-fours travel free.

Slow trains (*diretti, espressi, regionali* and *interregionali*) are cheap; fast services – InterCity (IC), EuroCity (EC), Eurostar Italia (ES) – are closer to the European norm.

You must stamp your ticket in the yellow machines at the head of the platform before boarding. You risk being fined if you don't.

Rome's main stations are **Ostiense** (piazzale dei Partigiani),

Termini (piazza dei Cinquecento), **Tiburtina** (circonvallazione Nomentana) and **Trastevere** (piazzale Biondo).

Public transport

Rome's transport system is co-ordinated by **ATAC** (06 57 003, www.atac.roma.it, disabled information helpline 800 154 451). You can download maps of the transport network from the website (click on *Linee e mappe*), which also has a useful journey planner.

City-centre and inner-suburb routes are served by the buses and trams of the **Trambus** transport authority. The system is relatively easy to use and as efficient as the traffic-choked streets allow.

Pickpocketing is a problem on buses and metros, particularly on major tourist routes, notoriously the 64 and 40 Express between Termini station and the Vatican.

Tickets

The same tickets are valid on all city bus, tram and metro lines, whoever the operator is. They are not valid on services to Fiumicino airport. Though the latest generation of buses has ticket dispensers on board, in most cases you'll have to buy before you board, from ATAC automatic ticket machines, information centres, some bars and newsstands and all *tabacchi*. Before purchasing a three-day ticket, consider whether the three-day **Roma Pass** (p12) might not be better value.

BIT valid for 75mins, during which you can take an unlimited number of city buses, plus one metro trip; €1.
BIG valid for one day, until midnight; covers the whole urban network; €4.
BTI three-day pass, covering all bus and metro routes, and local mainline trains to Ostia; €11.

ESSENTIALS

CIS valid for seven days; it covers all bus routes and the metro system, including the lines to Ostia; €16. You must stamp tickets on board. Under-tens travel free; older kids and pensioners must pay the adult fare. If you are caught without a stamped ticket, you'll be fined €51 on the spot, or €104.40 if you opt to pay later at a post office.

Buses

Bus is the best way to get around. The system is easy to use; a sign at each bus stop tells you the routes each line stopping there takes.

Most services run 5.30am-midnight daily, every 10-45mins. The doors for boarding (usually front and rear) and alighting (usually centre) are clearly marked. Note that 'Express' buses make few stops along their route: check before boarding so you don't get whisked past your destination.

Trams

Tram routes mainly serve suburban areas. An express tram service – No.8 – links largo Argentina to Trastevere and the western suburbs. Tram 3 has been replaced by a bus.

Metro

MetRo (06 57 531, www.metroroma. it) runs Rome's two metro lines, which cross beneath Termini train station. Line A runs from south-east to north-west; line B from EUR to the north-east. Both are open 5.30am-11.30pm (until 1.30am Fri & Sat). From 11.30pm (1.30am Fri & Sat) until 5am, buses N1 and N2 ply the same routes respectively.

Taxis

Licensed taxis are white and have a meter. Touts are rife at major tourist magnets; ignore them if you don't want to risk an extortionate fare.

Recent changes in taxi tariffs have made them super-complicated. When you pick up a taxi at a rank or hail one in the street, the meter should read zero. The minimum fare is currently €2.80 (€4 on Sundays and public holidays), or €5.80 if you board 10pm-7am. Each kilometre after that is 92c. The first piece of luggage put in the boot is free, then it's €1 per piece. Tariffs outside the GRA, Rome's major ring road, are much higher. There's a ten per cent discount for trips to hospitals, and for women travelling alone 9pm-1am, and a €2 surcharge for any trip starting at Termini station.

Fixed airport tariffs from anywhere inside the Aurelian walls (ie most of the *centro storico*) are €40 to/from Fiumicino; €30 to/from Ciampino. This is for up to four people and includes luggage: don't let taxi drivers tell you otherwise.

Most of Rome's taxi drivers are honest; if you think you're being fleeced, take down the driver's details from the metal plaque inside the car's rear door. The more obviously you do this, the more likely you are to find the fare returning to its proper level. Report complaints to the drivers' co-operative (phone number on the outside of each car) or, in serious cases, the police.

When you phone for a taxi, you'll be given the taxi code-name (always a location followed by a number) and a time, as in *Bahama 69, in tre minuti* ('Bahamas 69, in three minutes'). Besides the minimum fare, you'll be charged the following 'call' rates depending on how long your taxi takes to arrive: €2 (up to five mins), €4 (five-ten mins) or €6 (more than ten mins). If the meter shows more than this when the taxi arrives, the difference must be deducted at the end of the trip.

Cooperativa Samarcanda 06 5551/
www.samarcanda.it.
Cosmos Radio Taxi 06 88 177/
06 8822.
**Società Cooperativa Autoradio
Taxi Roma** 06 3570/*www.3570.it*.
Società la Capitale Radio Taxi
06 49 94.

Driving

Much of central Rome is off-limits
during the day for anyone without
a permit. Police and cameras guard
these ZTL (*zone a traffico limitato*)
areas; any car without a pass will
be fined €70 if it enters at restricted
times. A strict no-car policy applies
in the centre on some Sundays too;
check www.comune.roma.it or
www.atac.roma.it for info.

Most motoring associations have
breakdown service agreements with
either **Automobile Club d'Italia**
(24hr info and emergency toll-free
800 116, www.aci.it) or **Touring
Club Italiano** (06 3600 5281,
www.touringclub.it).

Remember:
* You are required to wear a seatbelt
at all times, in front and back seats,
and to carry a warning triangle
and reflective jacket in your car.
* You must keep your driving
licence, vehicle registration and
ID documents on you at all times.
* Traffic lights flashing amber mean
stop and give way to the right.

Parking

Residents park for free and visitors
pay to park in many areas. It's well
policed, so look for the blue lines.
Buy parking tickets (€1/hr; €1.20/hr
in ZTL areas) at pay-and-display
ticket dispensers or from *tabacchi*. In
most areas you can park for free at
certain times. Hourly parking cards
(*scheda per il parcheggio*), available
from *tabacchi*, save you the bother
of scrabbling for small change.

In zones with no blue lines,
anything resembling a parking
place is up for grabs, with some
exceptions: watch out for signs
saying *Passo carrabile* ('access at
all times') or *Sosta vietata* ('no
parking'), and disabled parking
spaces (marked by yellow stripes).
The sign *Zona rimozione* ('tow-away
zone') means no parking, and is
valid for the length of the street or
until the sign is repeated with a red
line through it. If a street or square
has no cars parked in it, assume it's
a strictly enforced no-parking area.

In some areas, self-appointed
parcheggiatori will 'look after' your
car for a small fee; it may be illegal
and an absurd imposition, but it's
worth paying up to ensure your
tyres remain intact.

Cars are safe in most central
areas, but you may prefer to use
a car park to keep your car off the
street. The following are central:
Parking Ludovisi *via Ludovisi 60 (06
474 0632)*. **Rates** €2.20/hr for first five
hours, €1/hr thereafter. No credit cards.
Terminal Park *via Marsala 20 (06
444 1067)*. **Rates** €2 for two hours;
€1.50/hr thereafter. No credit cards.

Vehicle removal

If your car is not where you left it,
it may have been towed. Phone the
municipal police (*Vigili urbani*) on
06 67 691 and quote your number
plate to find out which pound it's in.
Alternatively, check for it on
www.comune.roma.it, clicking on
'*Dipartimenti e altri uffici*', then
'*Corpo di Polizia Municipale*'.

Vehicle hire

Avis 06 481 4373/06 4521 08391/
199 100 133/*www.avisautonoleggio.it*.
Europcar 199 307 030/
www.europcar.it.
Maggiore 06 2245 6060/06 488
0049/199 151 120/*www.maggiore.it*.

ESSENTIALS

Resources A-Z

Accident & emergency

To call an **ambulance**, dial 118; for the **fire brigade**, dial 115; for **police**, see p185. The hospitals listed below offer 24hr casualty services. If your child needs emergency treatment, head straight for the Ospedale Bambino Gesù.

Ospedale Fatebenefratelli
Isola Tiberina (06 68 371).

Ospedale Pediatrico Bambino Gesù *Piazza Sant'Onofrio 4 (06 68 591/www.opbg.net).*

Ospedale San Camillo-Forlanini *Via Portuense 332 (06 55 551/ 0658701/www.scamillo forlanini.rm.it).*

Ospedale San Giovanni *Via Amba Aradam 8 (06 77 051/ www.hsangiovanni.roma.it).*

Policlinico Umberto I *Viale Policlinico 155 (06 49 971/ www.policlinicoumberto1.it).*

Pharmacies

Normal pharmacy opening hours are 8.30am-1pm, 4-8pm Mon-Sat. Outside these hours, a duty rota system operates. A list by the door of any pharmacy (and in local papers) indicates the nearest ones.

Farmacia della Stazione *Piazza dei Cinquecento 49-51 (06 488 0019).* **Open** 24hrs daily.
Piram *Via Nazionale 228 (06 488 0754).* **Open** 24hrs daily.

Credit card loss

The following are open 24hrs.
American Express *06 7290 0347/US cardholders 800 874 333*
Diners Club *800 864 064*
MasterCard *800 870 866*
Visa *800 877 232/800 819 014*

Customs

Travellers arriving from EU countries are not required to declare goods imported into or exported from Italy if they are for personal use, up to the following limits:
■ 800 cigarettes or 400 cigarillos or 200 cigars or 1kg of tobacco
■ ten litres of spirits (over 22% alcohol) and ten litres of fortified wine (under 22% alcohol).

For people arriving from non-EU countries the following limits apply:
■ 200 cigarettes or 100 cigarillos or 50 cigars or 250g of tobacco
■ one litre of spirits or two litres of wine; one bottle of perfume (50g)
■ 25 cl of eau de toilette or various merchandise not exceeding €175. Anything above will be subject to taxation at the port of entry. There are no restrictions on the importation of cameras, watches or electrical goods. Call Italian customs (*dogana*) on 06 5024 3260 or check its website (www.agenziadogane.it).

Dental emergency

For serious dental emergencies, use hospital casualty departments (see above). Children should be taken to the Ospedale Bambino Gesù.

Disabled

With cobbled streets, narrow pavements and old buildings, Rome is difficult for disabled people. That said, many city-centre buses are now wheelchair accessible and most museums and larger hotels have facilities.

Rome city council's Osservatorio Permanente sull'Accessibilità has an excellent (but very well-hidden) website, in English, showing accessibility and facilities in all the city's major tourist sites. Check out www2.comune.roma.it/Accacomune/osservatorio/default.asp.

The non-profit **CO.IN** (www.coin sociale.it) give details of disabled facilities at museums, restaurants, shops, theatres, stations and hotels. It also organises transport for disabled people (up to eight places), which must be booked several days in advance. It runs a phone service in Italian and English (toll-free 800 271 027, from within Italy only).

Roma per Tutti (06 5717 7094, www.romapertutti.it) is an info line run by CO.IN and the city council. English-speaking staff answer questions on accessibility in hotels, buildings and monuments. Guided tours with transport can be booked. Its site also contains useful information on events.

Electricity

Italy uses 220V – compatible with British-bought appliances (with a plug adaptor); US 110V equipment requires a current transformer.

Embassies & consulates

For a full list of embassies, see *Ambasciate* in the phone book.
Australia *Via Antonio Bosio 5 (06 852 721/www.italy.embassy.gov.au).*
Britain *Via XX Settembre 80 (06 4220 0001/ www.ukinitaly.fco.gov.uk).*
Canada *Via Zara 30 (06 854 441/ www.canada.it).*
Ireland *Piazza Campitelli 3 (06 697 9121/www.ambasciata-irlanda.it).*
New Zealand *Via Clitunno 44 (06 853 7501/www.nzembassy.com).*
South Africa *Via Tanaro 14 (06 852 541/www.sudafrica.it).*
US *Via Vittorio Veneto 119 (06 46 741/www.usembassy.it).*

Internet

Much of central Rome, plus major parks (*ville* Borghese, Pamphili, Ada, Torlonia), EUR and the Auditorium – Parco della Musica zone, is covered by the ever-growing city-sponsored free wireless network. When you open your browser in one of the 100+ hotspots, you'll be asked to log on. Initially, you'll need to register, giving a mobile phone number. For information, including a map of hotspots, see www.roma wireless.com.

Opening hours

For shopping hours, see p23; for pharmacies, see p184.

Most banks open 8.30am-1.30pm, 2.45-4.30pm Mon-Fri. Some central branches also open until 6pm Thur and 8.30am-12.30pm Sat. All banks work reduced hours the day before a holiday (many close by 11am).

Police

For emergencies, call one of the following helplines:
Carabinieri *(English-speaking helpline) 112*
Polizia di stato *113*
The principal *Polizia di Stato* station, the Questura Centrale, is at via San Vitale 15 (06 46 861, www.poliziadistato.it). Others, and the Carabinieri's *Commissariati*, are listed in the phone directory under *Polizia* and *Carabinieri*. Incidents can be reported to either.

Post

The once-notorious Italian postal service is now generally efficient (try the Vatican Post Office, run in association with the Swiss postal service, if in doubt). For postal information, call 803 160 (8am-8pm Mon-Sat) or visit www.poste.it.

ESSENTIALS

There are large post offices (*ufficio postale*) in each district; opening hours are generally 8.30am-6pm Mon-Fri (8.30am-2pm Aug), 8.30am-1.30pm Sat and any day preceding a public holiday. Many areas now have smaller branches, which shut at 2pm Mon-Sat. All offices close up to two hours earlier than normal on the last day of each month. Some services are available via the website (www.poste.it); check it first to avoid the queues.

Posta Centrale *Piazza San Silvestro 19 (info 803 160).*

Vatican Post Office *Piazza San Pietro (06 6988 3406).* **Open** 8.30am-6.30pm Mon-Fri; 8.30am-6pm Sat.

Smoking

A law introduced in January 2005 prohibits smoking in all public places in Italy except for those that provide a distinct, ventilated smokers' room. Possible fines of between €27.50 and €275 (or up to €550 if you smoke in the presence of children or pregnant women) are the reason why you'll find small groups puffing away *outside* most restaurants, pubs and clubs.

Tabacchi

Tabacchi, identified by signs with a white T on a black background, are the only places where you can legally buy tobacco products. They also sell stamps, phone cards, tickets for public transport and lottery tickets.

Telephones

Dialling & codes

▪ Land-lines have the area code 06, which must be used whether calling from within or outside the city. When phoning Rome from abroad, do *not* omit the initial 0.

▪ Numbers beginning with 800 are toll-free. Numbers starting with 840 and 848 are charged at low set rates but can only be called within Italy.

▪ Mobile numbers begin with a 3. GSM phones can be used on both 900 and 1800 bands; British, Australian and New Zealand mobiles work fine, but US phones (unless they're tri-band) don't work.

▪ For international calls, dial 00, followed by the country code, area code (omitting the initial zero, if applicable) and number. Codes include: Australia 61; Canada 1; Irish Republic 353; New Zealand 64; United Kingdom 44; United States 1.

Directory enquiries

This is a jungle, and charges for information given over the phone are steep. The major services are 1254 (Italian and international numbers, in Italian) and 892 412 (international numbers, in Italian and English, from mobile phones). Italian directory information can be accessed for free at www.1254.it and www.paginebianche.it.

Public phones

Rome has no shortage of public phone boxes, and many bars have payphones, which are rarely busy as locals are addicted to mobiles. Most only accept phone cards (*schede telefoniche*); a few also accept major credit cards. Phone cards cost €5, €15 and €30 and are available from *tabacchi*, some newsstands and some bars.

Tickets

For pre-booking tickets for sights, galleries and exhibitions, see p11, and Tourist Information, p187.

Expect to pay *diritti di prevendita* (booking fees) on tickets bought anywhere except at the venue on the night. **Feltrinelli Libri e Musica** (Galleria Alberto Sordi, piazza Colonna, 06 679 4957) sells tickets for classical concerts and for rock, jazz and other events.

Hello Ticket (800 907 080, www.helloticket.it) takes bookings over the phone and online for most concerts, plays and sporting events.

Time

Italy is on Central European Time, making it an hour ahead of GMT and six hours ahead of Eastern Standard Time. In all EU countries clocks move forward an hour in early spring, and then back again in late autumn.

Tipping

Foreigners are generally expected to tip more than Italians, but the ten or more per cent usual in many countries is seen as generous even for the richest-looking tourist. Anything between €1 and €5 is normal; some smarter places now include a 10-15% service charge. For drinks, leave 10¢-20¢ when ordering at the counter. Taxi drivers will be happy if you round the fare up to the nearest euro.

Tourist information

The city council operates well-stocked, green tourist information kiosks (**PIT**), 9.30am-7/7.30pm daily; the most central are in piazza Pia (by Castel Sant'Angelo), piazza delle Cinque Lune (by piazza Navona), via del Corso and piazza Sonnino (in Trastevere).

The fastest one-stop shop for tourist information, however, is a new phone service, 060608, sponsored by the city council. Information on sights, opening times, shows and much else is dispensed in English and Italian;

phone operators will put callers through to the appropriate booking agency if they want to reserve tickets or seats. The www.060608.it website is an excellent source of information.

The APT tourist board's website www.turismoroma.it is also worth checking out.

Ufficio Pellegrini e Turisti (Vatican Tourist Office)
Piazza San Pietro (06 6988 1662/www.vatican.va). **Open** 8.30am-6pm Mon-Sat.

Visas

EU nationals and citizens of the US, Canada, Australia and New Zealand do not need visas for stays of up to three months. For EU citizens a passport or national ID card valid for travel abroad is sufficient; non-EU citizens must have full passports. In theory, all visitors must declare their presence to the local police within eight days of arrival. If you're staying in a hotel, this will be done for you.

What's on

Listings mags *Roma C'è* (www.romace.it, out Wed) and *Trovaroma* (free with *La Repubblica* on Thur) are the best sources of information about shows, concerts and nightlife. The latter has an English section.

Major events are listed on the official tourist board website – www.romaturismo.it – and on www.060608.it. For an alternative look at Rome's nightlife, check out www.romastyle.info and www.musicaroma.it. For information on Rome's gay scene, contact **Arcigay Roma** (06 6450 1102, www.arcigayroma.it) or **Arci-Lesbica Roma** (www. arcilesbica.it/roma). For other gay organisations, see p28.

ESSENTIALS

Vocabulary

Pronunciation

a – like a in ask
e – like a in age or e in sell
i – like ea in east
o – like o in hotel or hot
u – like oo in boot
c – as in cat before a, o and u; otherwise like ch in cheat
g – as in good before a, o and u; otherwise like g in giraffe; **gl** – like lli in million; **gn** – like ny in canyon
h – not pronounced; after any consonant makes it hard (ch – cat; gh – good); **sc** – like sh in shame; **sch** – like sc in scout

Useful phrases

hello/goodbye (informal) *ciao, salve*; **good morning** *buon giorno*; **good evening** *buona sera*; **good night** *buona notte*; **please** *per favore, per piacere*; **thank you** *grazie*; **you're welcome** *prego*; **excuse me, sorry** *pardon*, (formal) *mi scusi*, (informal) *scusa*; **I don't speak Italian** *non parlo l'italiano* **do you speak English?** *parla inglese?*; **can I use/where's the toilet?** *posso usare/dov'è il bagno?*; **open** *aperto*; **closed** *chiuso*; **entrance** *entrata*; **exit** *uscita*

Transport

bus *autobus, auto*; **car** *macchina*; **coach** *pullman*; **plane** *aereo*; **taxi** *tassì, taxi*; **train** *treno*; **tram** *tram*; **bus stop** *fermata (dell'autobus)*; **platform** *binario*; **station** *stazione*; **ticket** *biglietto*; **one-way** *solo andata*; **return** *andata e ritorno*

Directions

where is? *dov'è?*; **(turn) left** *(giri a) sinistra*; **(it's on the) right** *(è a/sulla) destra*; **straight on** *sempre dritto*; **is it near/far?** *è vicino/lontano?*

Communications

attacco per il computer *dataport*; **broadband** *ADSL (adiesselle)*; **cellphone** *telefonino*; **courier** *corriere, pony*; **fax** *fax*; **letter** *lettera*; **phone** *telefono*; **postcard** *cartolina*; **stamp** *francobollo*; **a stamp for England/the US** *un francobollo per l'Inghilterra/gli Stati Uniti*

Days

Monday *lunedì*; **Tuesday** *martedì*; **Wednesday** *mercoledì*; **Thursday** *giovedì*; **Friday** *venerdì*; **Saturday** *sabato*; **Sunday** *domenica;* **yesterday** *ieri*; **today** *oggi*; **tomorrow** *domani*; **weekend** *fine settimana, weekend*

Numbers, weights & sizes

0 *zero*; **1** *uno*; **2** *due*; **3** *tre*; **4** *quattro*; **5** *cinque*; **6** *sei*; **7** *sette*; **8** *otto*; **9** *nove*; **10** *dieci*; **11** *undici*; **12** *dodici*; **13** *tredici*; **14** *quattordici*; **15** *quindici*; **16** *seidici*; **17** *diciasette*; **18** *diciotto*; **19** *dicianove*; **20** *venti*; **30** *trenta*; **40** *quaranta*; **50** *cinquanta*; **60** *sessanta*; **70** *settanta*; **80** *ottanta*; **90** *novanta*; **100** *cento*; **200** *duecento*; **1,000** *mille*; **2,000** *duemila* **I take (shoe/dress) size** *porto il numero/la taglia…*; **100 grams of…** *un'etto di…*; **300 grams of…** *tre etti di…*; **a kilo of…** *un kilo di…*; **five kilos of…** *cinque chili di…*

Booking & paying

booking, reservation *prenotazione* **I'd like to book…** *vorrei prenotare… …a table for four at eight* un tavolo per quattro alle otto **…a single/twin/double room** *una camera singola/doppia/matrimoniale* **how much is it?** *quanto costa?*

Menu Glossary

Sauces & toppings

aglio, olio e peperoncino *garlic, oil and chilli*; **alle vongole** *clams*; **al pomodoro fresco** *fresh/raw tomatoes*; **al ragù** *'bolognese' (a term that doesn't exist in Italian)*; **al sugo** *puréed cooked tomatoes*; **all'amatriciana** *tomato, chilli, sausage and onion*; **alla gricia** *as above without tomato*; **all'arrabbiata** *tomato and chilli*; **alla carbonara** *egg, bacon and parmesan*; **alla puttanesca** *olives, capers and garlic*; **cacio e pepe** *cheese and black pepper*; **in bianco** *with oil or butter and parmesan*; **(ravioli) ricotta e spinaci** *filled with curd cheese and spinach*.

Meat & meat dishes

abbacchio, agnello *lamb*; **animelle** *fried pancreas and thymus glands*; **bresaola** *thinly sliced cured beef*; **coda alla vaccinara** *oxtail in celery broth*; **coniglio** *rabbit*; **lardo** *fatty bacon*; **lingua** *tongue*; **maiale** *pork*; **manzo** *beef*; **ossobuco** *beef shins with marrow jelly inside*; **pajata** *veal/lamb intestines*; **pollo** *chicken*; **porchetta** *roast suckling pig*; **prosciutto cotto** *ham*; **prosciutto crudo** *Parma ham*; **straccetti** *thin strips of pan-tossed beef*; **trippa** *tripe*; **vitello** *veal*.

Fish & seafood

alici, acciughe *anchovies*; **aragosta, astice** *lobster*; **arzilla, razza** *skate*; **baccalà** *salt cod*; **branzino, spigola** *sea bass*; **calamari** *squid*; **cernia** *grouper*; **dentice, fragolino, marmora, orata, sarago** *forms of bream*; **cozze** *mussels*; **gamberi** *prawns*; **granchio** *crab*; **mazzancolle** *king prawns*; **merluzzo** *cod*; **moscardini** *baby octopus*; **ostriche** *oysters*; **pesce sanpietro** *john dory*; **pesce spada** *swordfish*; **polpo, polipo** *octopus*; **rombo** *turbot*; **salmone** *salmon*; **seppie** *cuttlefish*; **sogliola** *sole*; **tonno** *tuna*; **trota** *trout*; **vongole** *clams*.

Vegetables

asparagi *asparagus*; **broccoli siciliani** *broccoli*; **broccolo** *green cauliflower*; **broccoletti** *turnip tops*; **carciofo** *artichoke*; **cavolfiore** *cauliflower*; **cicoria** *green leaf vegetable, like dandelion*; **cipolla** *onion*; **fagioli** *beans*; **fagiolini** *green beans*; **fave** *broad beans*; **funghi** *mushrooms*; **insalata verde/mista** *green/mixed salad*; **melanzana** *aubergine, eggplant*; **patate** *potatoes*; **patatine fritte** *french fries*; **piselli** *peas*; **puntarelle** *bitter salad vegetable usually served with anchovy sauce*; **rughetta** *rocket*; **sedano** *celery*; **spinaci** *spinach*; **zucchine** *courgettes*.

Fruit & desserts

ananas *pineapple*; **anguria, cocomero** *watermelon*; **arance** *oranges*; **ciliegi** *cherries*; **fichi** *figs*; **fragole** *strawberries*; **mele** *apples*; **nespole** *loquats*; **pere** *pears*; **pesche** *peaches*; **uva** *grapes*. **gelato** *ice-cream*; **pannacotta** *'cooked cream', a thick blancmange-like cream*; **sorbetto** *water ice*; **torta della nonna** *flan of pâtisserie cream and pinenuts*; **millefoglie** *flaky pastry cake*.

Miscellaneous

antipasto *hors d'oeuvre*; **primo** *first course*; **secondo** *main course*; **contorno** *side dish, vegetable*; **dessert, dolce** *dessert*; **arrosto** *roast*; **alla griglia** *grilled*; **all'agro** *with oil and lemon*; **ripassato in padella** *(of vegetables) cooked then tossed in a pan with oil, garlic and chilli*; **formaggio** *cheese*; **pane** *bread*; **sale** *salt*; **pepe** *pepper*; **aceto** *vinegar*; **olio** *oil*.

Index

Sights & Areas

ESSENTIALS

ESSENTIALS

ROME

VIA VITTORIO VENETO 62 A/B

METRO STOP: PIAZZA BARBERINI

+39-06-4203051 • HARDROCK.COM

FOR INFO:

ROME_SALES@HARDROCK.COM

VIP Entrance- First available table

RESTAURANT • COCKTAIL BAR • ROCK SHOP